Elaine —

An addition to
your extensive
leadership knowledge
& skills

Ann Lucas
Aug 23, 1999

Strengthening Departmental Leadership

Ann F. Lucas
Foreword by R. Eugene Rice

Strengthening Departmental Leadership

A Team-Building Guide for Chairs in Colleges and Universities

 Jossey-Bass Publishers
San Francisco

Substantial discounts on bulk quantities of Jossey-Bass books are available to corporations, professional associations, and other organizations. For details and discount information, contact the special sales department at Jossey-Bass Inc., Publishers. (415) 433–1740; Fax (415) 433–0499.

For sales outside the United States, please contact your local Simon & Schuster International Office.

Jossey-Bass Web address: http://www.josseybass.com

TCF Manufactured in the United States of America on Lyons Falls Turin Book. This paper is acid-free and 100 percent totally chlorine-free.

Permission to reproduce the exhibits in Chapter 2 and figure 2.2 is hereby granted.

Library of Congress Cataloging-in-Publication Data

Lucas, Ann F.
    Strengthening departmental leadership: a team-building guide for chairs in colleges and universities/Ann F. Lucas—1st ed.
        p.   cm.—(The Jossey-Bass higher and adult education series)
    Includes bibliographical references and index.
    ISBN 0-7879-0012-5
    1. Departmental chairmen (Universities) 2. Educational leadership.
    I.Title. II. Series.
    LB2341.L83 1994
    378.1'11—dc20   94-21302
                                                                 CIP

FIRST EDITION
HB Printing   10 9 8 7 6 5 4 3   Code 9492

The Jossey-Bass Higher
and Adult Education Series

Dedicated to five people who have greatly
enriched my life—
my husband, Rawley Dean Lucas;
our children,
Mark Douglas, Kathleen Ann, and Paul Kevin;
and our grandson, Peter Gregory—
with deep love and affection

Contents

Foreword

Alfred North Whitehead, in a 1929 address inaugurating the new campus of the Harvard School of Business, reminded his audience: "Imagination is not to be divorced from the facts: it is a way of illuminating the facts. . . . The tragedy of the world is that those who are imaginative have but slight experience, and those who have experience have feeble imaginations."

Ann Lucas, more than anyone I know, brings to her work on academic departments years of rich and varied experience. She has been there as a faculty member and department chair—a critical requirement for anyone writing on this topic—and has worked with thousands of department chairs in colleges and universities across the various sectors of higher education. What makes *Strengthening Departmental Leadership* especially valuable, however, is that Lucas combines her extensive experience with a rich and fertile imagination. This book ought to be read by every provost, dean, and—especially—department chair.

The importance of a work is often established by the timing of its publication. This book is appearing at a particularly propitious moment in higher education and has the potential for having a significant impact on how we go about our work. The emphasis on the professional autonomy of faculty, misunderstood as being that of scholars who work individually on their disciplinary careers independent of institutional concerns and responsibilities, has been pressed to the limit. Trustees, legislators, accrediting associations, and even faculty colleagues are calling for greater accountability toward the institution on the part of faculty; a new priority is being placed on collective responsibility and faculty leadership. The time has come for us as faculty members to fundamentally reframe how we think about what we do and move from a focus on "my work" to one on "our work." Strengthening departmental leadership is key to making this critical transition in the faculty role.

Until very recently, the professoriate has approached the chairing of departments much as it has regarded teaching: with the assumption that explicit preparation is unnecessary. In relation to teaching, it has been widely assumed that attending to the intellectual content of one's specialization is all that is needed —quality teaching should naturally follow. This assumption about teaching is now being successfully challenged. Even some graduate schools are changing their priorities. Ann Lucas's years of organizational work in higher education and now her book hold forth promise that academic leaders may soon recognize the explicit preparation and thoughtful reflection about one's performance that chairing a department requires.

In the 1960s, in the democratizing spirit of the time, most academic departments instituted rotating chairs. Old curmudgeons who had ruled departments in authoritarian ways (or what passed for that) were summarily deposed, and the leadership—a word seldom used then because it smelled of power—of departments was passed around among colleagues in a comfortably egalitarian manner. In many cases, secretaries took over. What could have been seen as a leadership opportunity was systematically transformed into what we disparagingly talked about as a "paper-shuffling chore" or a "three-year sentence." Ann Lucas not only challenges the devaluing of the role of the department chair but offers ways of assessing what is needed and changing the situation—and then provides wise counsel on how to be an effective department chair. Especially helpful is her forthright discussion of the power of the department chair, its use and misuse, and the ways it differs across the sectors of American higher education.

Besides bringing to the writing of this book the combination of experience and imagination that Whitehead found so frequently lacking, Ann Lucas draws on her rich background in both clinical psychology and the field of organizational behavior. Theory and practice in these two immediately relevant areas of inquiry inform and enrich her understanding of what is needed to strengthen departmental leadership. To all of this, she adds a depth of common sense and a humane orientation to working with people that comes through in every page.

July 1994   R. Eugene Rice
Vice president and dean of faculty
Antioch College

Preface

In working with more than six thousand academic chairs at over 125 different campuses in this country and abroad over the past twelve years, I have found that chairs everywhere struggle with the same issues and that two common threads run through these issues: all chairs desire to enhance their effectiveness as leaders, but in order to achieve that effectiveness, they need a better understanding of small-group dynamics and team leadership. Specific areas in which I saw opportunities for growth were team building with members of the department; creating a supportive communication climate; facilitating faculty development; motivating faculty, particularly difficult colleagues, poor teachers, and midcareer faculty; handling faculty evaluations and making feedback interviews meaningful; managing conflict; developing an effective relationship with the dean; and developing coping mechanisms to ensure the chairs' own survival.

There are eighty thousand chairs and heads of department in U.S. colleges and universities (Green, 1988a, p. 54). The vast majority are appointed by the dean, provost, or president, following a departmental election. Because departments normally rotate the position among their qualified faculty members, chairs are usually elected by their colleagues for a renewable term of three or four years. When faculty members and the dean feel the department needs to move in a new direction, when a department is fragmented by conflict, or when no one in the department is willing to serve as chair, a faculty committee and the dean may select an external candidate to fill the post.

However they are selected, those who become chairs for the first time frequently find that their experience as faculty members has not equipped them for the transition. The move from the freedom and autonomy of a faculty position to the demanding and restrictive position of chair is a wrench that most faculty members have not envisioned. Chairs must move from performing the highly individual work of the teacher and scholar to getting work done through others, a task for which new chairs are monumentally unprepared. Motivating colleagues to be effective teachers and productive scholars and to accept a fair share of the work of the department creates a role conflict for chairs, as they are required to act against what they have perceived as the good of teachers and scholars for the good of the department or institution. This role conflict is most likely to happen in such areas of chair responsibility as scheduling course offerings, requiring accountability from departmental members, and increasing faculty productivity. Moreover, since much college and university communication is funneled through chairs, they also contend with the stress of role conflict as they represent both administration to the faculty and faculty to the administration. These conflicts contribute to the most difficult aspect for chairs of assuming their new positions, the loss of their collegial support network and the feeling of being alone in the trenches.

Purpose

Carroll and Gmelch (1992) have identified four independent roles that chairs perform: leader, faculty developer, manager, and scholar. My work with chairs during this past decade has led me to select the roles of leader and faculty developer as key to effective departmental functioning. They are also the roles for which new chairs are least prepared. *Strengthening Departmental Leadership* demonstrates how chairs can learn the skills that are essential to their becoming leaders and faculty developers and making a significant impact on their departments. In addition, the information presented here will assist chairs in building cohesive teams in their departments and facilitate their learning and using survival skills. It is designed to be highly practical, presenting sensible advice on handling problems that occur frequently in college and university departments. It is firmly grounded in research but free of jargon. Underlying all that I have written here is my recognition that chairs already feel overwhelmed by paperwork, so my intent is not to add more chores to a very full agenda. I view the chair as a leader, not a paper pusher, and I provide a goal-setting framework and action steps that result in leadership knowledge and skills for department chairs.

Overview of the Contents

Chapter One describes opportunities departmental chairs have to handle specific challenges confronting higher education and discusses barriers that prevent chairs from becoming leaders and team builders. Chapter Two presents the leadership matrix, an instrument used to measure nine major leadership and faculty development responsibilities of academic chairs. Because the matrix assesses both the current level of a chair's leadership development and departmental needs, it pinpoints leadership strengths and target areas for leadership development while also identifying areas that will make little impact on a department no matter how much energy the chair devotes to them. Chapter Three describes what we know about research on leadership that is also applicable to chairs in higher education. Using a transformational leadership model, I present a practical, step-by-step method that depicts how a chair can develop a vision that will elicit the commitment of the department.

Chairs must find ways to motivate and reward faculty, particularly such special groups as difficult colleagues, midcareer faculty, and burned-out faculty. Chapter Four focuses on a practical approach chairs can take to motivate departmental colleagues. It also illustrates how chairs can use performance evaluation as a tool for ongoing faculty development as well as for personnel decision making. Chapter Five deals with motivating faculty to teach effectively. It includes two dozen strategies a chair can initiate for improving teaching in the department and more than thirty significant topics in teaching worth discussing at department meetings.

Evaluation of colleagues' teaching is a new demand on most chairs. Chapter Six examines the reasons student evaluations provide incomplete assessments, describes the value of observation by colleagues, and presents steps for counseling a faculty member before and after a classroom observation, along with an example of an effective feedback interview. Chapter Seven provides a look at the chair's role in creating a departmental climate that actively encourages scholarship. I offer a series of recommendations in the context of the new definitions of scholarship, a process and practical suggestions to help faculty overcome barriers to the act of writing, and tips for getting everyone to take a fair share of responsibility for accomplishing the work of the department.

Creating a supportive communication climate empowers faculty, helps strong teams to perform, and prevents dysfunctional conflict. Chapter Eight focuses on conducting meetings effectively, encouraging healthy disagreement, and carrying out problem solving in groups, so that faculty willingly commit themselves to decisions they recognize as sound and comprehensive. Chairs are more effective if they can recognize when conflict can be used creatively and when it is destructive for the department. Chapter Nine addresses strategies for managing conflict and describes in detail how the chair can play the role of third-party facilitator.

Chapter Ten explains how chairs can increase the value of the interaction between the dean and the chair, as they use the leadership matrix together to determine the needs of the department and the chair's strengths. The dean and the chair's objective look at the leadership growth opportunities for the chair can result in joint goal setting and the development of effective action steps. Chapter Eleven offers a step-by-step sequence for developing goals and action steps based on feedback from faculty members. This process is the beginning of a team-building effort within the department.

Learning the leadership behaviors described in the first eleven chapters of this book will help chairs thrive, not just survive; so will the stress-reduction interventions presented in Chapter Twelve. The strategies covered include interventions in individuals' physical, behavioral, and cognitive systems, and specific suggestions for managing time and tasks, changing dysfunctional thoughts, and creating a support network.

Finally, in Chapter Thirteen I integrate the information from the previous chapters and recommend how chairs can use it to ensure that leadership development does occur during their terms of service. In addition, I suggest that chairs view their personal leadership development as action research, creating a public document that records accomplishments of the department under their leadership and that may be useful for merit consideration in the college.

Audience

Individual department chairs and heads can use this book as their personal guide to leadership development and team building, or it may be used by all the chairs in a college as the basis for a self-study course that includes regular meetings of the chairs to enhance their leadership effectiveness collectively over the academic year. Program directors, who, like chairs, function as team leaders, also will find the guidelines for facilitating teams valuable.

In addition, this book can be read with profit by those who have overall responsibility for colleges and universities, the deans and senior academic officers. Since academic institutions are more productive when chairs and deans perform as teams and when departments function effectively, deans and senior academic administrators will want to increase their understanding of how leaders can be developed and teams built in all the academic units.

Moreover, those who know they are fated to become chairs can equip themselves to be more proficient leaders. Using the measures suggested in this book, future chairs can determine how close the match is between their individual strengths and the leadership needs of their departments and sharpen the appropriate skills before taking on the role of chair. Finally, faculty developers who work with chairs will find concepts and material that can form the basis for developmental workshops for chairs.

The application of many of the processes I address will be immediately evident to those who hold leadership positions in comprehensive universities, liberal arts colleges, and community colleges. In research universities and other large institutions whose departments seem to be governed in a fairly objective and very professional way, the value and use of these processes may not be recognized so promptly. However, in consulting with departments in a number of large universities, I have uncovered compelling evidence that dysfunctional departments exist in these schools also, and that often conflict is swept under the rug, faculty feel they have not been treated fairly and lack agreed-upon methods for managing conflict, and chairs perceive that they have no power. Practical steps for dealing with such issues are discussed throughout the book.

Acknowledgments

Strengthening Departmental Leadership had its origins in my first formal work with department chairs in 1982, when I founded and directed the Office of Professional and Organizational Development at Fairleigh Dickinson University. R. Eugene Rice, in the capacity of external consultant, suggested that because of the significant role they have in the university community, I talk with department chairs and listen to their needs. I followed his advice. He was right, and I am grateful. This was the beginning of more than a decade of deeply involving research and practical work across the country with the chairs, heads, and deans from whom I have learned so much and to whom I am indebted.

My thanks also to Howard Altman, Robert Boice, and Larry A. Braskamp, who reviewed the manuscript. I greatly appreciate their careful reading and their positive feedback and scholarly and practical advice, which were so helpful in the revision stage.

I am also indebted to Gale Erlandson, senior editor of the Jossey-Bass Higher and Adult Education Series, for her insightful recommendations and extremely useful suggestions about style, and to her assistant, Ann Richardson, for her encouragement at a particularly important point in my writing.

Finally, my thanks to the periodicals staff of the Fairleigh Dickinson University Library and to the three gracious and dedicated librarians who constantly obtained materials essential to the writing of this book: reference librarians Judith Katz and Laila Rogers and the head of government documents, Edward Grosek.

Englewood, New Jersey   Ann F. Lucas
July 1994

The Author

Ann F. Lucas is professor of organization development and former campus chair in the Department of Management at Fairleigh Dickinson University (FDU), where she is founder and former director of the Office of Professional and Organizational Development. She has also been a full-time faculty member in the doctoral program in clinical psychology and has served as chair of the Psychology Department at FDU. Lucas has conducted a part-time practice in clinical psychology for more than twenty years and has served as consultant to more than thirty Fortune 500 companies, in addition to hospitals and federal and city government agencies.

Lucas has served on both the executive and core committees of the Professional and Organizational Development Network in Higher Education. For six years, she served as Department Chair Consultant in Leadership Development in Higher Education for the American Council on Education, and she has been a member of the Faculty Development Advisory Committee for the New Jersey Department of Higher Education. A consultant on leadership in higher education internationally as well as in this country, she has conducted workshops for more than six thousand chairs and deans, on more than 125 college and university campuses in the United States and in Australia, New Zealand, Canada, and Puerto Rico. She has been a presenter at more than one hundred professional and disciplinary conferences.

A licensed psychologist and a diplomate of the American Board of Professional Psychology, Lucas received her B.S. degree in psychology from Seton Hall University, and her M.A. and Ph.D.

degrees in psychology from Fordham University, Rose Hill Campus. She is the editor of *The Department Chairperson's Role in Enhancing College Teaching* (New Directions for Teaching and Learning, no. 37), published by Jossey-Bass in 1989, and her more than forty publications include chapters in books and articles about academic departmental leadership; the chair's role in enhancing faculty teaching effectiveness; ways to increase writing productivity, build teams, and motivate students; performance evaluation; conflict resolution; outplacement in a university setting; and faculty development.

Nominated by her department chair and supported by faculty members in the department, Lucas was selected for the Outstanding Educators of America award. She has also received the Zucker Memorial Award for outstanding teaching and dedication to higher education, for which she was nominated by the students in her college of the university.

Chapter One

Strengthening Leadership at the Departmental Level

The following examples of actual problems from different kinds of institutions may seem dissimilar at first glance, but they all reflect problems that occur when departmental leadership is not handled well.

In an English department of fifteen faculty members in a liberal arts college, tensions ran high. The department was fragmented, and several faculty members did not speak to one other. Because the department had historically rejected recommendations that were the result of committee deliberations, all issues were now dealt with by a committee of the whole. This fact, combined with a tendency for everyone to express an opinion on every subject discussed, contributed to monthly departmental meetings that often lasted three to four hours. Because conflict was usually dealt with indirectly, it surfaced primarily as heated disagreements about inconsequential issues. Faculty members reflected the stress they felt when they spoke about not being able to sleep the night before and the night after a departmental meeting.

In a forty-person management department in a large state university, faculty became disenchanted with an autocratic department chair, who had been appointed by the dean despite the fact that he had been listed as a third choice by department members. Although from the outside it looked as if the department were running smoothly, faculty members complained to one another about the chair's threats and intimidation tactics ("If you don't volunteer to handle these open houses for student applicants [or serve on the curriculum committee or . . .], I will keep that in mind when I arrange your teaching schedule"). After he had served two four-year terms, the chair rotated back into a faculty position, and the faculty, determined not to allow anyone again to have so much power, wrote a departmental governance document that created an executive committee to handle a number of responsibilities. However, since the governance document was somewhat ambiguous, both the chair and the executive committee often acted without consulting each other, and faculty were not sure who was responsible for what tasks. Conflicting messages from the chair and the executive committee on the departmental requirements for promotion and tenure increased the stress level for junior faculty. Even after this revised departmental structure had been in place for several years, faculty tensions were still running high.

A comprehensive university that had always valued excellence in teaching began to place more weight in personnel decision making on research and publication. The deans seemed to agree that the reputation of a university depends upon high visibility, and that that visibility is achieved through publication. However, the reality is that, in most departments, a few faculty members are productive researchers, and others publish an occasional article, but most faculty members have either not published for years or have never written an article. At chair meetings, the topic of what might be done at the departmental level to increase scholarly productivity is occasionally raised but never resolved.

In a large, unionized community college, the president announced a three-year goal of improving excellence in the college. Yet the chairs, who had many student complaints about poor teaching and the unavailability of faculty members who simply taught their courses and left campus, did not know where or how to begin. Salary increases were given simply on the basis of faculty members' academic degrees plus additional credits accrued above the master's degree level. Faculty also were required to serve on at least one committee each year, in addition to completing one service function chosen from a list of acceptable activities. The chairs were dissatisfied with the performance of faculty, but felt they had no authority to control unsatisfactory behavior.

The following underlying chair responsibilities were addressed in the interventions for these problems, and all these responsibilities are discussed in this book.

Motivating faculty
Being an effective faculty developer
Creating a supportive communication climate
Developing good listening skills
Facilitating faculty agreement on mutual goals
Clearly defining roles and responsibilities
Managing conflict effectively
Addressing a dysfunctional departmental culture
Evaluating performance and providing effective feedback
Team building

The interventions used in all four situations improved the chairs' abilities to deal with these responsibilities and made it possible for them to improve faculty performance, increase the achievement of department goals, work together with faculty, and manage conflict so that it was no longer dysfunctional.

Leadership in a Climate of Educational Criticism

Departmental leadership is especially important today, when more than ever before the public is suspicious of college faculty. The public seems to believe that college faculty are not productive enough, do not work hard enough on behalf of students, and are not interested in teaching. Such views have been reflected in a number of reports. One of the most recent, *An American Imperative: Higher Expectations for Higher Education,* released by the Wingspread Group on Higher Education in December of 1993, asserts that "opinion polls leave no doubt that Americans have a profound respect for higher education. . . . But simultaneously the polls reveal deep public concern. . . . Public confidence in the 'people running higher education' has declined" (p. 6). The report also finds that "it is hard not to conclude that too much undergraduate education is little more than secondary school material— warmed over and reoffered at much higher expense but not at correspondingly higher levels of effectiveness" (p. 7). "The simple fact is that some faculties and institutions certify for graduation too many students who cannot read and write very well, too many whose intellectual depth and breadth are unimpressive, and too many whose skills are inadequate in the face of demands of contemporary life" (p. 1).

Such skepticism about the value of what faculty do has resulted in interventions from outside the academy that have left higher education in a state of disequilibrium. Greater accountability has been demanded as many state agencies have become involved in assessing outcomes, closing programs, determining faculty workloads, developing policies for reviewing tenured professors, and setting standards, all of which were once the prerogative of individual institutions. This increasing emphasis on quality and institutional effectiveness has come at a time of financial constraints, when state and federal cuts have necessitated significant reductions in the budgets of many colleges and universities. Moreover, institutions of higher education are being forced to face challenges arising from U.S. demographic change and its impact on enrollment patterns and cultural diversity. Increasing competition for students and funding, the demise of literacy among entering freshmen in all but the most prestigious institutions, and a rapidly changing technological world for which colleges and universities must adequately prepare their graduates, all seriously affect faculty. When we add to these issues the necessity for the chair to attend to the orienting and mentoring of new faculty and the continuing needs of more experienced faculty members—who also require attention, nurturance, empowerment, help with professional development, and on occasion, confrontation over behavior that is dysfunctional for students and for the department—we see just how essential it is for department chairs to exercise creative, proactive leadership.

Increasing complexity and a corresponding need for change require that, at every level in higher education, there be leaders capable of creating a vision; communicating that vision to others; stimulating people to think in different ways; formulating problems in the sophisticated, knowledgeable fashion that inspires creative solutions; and providing an organizational climate in which people achieve and feel appreciated. Today's educational climate calls for leaders who are capable not only of preserving what is going well but also of functioning as agents of change. And such leadership is crucial not only in senior administrators but also in department chairs.

Higher education is a vast, $100 billion enterprise of 12 million students and 400,000 full-time faculty members on more than 3,000 campuses (Green, 1988a, p. 1). Since academic departments are the building blocks of any university, how well the necessary changes are developed and implemented will depend heavily on the leadership ability of department chairs. Because academic chairs are the leaders most intimately connected with the heart of their institutions, namely the quality of teaching and learning, they have the potential for the greatest impact. Their impact is felt in the selection of new faculty, the professional development of current faculty, the creation of departmental culture, the setting of departmental norms, the faculty's formulation of departmental goals that identify new directions, and the creation of a quality curriculum, responsive to major changes in the discipline. It is the academic chair who shares with the faculty members a perception of reality that has evolved from the way their shared discipline views the world. On the highly practical side, the chair is the only person in a leadership role in the institution who sees department members two or three times a week. Moreover, the 80,000 department chairs and heads in U.S. colleges and universities constitute a formidable number. With the help of their faculty, they can determine how to maintain what is good and implement what needs to be changed in higher education.

Myths That Make Chairs Believe They Are Powerless

Despite the colossal need for leadership at the departmental level, and the logic indicating that the department is the place to make the changes that must be made in our colleges and universities, chairs often refuse to take on departmental leadership responsibilities. On campus after campus, particularly in comprehensive universities and liberal arts colleges but sometimes in community colleges and large research universities as well, chairs have repeated to me a series of statements that are in fact myths to which they subscribe, often as a reason for avoiding actions that need to be taken by a strong leader.

These conversations usually begin with a chair's list of problems—particularly concerns about motivating difficult colleagues, midcareer faculty, and poor teachers who are tenured—proceed to the difficulties of getting faculty to accept a "fair share" of the work of the discipline, and finally advance to the departmental conflicts. The tone then shifts, as the chair describes his or her feeling of powerlessness in the face of such difficulties, primarily because faculty are tenured. A number of firmly believed myths are then articulated as justification for the chair's being unable to do anything.

A myth, particularly one in which there is a strong belief, is a fixed perception of a situation that indicates what an individual can and cannot control and change. When such fixed perceptions are held by department chairs, the rules of the department "game" will develop from these attributions. For example, the perception determines whether chairs will try to deal with difficult colleagues or will ignore the situation because they believe there is nothing they can do that will make a difference. In subscribing to such sets of beliefs, individuals build high walls around themselves and around circumstances, and these barriers not only control the individuals' behavior but justify how they choose to behave. Whenever an individual describes a situation as having no solution or sees it only as a dichotomy, having only two opposed alternatives, it is probable that he or she is engaging in premature closure. In other words, the individual has stopped trying to generate options for handling the problem and, as a result, often puts himself or herself in a no-win situation.

Here are the six most frequent fixed beliefs, or myths, that are dysfunctional for the chairs who hold them. Each myth is accompanied by a rebuttal.

Myth 1. I am elected by my colleagues to serve at their pleasure for only three or four years, then I will be a faculty member again. Therefore, there is nothing I can do to deal with the problems.

Rebuttal. The chair's belief that he or she is unable to do any problem solving as chair because a department chair is simply a peer among equals conveys an aura of humility and democracy in action, yet it effectively leaves a department without a leader. Particularly when a chair is elected by peers for a limited term, choosing to be a team leader is a valuable choice of leadership style. As team leader, the chair can take an active role in seeking meaningful input and full participation from everyone in the department, so that faculty members can plan and organize themselves to function most effectively. Being a team leader requires setting shared goals with all members of the department and individual goals with each faculty member, so that faculty can focus on how they can achieve departmental goals while realizing their own individual goals. Setting goals with individuals and providing feedback on performance in a supportive climate are the strongest forces a chair can use for motivating faculty. When chairs are passive because they feel there is nothing they can do, departments, and often faculty, stagnate.

Myth 2. It is my turn in the barrel. I do not particularly want to be chair, but we all have to take a turn.

Rebuttal. There are individuals who say that they do not want to be chair and are taking the job simply because it is their turn. Given the academic norm that administration of any sort is a necessary evil, such statements do not usually raise concern among faculty; on the contrary, faculty often worry that people who want to be chair may be seeking power. However, when someone does not want to be chair, neither the department nor the faculty will benefit by having that person as chair simply because it is his or her turn. The most likely outcome is that the unwilling individual will adapt a form of passive resistance and accomplish nothing for the department. Whenever he or she is chided for not taking some responsibility, the response can always be, "But I didn't ask to be chair."

Myth 3. I am simply a peer among equals. I am not a manager.

Rebuttal. This is a good example of generating a simple dichotomy from a complex situation. The chair believes that he or she must be either a peer or a manager; there is nothing in between. On the one hand, however, a chair can no longer be just a peer among equals. Chairs have responsibilities different from those of faculty members. And on the other hand, even though all chairs must perform some management functions, they do not have to become managers. They can become leaders.

Myth 4. I have neither carrot nor stick. It is not possible either to reward or punish faculty members.

Rebuttal. It is simplistic to think that rewards refer only to economic benefits and that the ability to punish means only the power to fire a faculty member. There are many more subtle and meaningful ways to reward people. As for the use of punishment, it has so many negative side effects that it is rarely an alternative of choice for motivating others. When chairs are respected colleagues, they have the ability to reinforce faculty for their work by taking that work seriously and showing appreciation for the quality of an individual's work. Such recognition from a colleague is both rewarding and motivating to faculty. Moreover, chairs usually have major input into decisions about personnel, schedules, and release time. The courses they teach and the times such courses are offered are high among faculty's concerns, and it is the chair who signs off on teaching schedules. Whether faculty receive time for research activities, and the quantity of time they receive, are also heavily influenced by the chair, as is the management of other departmental resources.

Myth 5. I am neither fish nor fowl. Being neither a faculty member nor an administrator, my role is not clear.

Rebuttal. Even though the resulting role conflict is stressful, a chair must be the conduit between faculty and administration, representing the needs of each to the other. Meeting this responsibility requires that chairs be articulate spokespersons for department members to administration and even public relations agents so that faculty members' accomplishments, their impact on their discipline at the state or national level, and their outreach to the community will be understood and appreciated by the rest of the university. However, because chairs also represent administration to faculty, they must at times be able to advance points of view that represent what is deemed to be good for the college or university but that may not be perceived as equally good for the department or its individual members. A good example that might be found in a large research university is a request by the chair that all faculty members teach at least one undergraduate course, when teaching undergraduates is not popular among department members. In comprehensive universities as well as in liberal arts and community colleges, faculty often strongly resist a chair's request that they teach an 8:00 A.M. class, a late evening course, or a course that meets three times a week. In each of these cases, faculty may feel that the chair has lost the ability to identify with colleagues and is behaving like an administrator. Chairs must handle such conflict in their roles with tact, fairness, and good humor.

Myth 6. I have no power. Therefore, I can do nothing.

Rebuttal. Many chairs feel they have no power, though this perception is not usually accurate. If we define *power* as "the potential or actual ability to influence others in a desired direction" (Gordon, 1993, p. 392), then power for a chair is the ability to influence faculty to achieve their own goals as they accomplish the work of the department. Chairs do have enough power to motivate faculty to teach effectively, increase scholarly productivity, and increase service or outreach activities. All chairs need is to know how to go about identifying and tapping this power. Practical action steps chairs can use to achieve departmental goals and help faculty reach individual goals are included throughout this book. Team leaders get things done, and this book is about that team leadership.

Power to Motivate Faculty

Chairs have three kinds of power through which they can motivate faculty: position power, personal power, and expert power. The following discussion explores each of these types and their specific significance for department chairs.

Position Power

Professor Brockport, a well-known scholar and author, tells a story about returning from sabbatical to attend a department meeting at which it would be determined who would be chair for the next four years. (Throughout this book, the names used in examples are pseudonyms.) He reports, "I went back to the department as one of the guys, but at the meeting it was decided that I would be the next department chair. It's amazing the difference, the very subtle but real difference, with which I was treated as we walked out of that meeting. Somehow, just the fact that I was going to be the next department chair gave me an edge, so that people looked at me differently and treated me with a certain amount of deference." The behavior of Professor Brockport's colleagues demonstrates their acknowledgement of the position power he had just acquired.

Position power, often also referred to as legitimate power, is the authority individuals have simply because of their positions or functions. The extent to which chairs control rewards and punishments, the trappings of position power, varies markedly from one institution to another, but when colleges and universities give weight to chairs' input on administrative matters, the chairs' position power is increased. Thus, chairs have strong position power when their judgment is given serious consideration in such personnel decision making as the allocation of release time for research and of travel money, the funding of requests for equipment or computer software, the determination of who will teach which courses and at what time, and the assignment of graduate research fellows and clerical assistants. The position power of chairs in research and some large state universities is usually greater than that of chairs in other schools. They may be permanently appointed to their posts and feel primarily responsible to administration. Their power in allocating resources, determining curriculum, scheduling, and deciding the direction that a department will take is also considerable. Permanently appointed chairs who are prudent find ways to diminish faculty concern about power by involving faculty in participative decision making. Such an approach also develops faculty commitment to departmental goals and policies.

However, faculty are sometimes troubled when a chair has considerable position power. Disagreement and resentment may not be dealt with openly. When invited to consult with large departments because there is an undercurrent of conflict, I have found a number of strategies that faculty have developed to diminish a chair's power. For example, as described earlier in this chapter, faculty in one department had mandated the formation of an elected executive committee as a strategy for diminishing the chair's power. Unfortunately, the descriptions of the responsibilities of the chair and of the executive committee were highly ambiguous, so the chair and the executive committee developed the habit of acting independently of each other, which often undermined the authority of each and created new tensions in the department. In a large department at another university, an advisory committee that comprised all the former chairs was set up to counsel the current chair. This strategy did not work, in part because it was not clear to what extent the current chair had to accept the committee's advice. Also, a former chair who had failed to win election to a second term seemed frequently to undercut decisions made by the present chair. Conflict between the chair and the advisory committee created factions and fragmented the department. However, these matters were considered indiscussible and were never raised at meetings, so conflict escalated. One symptom of conflict was that the department could not get faculty commitment to carry out decisions. When faculty voted on recommendations, those who lost the vote constantly undermined implementation of what the majority of faculty members had agreed to. Only when the department's problems were directly addressed, roles clarified, and procedures devised for making high-quality decisions, solving problems, and managing conflict was the department able to get back on track. In some large state universities, the position power of the chair has been somewhat diminished when the institution has been unionized and chairs made part of the bargaining unit, with their authority and responsibility specified in the collective bargaining agreement.

While not all colleges and universities will follow these patterns, in general, chairs in private liberal arts colleges frequently seem to function with a moderate amount of position power, often sharing it with strong departmental committees. In many comprehensive universities and community colleges, the position power of chairs has been eroded. And in the several state systems where I have consulted, chairs complain that they have little control over personnel decision making. Many of them indicate that it is customary for chairs to write positive evaluations for all faculty members during personnel reviews, because chairs who wrote more realistic faculty evaluations would be viewed as preventing their own faculty from gaining tenure and promotion.

In these same comprehensive universities in state systems, chairs and faculty are critical of school presidents' actions in sharply limiting the number of promotions granted each year. However, since it is unlikely that everyone who is recommended is worthy of being promoted, those at the top, faced with insufficient information, must exercise their own judgment. If all faculty members are rated excellent in all areas, excellent becomes synonymous with average. When those who work most closely with faculty do not exercise discriminating judgment, that responsibility consequently moves up to the highest administrative levels. Although faculty and chairs complain about this shift, they clearly bear some responsibility for the fact that control is no longer in their hands. Problems with poorly used position power arise in these institutions partly because the institutions themselves do not take the role of chair seriously enough. Full professors refuse the role, and assistant professors and untenured faculty are sometimes allowed to become chairs. Since these chairs know that they will be evaluated for promotion or tenure by faculty whom they are now evaluating, they cannot risk saying anything negative. So they must, even if unwillingly, describe everyone in glowing terms.

Many chairs argue that there are constraints placed on what they can accomplish in their departments, in other words that their position power is limited. Clearly, their complaints are often justified. However, as can be appreciated from the examples just discussed, chairs also need education and support in using their position power wisely, and this instruction needs to be undertaken throughout the entire institution to develop an amount of consistency that will support individual chairs' behavior. Moreover, problems in the system that permit untenured faculty members to become department chairs need to be resolved at the higher administrative levels in order for all chairs to function effectively.

Personal Power

Although position power varies from institution to institution, within an institution, it is by and large a given. It is personal power that varies considerably from chair to chair and that can be increased. Personal power comes from several different sources. Some individuals possess influential personal characteristics such as charisma, the ability to attract others to identify with them and follow them. The respect a chair has won from the college or the university at large, faculty perceptions of how much influence a chair has with the dean, a chair's fairness and reasonableness in dealing with faculty, the respect a chair is given within his or her own discipline, a chair's consulting experience, all of these factors contribute to the amount of personal power a chair possesses.

However, coercion is also part of personal power. Coercive individuals exert power because they are able to instill fear. This is not the same as having the power to exercise legitimate punishment, such as recommending no release time for research because a faculty member has produced nothing for two years. Such legitimate refusals are part of position power. Coercive power is not legitimate and may include threats such as, "If you don't agree to serve on that committee, I will give you an early morning and late night schedule"; or, "I will see that you do not get release time for research," even when objective criteria and the faculty member's prior productivity suggest that release time is warranted. Some chairs manage to get away with such tactics for years before faculty take things into their own hands and request that the dean poll department members to discover whether they have confidence in the chair.

Chairs can increase their personal power in a number of legitimate ways. If chairs are equitable in their distribution of departmental resources, treat everyone with respect, are perceived as working for and fighting for the well-being of their faculty members when the cause is just, create a supportive climate in the department, and give people recognition and visibility for achievements, their personal power becomes greater.

In particular, the typical structure of colleges and universities also provides an opportunity for chairs to increase their personal power. As long as colleges and universities function as bureaucracies, characterized by short career ladders and limited reward systems, faculty find that excellence rarely pays off. Most individuals with doctorates begin their academic careers as assistant professors, and most do not become administrators; therefore, they can receive only two promotions during a career lifetime. Since the 1960s, when rotation of the chair's job became commonplace, most individuals have not retained that job for more than one or two terms. (Chairs at large state universities often provide an exception to this statement.) Moreover, once faculty members become tenured full professors, recognition within their own university is a relatively rare occurrence. Merit increases for faculty are given in some institutions, but when the criteria are not clear and objective, or when there are more losers than winners, merit salary awards have a negative impact on morale. A faculty member who does not receive a merit increase is likely to think, What I am being told is that all of the work I have done for this institution during the past year is worth nothing.

Under such circumstances, when there is a vacuum of reinforcement for good work, department chairs serve a unique function when they demonstrate respect for and acknowledgment of the work in which faculty members are engaged. Colleagues need recognition, and chairs are in a good position to supply it. When they do so, in addition to providing greatly needed positive feedback to faculty, they increase their personal power. When an organization provides little reinforcement, people in that organization want to please those individuals who do provide recognition. Increasing personal power in this way is not manipulative. The responsibility of a chair as leader of a department is to achieve departmental goals. When that chair can influence faculty to match their own goals with departmental goals, so that both sets of goals are achieved at the same time, he or she unleashes an enormous motivational force.

Rewarding faculty does not require financial remuneration. Recently, working with about fifteen deans in a large state university, I asked what they could do to reward their chairs. The immediate, almost unanimous response was, "We can't reward them because all increases in salary are given as a percentage of their professorial rank." But when I asked the deans how their vice president could reward them, instantly, from various places in the room, came suggestions: "Recognition for increasing enrollment in these tough economic times"; "A simple thank-you for having accomplished an outstanding accreditation review in my college"; "Some appreciation for an adroit handling of a near-revolt when students read misinformation in the student newspaper that a department had been threatened with closure by an accrediting organization because equipment was obsolescent." Then, the light went on: "What you're saying is that we can acknowledge what chairs have accomplished; let them know we appreciate them." And, yes, that was the message.

People need honest recognition of their work. I am not recommending insincerity but genuine acknowledgment of what it is that faculty are doing. Chairs need to talk with faculty about their teaching, their research, their outreach efforts, their committee work, recognizing whatever they have done that is of value. Chairs who value effective teaching need to pass along the good things they hear about faculty members' teaching. If a syllabus has a particularly good reading list or includes an innovative idea about how a course will be structured to increase learning, the chair should compliment the instructor. So often, individual contributions, sometimes heroic in terms of time commitment, are taken for granted. The message a faculty member gets is, Nobody thinks what I have done is important.

Since a chair's personal power is also based on faculty perceptions of how highly the dean regards the chair, chairs can also increase their personal power by increasing their credibility with the dean. Chairs can demonstrate that they are knowledgeable and reasonable people by their behavior at chair meetings and their judicious responses to topics raised by the dean. Keeping informed about essential issues related to the functioning of the department, making positive rather than negative statements, resisting any tendency to complain about faculty, and responding to questions thoughtfully with answers based on evidence rather than hearsay or guesses raises a chair's credibility. Chairs should also prepare carefully for meetings with their deans, obtaining an agenda in advance so that they come prepared to discuss the appropriate issues and avoid what happened to the chair whose department lost six elective credits because he had not informed himself about the agenda in advance of a meeting with a new dean. At the meeting, the dean asked him to give up six credits that had previously been colisted with another department. Because the other department was small and had too few majors, the dean asked the chair to give those courses to the other department. Faced with no opportunity to think about it but not wanting the new dean to think he was uncooperative, the chair agreed. Only afterwards did he realize that his department would have to terminate the two adjuncts who had been teaching those specialized courses for years. This was one of several events that caused faculty to lose faith in him and his ability to represent them.

Expert Power

Expert power is based on knowledge and control of resources. Chairs usually know better than faculty how to get things accomplished in a college or university, particularly how to do things that are not described in faculty handbooks and other formal documents. Through meetings with the dean, chairs also hear about plans for the college, changes that will take place, and other major and minor events before faculty do. This knowledge, plus knowledge about and control over resources, such as knowing in advance about a source of additional funding for faculty research, gives chairs expert power. Faculty members recognize this dimension of a chair's power, though they may sometimes overestimate what the chair can do, particularly when they are seeking exceptions to rules.

Making the Most of Power

In short, a chair's position, personal, and expert power can be used to influence faculty to create a match between achieving departmental goals and attaining individual goals. Chairs can increase their personal power by recognizing faculty members' accomplishments, behaving fairly, and striving to be creditable in their relations with the dean, particularly through accepting responsibility for problems (instead of blaming or denigrating department members), doing homework on agenda items, and avoiding off-the-cuff, ill-informed statements.

The myths that chairs believe about powerlessness undoubtedly reduce chairs' effectiveness. However, institutions also have great responsibility for enhancing competent leadership at the chair level. If chairs are to be strong leaders, their role must be taken more seriously by colleges and universities. Although chairs constitute a body of leadership and influence that has the potential to drive change in sophisticated and knowledgeable directions, too often they are overlooked as valuable resources. The evidence suggests that insufficient care is given to selection and training of people to fill the role of chair. Moreover, the attention and resources allocated to professional development and support of chairs by deans and academic vice presidents are often minimal. If beneficial changes are to occur in higher education, the role of the department chair must be elevated to a significant function in the college and university. Chairs must be given more position power, that is, more authority, so that they can truly make a difference.

Furthermore, if chairs are to be team leaders, they need assistance in developing skills in participatory decision making and goal setting. They must learn how to confront and change departmental cultures that maintain negative norms of behavior for faculty and staff. They need to learn more about motivating faculty, mastering skills in creating a supportive communication climate, evaluating faculty, managing constructive feedback, resolving conflict, and engaging in their own ongoing leadership development. In addition, some of the mind-deadening paperwork—the primary complaint of chairs—must be handled by computer or delegated to a technical assistant or a competent secretary so that chairs have time to be leaders.

In the preface to their book *The Leadership Challenge: How to Get Extraordinary Things Done in Organizations*, Kouzes and Posner (1987) state that "the domain of leaders is the future. The leader's unique legacy is the creation of valued institutions that survive over time. The most significant contributions leaders make is not to today's bottom-line but to the long-term development of people and institutions who prosper and grow. But more than that . . . leadership is important not only in your dealings with others but equally in your own career. It is the leader who reaches the summit in any field. Because leadership development is ultimately self-development, the leadership challenge is a personal challenge" (p. xxi).

This view clearly underlines the responsibility that chairs, as leaders, must take for their own professional development. Chairs must know, or discover with the help of strategies provided in this book, their own leadership strengths and weaknesses. This self-knowledge is the first step in a systematic approach to leadership development.

Overview of the Leadership Matrix

As a way of providing structure for the work of chairs, I have developed a leadership matrix, a tool that visually represents the most important current needs of a department and the leadership strengths that must be developed to handle them (see Figures 2.1 and 2.2). Chairs can use the leadership matrix to assess their strengths and opportunities for improvement. Since the matrix is intended as an approach to goal setting and team building, a mechanism is also described for gathering information from department members and deans about their views of departmental needs and important leadership strengths, so that the matrix becomes a vehicle for goal setting and team building with faculty and with the dean.

The matrix examines nine major leadership and faculty development responsibilities of chairs. Chairs evaluate for themselves the importance of each of these leadership responsibilities to the department at this point in time; what their own level of development is in each of the nine leadership areas; and which of these responsibilities they will target for their own professional development while they are chairs. Next, they may get input from all the faculty members as individuals and share that feedback with the department as a whole, setting goals and developing action steps. When goals are set with department members, responsibility for the work needed to reach those goals is shared by everyone. The dean may be involved both as a source of a perspective on departmental needs and the chair's leadership skills and as someone who can link college and departmental goals. Resources for achieving goals that are set are identified with the dean so that the chair and dean become partners in a supportive problem-solving approach to handling departmental needs and the chair's leadership growth. The chair monitors progress on an ongoing basis; an evaluation of progress also takes place with the department and the dean at the end of the year. Chairs secure needed feedback on accomplishments, have an occasion to savor success, and discover what could make their leadership behaviors even more effective.

Chairs accepting responsibility for their own professional development steadily enhance their understanding of leadership concepts and increase their level of skill and are thus able to employ enhanced leadership behaviors for the good of the department and the college. By the end of a term in office, a chair should have developed a leadership portfolio. Based on action research, this portfolio is a statement of leadership accomplishments and professional development that, in some institutions, might be used in personnel decision making such as merit increases.

The leadership matrix can be used in all types of colleges and universities even though their policies, culture, tradition, and politics will differ. However, there may be a difference in the order in which a chair requests input from faculty and from the dean. Whether the next step after chairs have completed their own ratings is goal setting with the dean or with department members, and how conflicting goals from these two sources are resolved, will depend upon the nature of the institution and how well the department is functioning.

In those colleges and universities where departments are strong, chairs may choose to engage first in goal setting with the faculty and then to make a strong case with their deans for budgetary and administrative endorsement, confident that they are speaking for faculty who strongly support them. However, in institutions in which control and accountability tend to be vested more in senior administrators than in departments, goals that are set by the chair and the dean may be given equal weight or more than goals set with the department. Moreover, it is not unusual, particularly within large state universities, to find that great differences in policy and control exist from one college to another in the same institution. Often medical schools, engineering schools, and dental schools are more likely to have a top-down leadership style and more administrative power over goals and budgets than are colleges of liberal arts in the same institution.

So although I recommend that chairs engage in goal setting with both department members and the dean, chairs must decide how conflicting goals that emerge can be resolved. For example, in departments where faculty members have all been teaching for many years, faculty may generally believe that there is no reason for them to set a goal of improving teaching effectiveness. They may also believe that the poor to average student evaluations many of them receive come about because students are incapable of evaluating faculty. Moreover, they may state that colleague observations are unacceptable because classroom visits would be an infringement of academic freedom. In such a case, a chair and a dean, appreciating the need for teaching improvement in that department, might set goals that use many of the steps recommended in Chapter Five to improve teaching. To be effective, such an approach would address an indirect rather than a direct change in the departmental culture. Clearly, however, the relative priorities of the dean's and the faculty's goals would have to be determined by the chair.

I ask readers to keep these factors in mind as they peruse Chapter Two and the basic method of applying the leadership matrix. At all times, they should be guided by their knowledge of what will work in their own institutions.

Roles and Responsibilities of Chairs

Academic chairs often say that they have no clear idea of what the dean or their department members expect of them. More than 80 percent of the many chairs with whom I have worked have never participated in formal goal setting, and more than 90 percent have never been evaluated in their role as chair. This lack of feedback increases role ambiguity for chairs, who often feel uncertain about how others perceive their performance and unsure about how far to go on their own in determining departmental direction.

For new chairs, the breadth of the job becomes clear only after they have been engaged in it for several months. Once in the position, they spend so much time putting out brushfires, attending meetings, handling paperwork, trying to find uninterrupted periods for class preparation, and endeavoring to continue their work as scholars that there seems to be little opportunity to detach themselves long enough to think about new directions that require a proactive leadership role.

This chapter is intended to help chairs become proactive leaders. It describes the leadership matrix, which helps chairs determine in which of nine areas well-developed leadership skills will be most useful, and it also lists and defines seven managerial or administrative functions. My primary focus remains on leadership and faculty development responsibilities rather than on departmental management, for it is in the area of leadership that systematic guidance has not previously been available to chairs; however, separating the work of the chair into leadership and managerial tasks is useful for it encourages chairs to think clearly about the role they want to take, and what knowledge and skills they will need to develop during their terms of office.

The Leadership Matrix and Leadership Responsibilities

As I described in Chapter One, the leadership matrix provides a visual representation of departmental needs in relation to a chair's leadership characteristics. It is a structured approach for identifying the most important requirements of a department and the opportunity each need creates for the chair to develop specific aspects of leadership. Use of the leadership matrix enables chairs to take charge of their own professional development by assessing their own strengths and the areas in which they can increase their effectiveness. In addition, they can use the matrix as the first step in a goal-setting and team-building process with faculty and the dean.

Various authors have listed an extensive array of activities in which department chairs engage. Tucker's 1992 edition of the encyclopedic *Chairing the Academic Department* catalogues fifty-four separate duties. In a study of heads of department in eight Australian universities, forty functions were identified from an analysis of questionnaires and in-depth interviews (Moses & Roe, 1990). Building on such findings in order to distinguish the significant roles of chairs, the Carroll and Gmelch (1992) factor analytic study of 539 questionnaires from chairs in research and doctoral granting institutions identified four independent roles that chairs perform: leader, faculty developer, scholar, and manager.

As described earlier, I have chosen to focus on two of these roles, leader and faculty developer, which require both conceptual knowledge and interpersonal skills, and I have divided these two roles of leader and faculty developer into nine major responsibilities, each of which can be assessed for importance to the department and skill development of the chair by the leadership matrix.

My own work indicates that the issues with which chairs are struggling do fall into the areas of leading the department and motivating faculty. Therefore, I began with the two lists of chair activities identified in the research by Tucker (1992) and Moses and Roe (1990) and selected those tasks that related specifically to leadership and faculty development. Guided by the literature distinguishing management from leadership functions (Bass, 1990a; Conger, 1989; Tichy & Devanna, 1990), I then grouped the activities under nine chair responsibilities, all of which related to leadership and faculty development.

Support for my selection of responsibilities for leadership and faculty development roles comes from the Carroll and Gmelch factor-analytic study (1992, pp. 6–7), which finds that the faculty developer role includes practicing an informal leadership style; maintaining a favorable work climate, for example by reducing conflicts; encouraging development factors; evaluating faculty performance; and developing long-range department goals. Carroll and Gmelch find that the role of leader involves soliciting ideas to improve the department, conducting department meetings, and informing the faculty about department, college, and university concerns. I discuss all these chair responsibilities in *Strengthening Departmental Leadership*.

Responsibility 1: Leading the Department

A department chair is a team leader who creates a shared vision that challenges faculty members intellectually and emotionally. A chair empowers others by creating a learning environment in which individual self-development, encouraged and stimulated by colleagues, is enhanced through achievement of department and university goals. Problems come to be viewed through a positive, sophisticated lens that enables individuals to find opportunities in problems and identify resources for problem resolution. Department members feel a sense of accomplishment as goals that they have set jointly are achieved.

Responsibility 2: Motivating Faculty to Enhance Productivity

Individuals are motivated to do those things that are rewarded. Although faculty are also influenced by individual and background factors, the focus here is on the chair's role in creating a climate that is conducive to ongoing faculty learning and accomplishments. The key productivity enhancing approaches available to a chair are setting goals jointly with faculty members and giving feedback on performance in a positive supportive climate. Department chairs must give special attention to faculty at certain career stages and with certain problems: for example, new and midcareer faculty and difficult colleagues.

Responsibility 3: Motivating Faculty to Teach Effectively

Chairs need to create a departmental culture in which faculty improve their teaching effectiveness on an ongoing basis. There are many approaches by which chairs can motivate faculty to assume this development responsibility, such as making teaching excellence a high-priority goal in the department, requiring all applicants for faculty positions to make at least one presentation to faculty and students before receiving a faculty appointment, sponsoring workshops or sharing information on different aspects of teaching, developing a mentoring system, and using student evaluations as part of a process for instructional effectiveness.

Responsibility 4: Handling Faculty Evaluation and Feedback

Chairs should create a learning environment that encourages colleague mentoring and observation and that values feedback as an opportunity for celebrating the things faculty are doing competently, for sharing teaching strategies that work, for determining effectiveness in scholarship and service, and for stimulating ideas for professional development.

Responsibility 5: Motivating Faculty to Increase Scholarship

Chairs should create a departmental climate that is appropriate to the institutional and departmental missions of encouraging scholarship, whether as in the traditional view, or as recently defined in *Scholarship Reconsidered* (Boyer, 1990), which broadens the scope of acceptable research. In some colleges with a clearly defined teaching mission, the scholarship required may be simply that faculty be on the cutting edge of their disciplines. In those comprehensive universities that are placing an increasing emphasis on research and publication, the chair is responsible for introducing techniques that address the process of writing, as an aid for those who have not recently published.

Responsibility 6: Motivating Faculty to Increase Service

The chair should get everyone to take a fair share of responsibility for accomplishing the work of the department and of the discipline. Effective chairs encourage the faculty to assume the roles of consultant, mentor, leader, adviser, or departmental or disciplinary representative and to see that these activities balance teaching and scholarship and are consonant with the mission of the department. Typical service areas outside the department include advancing the profession beyond the institution, engaging in outreach activities, contributing to the community, and consulting with industry, government, and health services.

Responsibility 7: Creating a Supportive Communication Climate

Supportive communication is descriptive rather than judgmental, problem oriented rather than accusatory and blaming, able to relate to others as equals rather than inferiors, and open to new information rather than dogmatic. In this supportive communication climate, the chair who has good listening skills demonstrates respect for and empowerment of faculty and students. In addition, departmental meetings are well planned and effectively conducted and problem solving is conducted in groups whenever appropriate.

Responsibility 8: Managing Conflict

Conflict can energize a group and assist its members in coming to a thoughtful, comprehensive decision characterized by ownership and commitment. However, chairs must manage conflict effectively, so that it does not become dysfunctional, and they must recognize the many levels of conflict. In an academic department, conflict may occur between colleagues or factions, creating a fragmented department; between faculty member and student; between faculty members and the dean; and between the chair and the dean.

Responsibility 9: Developing Chair Survival Skills

Chairs should have two sets of survival skills: time management and stress management. Good time management requires chairs to monitor how their time is spent, set priorities, handle paperwork efficiently, use their time to achieve important goals, and confront and overcome time wasters. Stress management includes three sets of strategies: somatic, or physiological (for example, relaxing, exercising, and watching one's diet); behavioral (for example, planning, organizing, creative problem solving, keeping the department informed, using low-stress communication, being a public relations agent for the department, delegating, and developing a support network); and cognitive (checking one's internal dialogue and developing realistic, positive self-messages).

Administrative Functions of Chairs

Chairs must also perform or delegate a number of administrative functions. Although these are not leadership functions per se, and are not measured directly by the leadership matrix, they must be performed well. Faculty must be treated equitably, care given to secretarial and staff needs, and sufficient time and respect given to student requirements. In considering which responsibilities are important and how well chairs' skills are developed, effective chairs will want to give attention to the administrative tasks listed here to ensure that faculty, staff, and student morale are not negatively affected.

Considerable portions of several of these tasks can be computerized and some of the chair's time-consuming, uninteresting burden of paperwork can be eliminated. Roper (1993, p. 8) has categorized the types of data that come across a chair's desk and has shown what can be handled by computer.

Budget: observing how different budget categories are being depleted.

Teaching: keeping track of enrollments, grades, and teaching assignments.

Students: keeping track of progress.

Alumni: updating alumni addresses, jobs, and donations to the department.

Faculty: evaluating faculty and tracking faculty data

Space: easy alteration of building plans showing locations of people and equipment.

Once the information for such activities is computerized, new chairs can have the necessary computer skills built into their orientation sessions. Roper (1992), who is head of a physics department, has also listed and discussed the software packages he has used for data-based management. Software for the user-friendly Macintosh is also available for such tasks as developing departmental teaching schedules. Of course, considerable variability is to be expected in terms of chair preferences for using computers for tracking departmental data. Another possibility is simply delegating the computerized portion of the paperwork to a computer technician, an assistant, or a secretary.

Here are the chair's seven major administrative tasks. While some can be delegated, others require the chair's ongoing insight and judgment.

1. *Prepare teaching schedules.* What a faculty member teaches and when he or she teaches it are high-priority items to faculty. In setting up course offerings, a chair must deal with faculty preferences, the number of sections offered, the time slots for courses, student needs, conflicting needs and desires of other departments, and input from the dean, who tries to establish equity.

2. *Ensure teaching effectiveness of adjunct and part-time faculty.* This administrative activity includes recruitment, selection, assignment, and orientation of adjunct and part-time faculty. In addition, chairs must find ways of helping these faculty members feel a part of the department and must evaluate their classroom effectiveness.

3. *Manage graduate assistants.* Skills for recruitment, selection, assignment, orientation, training, integration of assistants into the department, observation and feedback, and evaluation are all needed to work with these junior colleagues.

4. *Manage administrative assistants, a department secretary, and clerical assistants.* In large departments, a chair often depends heavily upon the responsibility and competence of an administrative assistant, the department secretary, and clerical staff for smooth, effective functioning of the department. In smaller departments, staff will be more limited. But whatever the departmental size, defining responsibilities, motivating, developing commitment, providing feedback, and evaluating are all part of effective supervision of all nonacademic personnel. When staff are unhappy, productivity in the department is affected and students are poorly served.

5. *Perform personnel decision making.* In almost all institutions, chairs have the responsibility of providing the administration with data about faculty activities and other evaluation information for personnel decision making. The chair is also responsible for keep-

ing faculty informed about criteria for personnel decision making and what the chair will require in order to recommend a faculty member for continuation, tenure, or promotion. Documenting this information and the writing of recommendations are also significant administrative tasks the chair must perform.

6. *Revise the curriculum.* One of the chair's key administrative tasks is to initiate a periodic review of the curriculum. This typically involves updating courses, eliminating overlap, ensuring that the curriculum is consonant with the goals of the department, and frequently, resolving territorial issues among faculty.

7. *Manage the budget.* Obtaining necessary resources for the department is often perceived as one of the chair's most important tasks. While there is considerable variation in the way institutional budgets are prepared and the actual role a chair may have, preparing the departmental budget, sharing information with faculty, and allocating resources are basic steps in the process.

These lists of leadership responsibilities and management tasks to be accomplished by department chairs may be used in several ways. Our focus here is on how chairs and others can use them to determine the leadership responsibilities that ought to be a high priority in their departments. Then chairs must determine which of their needed leadership skills are well developed and which ones need further work. When one or more of the administrative tasks has particular importance in a chair's department, or if compelling circumstances make an administrative task a significant issue, work on that task can be included in the chair's leadership portfolio as a way of documenting what was accomplished during his or her term of office.

Rating the Nine Leadership Responsibilities on the Leadership Matrix

Whether the individual rating the leadership responsibilities is a chair, a dean, or a faculty member, the steps involved in determining what is important in a department and how satisfied the rater is with the chair's current level of leadership development remain the same.

1. The individual rates each of the nine leadership responsibilities on a scale from 1 to 4, in terms of their importance to the department. A rating of 4 means that the responsibility is very important to the department at this time. A rating of 1 means that the responsibility is not currently important to the department. The rater enters this number on an individual rating sheet (see Exhibits 2.1 to 2.9).

2. The rater reviews the nine leadership responsibilities again, this time rating his or her degree of satisfaction with the chair's current level of skill development in each responsibility. Again, a rating of 4 means that a rater is very satisfied that a chair's skills are well developed; a rating of 1 indicates low satisfaction. The rater also enters this number on the individual rating sheet.

3. The rater plots the intersection of the two ratings, responsibility importance and rater satisfaction, for each of the nine leadership responsibilities, plotting each intersection on a separate copy of the leadership matrix. For example, if a rater feels that leadership responsibility 1, Leading the Department, is quite important at this time, he or she might rate it 4. That rating would place it near the top of the matrix on the vertical axis (see Figure 2.1). If the rater also feels that the chair's leadership ability in leading the department is excellent, that rating will be a 4 on the horizontal axis of the matrix. The intersection of the two numbers will fall high in cell B. The message to the chair in this case is, savor your success and maintain your effectiveness in overall leadership of the department.

The ratings plotted on the matrix for each responsibility enable a chair to compare a rater's perceptions of how important a responsibility is with the rater's satisfaction with the chair's skill development in each leadership responsibility. The results of each comparison will fall into one of the four cells. A result in cell A indicates an opportunity for leadership development, that is, the rater finds the responsibility to be of high importance to the depart-

Figure 2.1. Completed Leadership Matrix.

Leadership Matrix 1: Leading the Department
Importance of Leadership Responsibility and Perceived Skill Level of Chair
(Plot Ratings in Appropriate Cells)

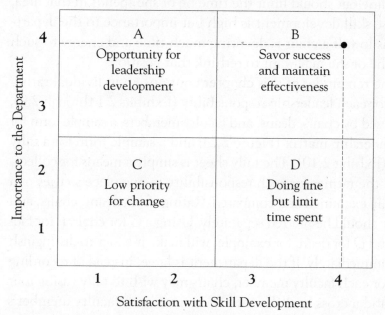

Satisfaction with Skill Development

ment but also finds that the chair's skills for taking on that responsibility are low. Cell A rankings deserve the most thoughtful attention of the four cells and require the generation of ideas for creating change.

A result in cell B, as in the earlier example, indicates that chairs have highly developed skills for handling the leadership tasks being rated and that these tasks are important to the department. Chairs should, however, continue to think about ways to maintain their competence in handling these responsibilities.

When the intersection of ratings falls in cell C, it indicates a low priority for change. This cell includes responsibilities in which the chair's skills are considered low but the responsibilities themselves are not rated as particularly important. A chair does not necessarily have to be concerned about change in these areas. However, if this evaluation is based only on the chair's judgment, it may be useful to secure the perceptions of faculty and the dean about these items.

Finally, a result that falls in cell D suggests that the chair is doing fine but should limit the time he or she spends in that area, because skill development is high but importance to the department is low. If a chair is devoting much time and energy to such areas, he or she may want to rethink that position.

The remainder of this chapter contains an individual rating sheet for each leadership responsibility (Exhibits 2.1 through 2.9), to be used by chairs, deans, and faculty members; a sample form for the leadership matrix (Figure 2.2); and a sample form for a tally sheet (Exhibit 2.10). The tally sheet is simply a means for collecting all the ratings for each responsibility in one place so they can be easily examined and compared. Ratings from deans, chairs, and faculty should be plotted separately. Using a C for chair, F for faculty, and D for dean, for example, will make it easier to distinguish them immediately. If the department is large, instead of recording an F for each faculty member, chairs may wish to tally (using four ones and a cross bar) the intersection of each faculty member's scores (importance and satisfaction) in the appropriate cells. Finally, chairs should not compute means or averages, because the results of such computations will be meaningless.

Exhibit 2.1. Individual Rating Sheet 1: Leading the Department.

Leading the Department

A department chair is a team leader who creates a shared vision that challenges faculty members intellectually and emotionally. A chair empowers others by creating a learning environment in which individual self-development, encouraged and stimulated by colleagues, is enhanced through achievement of department and university goals. Problems come to be viewed through a positive, sophisticated lens that enables individuals to find opportunities in problems and identify resources for problem resolution. Department members feel a sense of accomplishment as goals that they have set jointly are achieved.

Importance Rating _____   Satisfaction Rating _____

Exhibit 2.2. Individual Rating Sheet 2: Motivating Faculty to Enhance Productivity.

Motivating Faculty to Enhance Productivity

Individuals are motivated to do those things that are rewarded. Although faculty are also influenced by individual and background factors, the focus here is on the chair's role in creating a climate that is conducive to ongoing faculty learning and accomplishments. The key productivity enhancing approaches available to a chair are setting goals jointly with faculty members and giving feedback on performance in a positive supportive climate. Department chairs must give special attention to faculty at certain career stages and with certain problems: for example, new and midcareer faculty and difficult colleagues.

Importance Rating _____   Satisfaction Rating _____

Exhibit 2.3. Individual Rating Sheet 3: Motivating Faculty to Teach Effectively.

Motivating Faculty to Teach Effectively.

Chairs need to create a departmental culture in which faculty improve their teaching effectiveness on an ongoing basis. There are many approaches by which chairs can motivate faculty to assume this development responsibility, such as making teaching excellence a high-priority goal in the department, requiring all applicants for faculty positions to make at least one presentation to faculty and students before receiving a faculty appointment, sponsoring workshops or sharing information on different aspects of teaching, developing a mentoring system, and using student evaluations as part of a process for instructional effectiveness.

Importance Rating _____   Satisfaction Rating _____

Exhibit 2.4. Individual Rating Sheet 4: Handling Faculty Evaluation and Feedback.

Handling Faculty Evaluation and Feedback

Chairs should create a learning environment that encourages colleague mentoring and observation and that values feedback as an opportunity for celebrating the things faculty are doing competently, for sharing teaching strategies that work, for determining effectiveness in scholarship and service, and for stimulating ideas for professional development.

Importance Rating _____   Satisfaction Rating _____

Exhibit 2.5. Individual Rating Sheet 5: Motivating Faculty to Increase Scholarship.

Motivating Faculty to Increase Scholarship

Chairs should create a departmental climate that is appropriate to the institutional and departmental missions of encouraging scholarship, whether as in the traditional view or as recently defined in *Scholarship Reconsidered* (Boyer, 1990), which broadens the scope of acceptable research. In some colleges with a clearly defined teaching mission, scholarship required may simply be that faculty be on the cutting edge of their disciplines. In those comprehensive universities that are placing an increasing emphasis on research and publication, the chair is responsible for introducing techniques that address the process of writing, as an aid for those who have not recently published.

Importance Rating _____   Satisfaction Rating _____

Exhibit 2.6. Individual Rating Sheet 6: Motivating Faculty to Increase Service.

Motivating Faculty to Increase Service

The chair should get everyone to take a fair share of responsibility for accomplishing the work of the department and of the discipline. Effective chairs encourage the faculty to assume the role of consultant, mentor, leader, adviser, or departmental or disciplinary representative and to see that these activities balance teaching and scholarship and are consonant with the mission of the department. Typical service areas outside the department include advancing the profession beyond the institution, engaging in outreach activities, contributing to the community, and consulting with industry, government, and health services.

Importance Rating _____   Satisfaction Rating _____

Exhibit 2.7. Individual Rating Sheet 7: Creating a Supportive Communication Climate.

Creating a Supportive Communication Climate

Supportive communication is descriptive rather than judgmental, problem oriented rather than accusatory and blaming, able to relate to others as equals rather than inferiors, and open to new information rather than dogmatic. In this supportive communication climate, the chair who has good listening skills demonstrates respect for and empowerment of faculty and students. In addition, departmental meetings are well planned and effectively conducted and problem solving is conducted in groups whenever appropriate.

Importance Rating _____   Satisfaction Rating _____

Exhibit 2.8. Individual Rating Sheet 8: Managing Conflict.

Managing Conflict

Conflict can energize a group and assist its members in coming to a thoughtful, comprehensive decision characterized by ownership and commitment. However, chairs must manage conflict effectively, so that it does not become dysfunctional, and they must recognize the many levels of conflict. In an academic department, conflict may occur between colleagues or factions, creating a fragmented department; between faculty member and student; between faculty members and the dean; and between the chair and the dean.

Importance Rating _____   Satisfaction Rating _____

Exhibit 2.9. Individual Rating Sheet 9: Developing Chair Survival Skills.

Chairs should have two sets of survival skills: time management and stress management. Good time management requires chairs to monitor how their time is spent, set priorities, handle paperwork efficiently, use their time to achieve important goals, and confront and overcome time wasters. Stress management includes three sets of strategies: somatic, or physiological (for example, relaxing, exercising, and watching one's diet), behavioral (for example, planning, organizing, creative problem solving, keeping the department informed, using low-stress communication, being a public relations agent for the department, delegating, and developing a support network), and cognitive (checking internal dialogue and developing realistic, positive self-messages).

Importance Rating _____   Satisfaction Rating _____

Exhibit 2.10. Tally Sheet.

Leadership responsibility to be evaluated:

　　Record ratings of chair, dean, and all individual faculty members on this sheet.

Chair's Importance Rating _____   Satisfaction Rating _____

Dean's Importance Rating _____   Satisfaction Rating _____

Individual Faculty   *Individual Faculty*
Importance Ratings   *Satisfaction Ratings*

  1. _____   _____
  2. _____   _____
  3. _____   _____
  4. _____   _____
  5. _____   _____
  6. _____   _____
  7. _____   _____
  8. _____   _____
  9. _____   _____
 10. _____   _____

Individual Faculty
Importance Ratings, Cont'd.

Individual Faculty
Satisfaction Ratings, Cont'd.

11. _____   _____
12. _____   _____
13. _____   _____
14. _____   _____
15. _____   _____

Use additional sheets as needed.

Figure 2.2. Leadership Matrix.

Leadership Responsibility to be evaluated: _____

Importance of Leadership Responsibility and Perceived Skill Level of Chair
(Plot Ratings in Appropriate Cells)

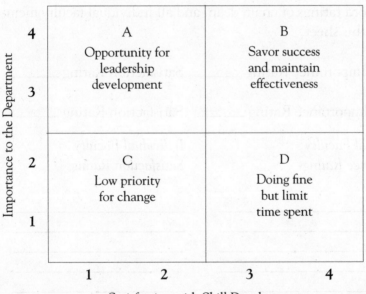

Satisfaction with Skill Development

Permission to reproduce the exhibits in this chapter and figure 2.2 is hereby granted.
Source: *Strengthening Departmental Leadership* by Ann F. Lucas. San Francisco: Jossey-Bass. Copyright © 1994.

Using Information from the Leadership Matrix to Identify Opportunities for Development

Once chairs have reviewed the completed matrices and looked at cell B to see where the match is good between the leadership responsibilities needed by their departments and the areas in which they have well-developed leadership skills, they will want to take time to celebrate the good news. This step is important and should not be skipped. Next, chairs should look at those ratings that intersect in cell A. The task facing chairs as they review the results in this cell is to think creatively about how they can enhance the leadership skills in which raters said the chair was not as strong as she or he should be. However, the chair should not try to work on enhancing too many leadership responsibilities at once, focusing instead on no more than two or three of the opportunities for leadership development that are shown in cell A. In addition to reviewing the appropriate chapters in this book, the chair can work on leadership development by attending workshops, reading books and articles, viewing videotapes, listening to audiotapes, seeking out knowledgeable colleagues who possess the skills the chair wants to develop or whose formal training gives them expertise, working closely with another experienced chair who is willing to serve as a mentor, and getting advice from the dean. When an institution wants to help a number of departmental chairs develop their leadership skills, a useful strategy is to arrange an on-site workshop taught by a consultant who knows both how to help chairs develop the necessary skills and how to tailor the workshop to satisfy the needs of chairs at the particular college or university. This is less expensive than paying for chairs to attend national or regional conferences, and small colleges could jointly sponsor a workshop facilitator.

Certainly, chairs will want to discuss some of these developmental tools with their deans, who may have additional suggestions for enhancing chairs' leadership competencies. Deans can perform specific interventions to assist chairs' leadership development—such as broadening chairs' assignments, suggesting individual development activities, and coaching chairs on the job—in order to give chairs experience in putting knowledge and skills into practice as they are acquired.

The Importance of Others' Perceptions

It is undoubtedly possible for chairs to develop and sharpen their leadership knowledge and skills entirely on their own. However, it will take longer than assisted development, and chairs may find that their perceptions about the impact of their behavior are not totally accurate. Clearly, members of any department have different judgments about task importance and their chair's demonstrated skill level; therefore, feedback is always useful. If a faculty member perceives his or her term as department chair as a professional growth experience and is willing to put a reasonable amount of trust in the department, he or she can benefit greatly from inviting faculty to share their perceptions. At the same time, this process of sharing views can also increase departmental team building.

Deans will also have a set of perceptions about how important these leadership tasks are for chairing a department and some thoughts about a chair's skill levels in each of these responsibilities. Deans can complete a set of leadership matrices then discuss similarities and differences with chairs. Out of this discussion should come an identification of the goals, action steps, timelines, and resources that will facilitate the chair's leadership development.

Conclusion

Using the leadership matrix brings structure to chairs' leadership development and typically has the following beneficial results for chairs, their departments, and their schools.

Departments and institutions reap the benefits of the enhanced productivity and accomplishment that are usually an outcome of goal setting.

Chairs, faculty, and deans are supplied with a process that encourages the sharing of expectations and needs. As chairs and deans share their perceptions at the beginning of each academic year their discussions can form the basis for team building, problem solving, and identification of needed resources.

Deans and chairs discuss and pinpoint areas for development for the next year or for a three- or four-year period. When such areas are behaviorally defined, they can be monitored and rewarded as departmental accomplishment as well as realistically based personal and professional development for the chair.

At the outset of the academic year, chairs and faculty members have a basis for discussing their perspectives on the leadership responsibilities of the chair and the leadership skills that might be targeted for development. Chairs and faculty have an opportunity to resolve differing points of view, request assistance, ask for ongoing feedback, and perform goal setting together. Communication about previously undiscussable issues is opened up. Adversarial postures are diminished, and a basis for team building can be established.

Ongoing feedback meetings with the department and the dean and a review of progress at the end of the academic year are encouraged. The benefits of these meetings are increased team building; provision of needed feedback to the chair, the department, and to the dean; maintenance of a supportive communication climate in the department and in the college; and a renewed commitment to or revision of the goals set through participative decision making.

Faculty members will be more willing to serve as department chair once the position is taken more seriously by the institution and the department and once professional leadership growth opportunities are built into the role. Moreover, any ambiguity about the responsibilities of the chair and the different perceptions the dean and the faculty have of the position will be openly discussed as an issue requiring problem solving.

Deans can become facilitators for developing pools of leadership talent in their colleges and universities, thus increasing the number of individuals who will go back into the department after a term as chair able to identify with the needs of their institution as well as of their department. These faculty with well-developed leadership skills will also be effective in conducting committee meetings, using appropriate problem-solving approaches to departmental issues, enhancing team building, and resolving conflict in the department and in the college.

Chairs, whether tenured full professors or untenured assistant professors, can view their time in office as a leadership growth opportunity, one from which they will profit no matter whether they choose to continue their development in preparation for further leadership roles in the academy or to become informal leaders in their institutions. They will have a leadership portfolio, based on action research, that they can present to college personnel committees and that might be given some weight in personnel decisions, such as merit increases.

In the next chapter, I discuss a transformational leadership model that distinguishes leaders from managers. Effective behaviors of academic chairs as leaders are described, along with the extraordinary impact that transformational leadership can have on a department.

Chapter Three

Leading the Academic Department

In colleges and universities with high-quality departments, professional development of faculty members is viewed as an important ongoing activity. Faculty teach effectively, share their successes, and view failures both as topics for problem solving with colleagues and as events from which they can learn. The department becomes a learning environment for both faculty and students, and faculty are involved in scholarly activities congruent with the institutional mission. (These activities are discussed in Chapter Seven.)

When departmental leadership is strong, the climate exudes excitement and enthusiasm about the work in which the department is engaged. It is the chair, functioning as a team leader, who creates this climate in which faculty members can be supportive of each other rather than defensive. The chair uses participative decision making so that faculty feel committed to the direction the department is taking and are, therefore, willing to take on their share of the work and feel a sense of accomplishment as goals that they have set jointly are achieved. Problems come to be viewed not as reasons for people to take sides and disrupt the department but as situations for individuals to find opportunities and identify resources for problem resolution. When conflict emerges, disagreements are fully aired because faculty recognize that, when different points of view are explored, the quality of decision making will be improved.

The chair has the major role in creating this kind of department. A chair empowers others by creating a learning organization, one characterized by individuals striving for personal mastery and team learning and a chair committed to self-discovery and self-growth. Learning, both personal and professional, is intentional in this department and goes far beyond knowing the discipline for which one has been educated. This learning is a commitment to excellence and to ongoing development as a lifelong enterprise. As Senge (1990, p. 153), the highly regarded author of *The Fifth Discipline*, has said so well, "Truly creative people use the gap between vision and current reality to generate energy for change." That energy to change is also the energy to learn.

Leadership Theories and Research and Academic Chairs

Although leadership is a well-researched topic about which much has been written and theorized in social and organizational psychology, history, and business, the complexity of the research makes it difficult to develop a final version of a leadership model that will apply specifically to academic chairs. Recent comprehensive review articles indicate some of the knotty issues to be resolved (Hollander & Offermann, 1990; Yukl, 1989), such as the integration of power and leadership and the methodological problem of measuring power. One unresolved issue to which academics can relate is the view of leadership as an interactive model in which leaders influence followers, while followers also influence leaders. An example of how a view of leadership as a two-way process of influence affects academic institutions is that the tradition of faculty autonomy has sometimes caused chairs and academic administrators to tread lightly in dealing with the poor performance of faculty members. Yet, as sometimes happens, if faculty justify poor teaching or lack of productivity under the rubric of academic freedom, chairs and administrators may adopt an increasingly autocratic leadership style. However, as department chairs look for a leadership model that might provide practical guidelines, the potential of transformational leadership, compared to transactional leadership, is impressive (Bass, 1990b). In the following discussion, we will look at three sources in particular for the characteristics of transformational leaders: Bass and his associates, Tichy and Devanna (1990), and Kouzes and Posner (1987).

Transformational leaders create a shared vision, energize others by communicating that vision at many levels, stimulate others to think in different ways and to excel, give individual consideration to others, and provide an organizational climate that helps others to accomplish activities of value and feel appreciated. In contrast, transactional leaders are managers who plan, organize, lead, staff, and control or monitor progress toward organizational goals. Although department chairs must perform some managerial functions, these functions are not a substitute for transformational leadership. Chairs must learn to be leaders and to view themselves as leaders. Moving the organization toward a shared vision characterizes transformational leaders, that is, their current choices are directed by their future goals. Maintaining the status quo characterizes transactional leaders or managers, that is, their decision making is guided by past practices—"how things are done around here." As they maintain a steady-state organization, transactional leaders generally motivate desired performances by offering rewards. The transactional department chair might say, "If you publish four articles in refereed journals, I will recommend you for promotion"; or (in a community college), "If your teaching is excellent, if you complete ten additional graduate credits, if you chair a committee on curriculum revision, and contribute sufficient additional service to the department, I will recommend you for promotion."

Amid all the complex theorizing about leadership, Bass and his associates have been studying transformational leaders and collecting some hard data. Bass has found that transformational leaders have followers who perform at a higher level and who are more satisfied with their work than other employees (Bass, 1985a, 1985b; Hater & Bass, 1988). Such leaders are also more likely to be judged to be top performers (Hater & Bass, 1988) and to have potential for advancement by the people to whom they report (Bass & Avolio, 1990).

Tichy and Devanna (1990, pp. 271–280) have described a similar set of characteristics that differentiate transformational from transactional leaders. Transformational leaders identify themselves as change agents; are courageous risk takers; believe in people and work toward the empowerment of others; are value driven; are lifelong learners; have the ability to deal with complexity, ambiguity, and uncertainty; and are visionaries.

Thus, the chair in the psychology department in the following example was clearly functioning as a transformational leader when she helped a faculty member keep the department's shared vision in mind while she also made him feel appreciated. The department, in a comprehensive university, was preparing for a American Psychological Association accreditation visit to the department's new doctoral program. The faculty member arrived about twenty minutes late for a meeting on curriculum revision. He was very agitated and his opening statement was, "I've been driving around the parking lot for thirty minutes looking for a parking space. If the university can't provide me with a space, I'm going to resign from this committee." The department chair, who was leading the meeting, responded slowly and with dignity, "Ken, I know that the parking situation is abominable! We're all having problems with it. But the work of this committee is a high priority for all of us, and we value the contributions you make to our decisions." The faculty member, somewhat mollified, sat down, seemingly more in control of his anger. While acknowledging the reality of the problem that had exasperated the faculty member and expressing recognition for his work on the committee, the chair had still emphasized the importance of the vision for all of them.

This example shows only one of the many types of people problems chairs must deal with as department leaders. Unproductive faculty, difficult colleagues, midcareer faculty, and poor teachers represent particularly important challenges for any chair. Responding to questionnaire surveys I have conducted, more than two-thirds of 2,500 chairs have asserted that they have been unsuccessful in motivating one or more faculty members who fall into these categories. For chairs, the most frustrating department members seem to be those faculty who simply teach their classes—often not well—and then leave campus. These individuals seem not otherwise engaged in either scholarly or service activities of any kind. Further, chairs report that such behaviors are not confronted by anyone in a leadership position and, thus, might be said to be supported by the culture of the institution. How can a chair motivate unproductive faculty? In two studies that compared leaders who create a shared vision and communicate this vision to others to either high-task or high-relationship leaders, the only ones able to break down the negative culture of unproductive individuals were those who created and shared a vision, a trait characteristic of transformational leaders (Howell & Frost, 1989; Yukl & Van Fleet, 1982). Developing a vision for a department is one approach to involving faculty in setting goals.

Unless thoughtful departmental planning and goal setting are undertaken by a leader who believes in participative decision making, a department may simply maintain the status quo even when universities need to cope effectively with change. Furthermore, it is important that a chair be a transformational leader, since that is precisely the kind of leader who can perform these essential tasks: revitalize faculty and improve their professional development, act as a catalyst to improve the departmental culture, use the untapped talents of faculty, help faculty formulate departmental goals identifying new directions, and create a quality curriculum responsive to major changes in the discipline.

Given the promising research findings about transformational leadership, I have applied the transformational leadership model to the position of department chair. Specifically, because the model of transformational leadership presented by Kouzes and Posner (1987) is an excellent summary of the five major characteristics of such leaders, I have simply applied the headings they use and their model for the use of department chairs. (I presented an earlier version of this adaptation at the 1991 Kansas State University National Conference for Academic Chairpersons [Lucas, 1991].)

Of course, as discussed in Chapter One, chairs may hesitate to accept necessary leadership roles such as the professional development of faculty, feeling that such attempts would be unwelcome. Therefore, it is important that chairs consult with department members and with the dean (using the leadership matrix) about the chair's role as team leader.

A Model of Transformational Leadership for Departmental Chairs

The following behaviors are characteristic of academic chairs who become transformational leaders.

Challenging the Process

There is an old maxim in organizations that says, If it ain't broke, don't fix it. But a transformational leader engages in an ongoing quest for quality, looking for opportunities to make things better, whether or not they are obviously broken. In academe, as in most organizations, the way people function is a result of both formal and informal rules and procedures that their group follows. These rules and procedures are the norms that guide faculty behavior and have evolved over time from the departmental culture. Schein (1992, p. 12), who has written extensively on organizational culture, defines this culture as "a pattern of shared basic assumptions that the group learned as it solved its problems of external adaptation and internal integration, that has worked well enough to be considered valid and, therefore, to be taught to new members as the correct way to perceive, think, and feel in relation to those problems." The norms that evolve from the culture are typically not written down, but are tapped in such statements as, "In this department, it is all right to . . . ," or, "Something like that would never work in a place like this": statements that indicate a strong norm that would be hard to change. Departmental norms cover how acceptable colleague or chair observation of classroom teaching is, how grading is regarded, what a syllabus should look like, and whether faculty need to take office hours seriously. Norms also guide how faculty handle conflict and whether the chair can effectively confront a departmental member who is arbitrary and capricious in dealings with students.

Even within a university, there may be considerable variability in the norms that exist from one department to another. The extent to which departmental responsibilities are shared by faculty, for example, will differ greatly from department to department. There are departments in some universities in which it is rarely necessary to cancel a class because faculty conscientiously substitute for a colleague who is ill or attending a conference. If a guest should visit faculty offices over a weekend in some departments, at least several faculty members will be there working on their research. These are behaviors guided by norms.

Much of individuals' resistance to change comes from their experience within the life of a group; they understand about previous methods of doing things that have solved certain problems, mutual expectations, and longstanding relationships that have developed over time. For example, if a department has once witnessed a shouting match between two faculty members at a department meeting, an incident uncomfortable for all who witnessed it, that department may well have developed a norm of going to great lengths to avoid conflict.

Such well-established methods of handling issues are created not only through the evolution and history of a department but also by the kind of leaders it has had. Departmental chairs have a significant role to play in motivating faculty because they can either perpetuate the existing climate or confront it and its positive and negative norms. A challenging task for the chair is to help faculty identify departmental norms and to ask whether these norms work to the good or the detriment of the department. A transformational leader will know his or her organization's norms and culture very well but will also be willing to risk challenging those norms when they are negative or dysfunctional. Offering what could be useful advice for chairs, Schein (1992, p. 15) writes, "The bottom line for leaders is that if they do not become conscious of the cultures in which they are embedded, those cultures will manage them. Cultural understanding is desirable for all of us, but it is essential to leaders if they are to lead."

Sometimes, norms exist in a culture about which faculty are resentful, but the culture and its norms are not questioned because they are considered undiscussible. For example, a difficult matter for a new chair to handle is the faculty member who has a feeling of entitlement and who expects special privileges. Consider the case of Randolph Erwin, an untenured member of a history and political science department. Through family connections at the United Nations, he is often able to invite to his class diplomats and others who function at second- or third-level positions in representing their countries. These individuals' lectures at the university have been the subject of articles in local newspapers, increasing the public visibility of the institution. On occasion, the president of the university has even telephoned the department to talk to Erwin about making arrangements for the president to have dinner with Erwin and his guest. However, in return for sharing his connections with the university, Erwin expects special privileges. Although the university requires all faculty members to have at least a three-day schedule on campus, Erwin insists that he teach only two days a week. He also will not teach more than one evening, and that evening must fall on one of the two days he is on campus. Erwin also wants two sections of the same course to be offered back to back in the daytime. However, student enrollment for his sections, which was excellent the first year he was at the university, has plummeted. Based on enrollment for these sections during the same semester last year, offering two sections of the same course is not justified. Erwin does not accept this reasoning; instead, he states with conviction that more students will be taking his course next semester, though he offers no evidence for his belief. When the new chair refused to give him a two-day schedule, Erwin accused the chair of being unreasonable and pointed out that the former chair always gave him such a schedule. The new chair's response was, "That may be, but projected enrollment warrants that only one section be offered."

Requests for special treatment occur at many institutions for many reasons unconnected with scholarship. Because such special treatment for nonacademic reasons is unfair, other faculty resent these exceptions yet dare not object too openly. In this case, the chair confronted the norm that had existed, gave a rationale for the new decision, and refused to budge. When Erwin complained to other faculty members about this treatment, a few sympathized, but most reinforced what the chair had told him, that enrollment figures did not justify offering the two sections he wanted. Thus, the established norm of giving special entitlements for nonacademic reasons was confronted and changed.

In order to challenge norms that are deeply embedded in the culture, chairs must take risks. It is easier to take a stand when a chair can refer to an objective statement of principles that is available in a printed document that applies to all, a faculty handbook for example. Without such support, there is always the risk that an individual may indeed have leverage with a higher authority and the chair will be forced to back down. Thus, chairs who are leaders must be courageous individuals. In taking positions, they must be prudent risk takers, willing to stand against the status quo in the larger interest of the organization. Moreover, when chairs encourage faculty to confront negative or dysfunctional norms, they must be prepared to be supportive, because the confrontation process is often painful for faculty.

In encouraging faculty to be think creatively and to take risks, chairs need to have a high tolerance for mistakes, both their own and those of others. Not every new thing that is attempted will work in practice, but the important thing is to establish a climate in which an idea that appears reasonable will be tried. Indeed, one of the differences between effective and ineffective leaders is that effective leaders learn from their mistakes. Ineffective leaders make the same mistake again and again (Kouzes and Posner, 1987, pp. 284–286). Failure must be regarded as "simply, a shortfall, evidence of the gap between vision, and current reality. Failure is an opportunity for learning—about inaccurate pictures of current reality, about strategies that didn't work as expected, about the clarity of the vision. Failures are not about our unworthiness or powerlessness" (Senge, 1990, p. 154).

Inspiring a Shared Vision

Researchers who have used the transformational leadership model, as well as many who simply describe effective leadership during a period of change, agree that an important leadership characteristic is the ability to create a shared vision. A vision in this instance is simply a picture of the future that individuals want to create; in other words, it describes what the department would look like if it were all the things chair and faculty want it to be. A vision motivates because it provides a challenge that can mobilize the organization and its people and because it increases self-esteem among the faculty. A vision can provide both a dream of what the organization will be in the future, and a look at what is required in order to get there. An effective vision appeals to both the intellect and the emotions; the two combined can create strong positive motivation.

How does a chair create a vision? Although creating a vision or a mission sounds very abstract, it is a process frequently used in the nonacademic world, and it can be replicated step by step in an academic department. Chairs need to plan the process carefully, however, and anticipate some faculty resistance. Thus, faculty need to be prepared for and supported in creating a dream out of which a mission statement can be developed.

The leadership literature tells us that people are more creative when they are looking at the future as they want it to be rather than retelling war stories about how bad things are. Thus, chairs must move toward a dream, not just away from pain. Out of this dream or vision will come some concrete plans and implementation steps, with assignment of particular responsibilities and agreed-upon methods for assessment of results.

Initially, the chair must talk about the process with several informal leaders in the department. He or she gets their support before announcing at a departmental meeting the purpose of the process, what is to be accomplished, and the methodology to be used. Next, the chair forms a committee of three or four individuals to help plan for and set up the departmental meeting. Some departments have funding available for an off-site retreat to formulate or revisit a mission statement and set goals. Others must make do with one all-day meeting in a classroom and several shorter follow-up meetings. Wherever the meeting is held, preparing faculty and developing faculty ownership by getting them involved in planning the meeting, and conducting the meeting in ways that encourage openness and cooperation are crucial elements for success. Setting an agenda for a one- or two-day meeting helps allay any faculty concerns about meeting to create a vision. Items for inclusion might be

1. How do we want things to be? How are they now? Analyze gaps.
2. Evaluate data. Prioritize issues.
3. Set goals for each issue. Develop action steps and time lines.
4. Evaluate progress.
5. Identify follow-up steps. Who has responsibility for what? Set dates for progress reports.

If a chair does not think that he or she can pull this off, another member of the department or an outside facilitator can be asked to handle the meeting. When the faculty come together, the chair must create an environment conducive to the success of this kind of participative meeting, paying attention to such details as seating (arranging chairs in a U-shape allows all attendees to see each other and leaves a space for the chair or facilitator to conduct the meeting and record ideas on a flip chart), serving tea and coffee, and personally greeting people as they arrive.

The chair opens the meeting by setting a framework and describing to faculty the goals and ground rules of the meeting. The chair states that, since an ongoing goal is to create a quality department, this meeting has been set aside for that specific purpose. One way to approach that purpose is to look at what might be, to do some "visioning" and to think about what advances have been made in the discipline, what might be done to stay on the cutting edge, and whether there are directions that might more completely utilize the talents of the faculty.

The chair, or the facilitator, then leads a brainstorming discussion, first discussing, if need be, the value of brainstorming in unleashing creativity. Faculty members need to be reminded that, while everyone is creative, creativity is frequently inhibited because people have been educated and socialized to be self-critical and to criticize the ideas of others. Moreover, making spontaneous comments that have not been carefully evaluated ahead of time, in a group of one's colleagues, particularly when these colleagues are perceived to be critical, is risk taking.

Participants are then given specific permission to participate. They are told that all ideas are acceptable and that they will be experimenting in the departmental use of the brainstorming method, which is used widely in developing mission statements. Afterwards, they will have a chance to evaluate its effectiveness. The introduction should encourage each person to feel free to offer ideas without defending them and without being critical of any other individual. This is the primary guideline for encouraging creative thinking. Participants should be told that ideas will be recorded on the flip chart to develop a permanent record of the discussion that can later be computerized. The goal is to generate as many ideas as possible. Because critiquing dries up the creative juices, the critique will come after the brainstorming.

Chairs can use the following questions, which are often posed to stimulate thinking about how things might be, to guide the brainstorming session.

What would this department look like if it were functioning better?

What dysfunctional behavior would disappear and what positive behaviors would take its place? What would these behaviors look like, sound like, feel like? (For example, I would not feel tense before a departmental meeting.)

You're looking at this department two years down the road, two good years. What do you see?

Discussion of such questions can develop a departmental vision, create excitement, mobilize energy and effort, and motivate faculty to search for strategies to accomplish the scenarios they imagine. The vision will contain an implicit mission statement, for embedded in every vision is a sense of what kind of department faculty want at some point in the future.

Once quite a few ideas have been generated and the group seems to have "run dry," the chair distributes one or two pages of the flip chart on which ideas have been recorded to each of several small groups. Each of the groups categorizes the ideas into three or four areas or issues. Finally, representatives from each group meet in another small group to develop consensus on goals and to prioritize them. The results are then presented to the entire group of participants for agreement and for conversion into goals and action steps.

This scenario building allows faculty to see things not as they are but as they could be. It spurs creativity and generates excitement. Once scenarios have been generated and preferred goals selected, action plans can turn those scenarios into a viable agenda. In this step, initial formulations should be stated as outcomes; for example, a management department might sum up a goal this way: "Create a Human Resource Development Program as a center of excellence"; a chemistry department might say, "Establish closer ties with local pharmaceutical companies so mutual benefits can result." The action steps that follow need to be specific, measurable, realistic, and set in a reasonable time frame.

Finally, the chair and the faculty turn goals into action plans, with faculty deciding who will be responsible for what and how success will be measured. For example, the implementation steps for one of the chemistry department's goals were to set up an advisory board from pharmaceutical companies for a discussion of the curriculum, to exchange lecturers, and to start a monthly newsletter for "Friends of the Chemistry Department." The ultimate result of setting this goal was that pharmaceutical houses donated equipment to the university, faculty engaged in collaborative research with industry, adjunct faculty from industry were hired, faculty consulting increased, department graduates were placed in jobs, and sabbatical internships for faculty were arranged.

The people who have been most involved during the brainstorming phase often become so enthusiastic that they are quite willing to volunteer to assume important responsibilities for parts of the action plan. (However, if a chair knows from past experience that some individuals lose their enthusiasm for new ideas quickly, they can be teamed with others who have more staying power.)

When a chair decides to conduct a departmental meeting to create a vision, mission statement, goals, and action plans, he or she should follow the rule of never letting the person to whom one reports be surprised. It is clearly appropriate, and advantageous, to discuss such a meeting with the dean before beginning. The dean can give the chair a clearer idea of available resources for both holding the meeting and achieving the goals that are set. Moreover, letting the dean know the chair's purpose and goals in this undertaking ensures that the dean will not hear a distorted version of it first from someone else.

However chairs go about it, there is an important value in developing departmental goals faculty have participated in formulating. Such activities can be revitalizing, even for faculty members who have been apathetic, and creating a vision can set fire even to a previously unproductive group.

Enabling Others to Act

The third characteristic of chairs as transformational leaders is their ability to recognize that exciting ideas can be generated by faculty and students as well as by those appointed to leadership positions. When individuals with creative ideas approach chairs, all chairs need to do to translate innovative thoughts into actions is to empower these individuals to act. Along with transformational leadership, empowerment is an important concept that is being actively developed in theories of organizational psychology at present. Power is the ability to influence others to accomplish goals, and it is important to recognize that, in this view, power is not a zero-sum game. It is not a finite resource like energy. It does not come in fixed amounts, so that the more power a given faculty member has, the less power is left for the chair. Rather, power can be increased when it is shared, and when two individuals have power, they can accomplish more than either could alone.

Faculty can be empowered when a chair simply listens to their ideas, and then asks, What would it take to do that? How would you begin? How can I help you do that? and, How will you know if it has worked? Such questions often push a faculty member to think ideas through more completely. There are times when innovative ideas can simply be implemented without anyone's permission, but without support a creative idea often dies aborning. When someone an individual respects takes what that individual has to say seriously, that is an empowering act. Under this circumstance, individuals often discover there is nothing to stop their doing what they think should be or could be done.

An example of empowerment of a faculty member in a community college occurred when the chair of a management department asked a full-time faculty member, Suzanne Bright, to observe a class taught by a new part-timer, Michael Enright. During the classroom visit, Bright observed that, while Enright had very good potential as an instructor, several things, which were simply a reflection of his inexperience, reduced his teaching effectiveness. When Bright conducted the feedback interview with Enright, she discovered that he had several questions about teaching she could easily answer. In turn, Bright discovered that Enright used materials developed by his full-time employer that Bright felt would be useful in her classes. The interview went very well, and Enright was very receptive to Bright's suggestions. When Bright reported this observation and discussion to the chair, she was so enthusiastic she suggested that each department member work closely with one part-timer in his or her area of specialization. The chair asked her to present the idea at the next department meeting. Bright did and became coordinator of an adopt-an-adjunct project, which then resulted in closer ties between full- and part-time faculty and a drop in the turnover rate of adjuncts.

Other empowering behaviors that develop self-efficacy in others are described by Bandura (1982), who suggests four means of providing empowering information to others: by providing positive emotional support when others are under stress; by generally being supportive and offering words of encouragement; by providing successful role models; and by creating actual successful experiences or small steps taken toward the accomplishment of a goal.

The latter method, creating and rewarding small wins, is the most effective method of empowering others. For example, Kevin

Sinclair, a junior faculty member, was trying to establish himself as a researcher. However, during the same week that he was scheduled for his interview with the chair about his progress towards tenure, he received his third rejection for an article submitted to a prestigious journal. Although Sinclair recognized that the journals he had applied to were highly selective, he felt that having his work accepted by a well-regarded journal would provide quick prestige for him. Therefore, his strategy had been to send his paper to the most prestigious journal first, then to the next, and so on down the line. However, several months passed before he received a response from each journal and went on to the next, and he was now in a position of not having published anything for two years. When the chair asked if she could read the article Sinclair had submitted, she was able to give him some very positive feedback about the quality of what he had done and to suggest a few changes that would enhance its acceptability. She was also able to recommend other journals, which had a higher acceptance rate, to which he could submit the paper. Lastly, she indicated that once he had a publication record, it would be easier for his work to be accepted by more highly regarded journals. When Sinclair's paper was accepted by one of the journals she had recommended, she sponsored a small wine and cheese party in the department to celebrate his success.

Modeling the Way

One difficult challenge for chairs is the need to model the positive norms that they would like to characterize the departmental culture. Whether these norms be in teaching, research, or service, part of the way in which chairs establish a healthy, positive culture into which new faculty can be integrated is to demonstrate effective behaviors themselves.

Chairs who are generally upbeat and positive in their thinking and in conversations with faculty can create a climate that discourages dwelling on the old stories about unresponsive administration, budget cuts, or "the impossible task of working with the kind of students we get." Such negativity can keep everyone feeling discouraged about accomplishing anything. A positive climate is created when a problem-solving approach is developed that has an underlying theme that might be stated this way: we are an intelligent group of people who know how to solve problems. Let us put our heads together to see what we can come up with.

Instead of fixing blame, creative problem solvers confront difficulties directly, involve others in identifying the core problem, and then brainstorm alternatives until they come up with high-quality solutions that generate ownership and commitment from faculty. Since little time and energy are wasted on fixing blame, such an approach also eliminates a good chunk of the conflict that goes on in a department. (This approach of looking at processes and procedures to discover what needs to be changed, rather than blaming individuals, is also an important part of Total Quality Management.) (Additional examples of the chair as role model will be found in Chapters Five and Seven.)

Encouraging the Heart

The final characteristic of transformational leaders to be discussed here is that they believe in people. They find ways of celebrating accomplishments and reinforcing small wins. They recognize that change occurs through the experience of success with new behaviors. In short, they encourage the heart, or as Irwin Federman, CEO of Monolithic Memories, a very successful high-tech company puts it, "If you think about it, we love others, not for who they are, but for how they make us feel. In order to willingly accept the direction of another individual, it must make you feel good to do so. . . . If you believe what I'm saying, you cannot help but come to the conclusion that those you have followed gladly, passionately, zealously—have made you feel like somebody. . . . This business of making another feel good in the unspectacular course of his daily comings and goings is, in my view, the very essence of leadership" (Bennis & Nanus, 1985, pp. 64–65).

In some departments, colleagues give little recognition to one another for an accomplishment. A couple of years ago, I met on a campus a professor whom I recognized because I had seen her on a recent talk show. The author of a number of scholarly books, she had been invited to be a guest on a television program because her latest book contained a vast amount of information useful to several professional groups and also of interest to the general public. I stopped her, introduced myself, and congratulated her on the book. After thanking me, she said that no one in her department had spoken to her about her publication and the interest it was generating. It seemed clear that, despite her accomplishment and the public recognition she had received, lack of recognition from her departmental colleagues had left a vacuum.

Contrast this with an incident at a state university. A young faculty member had just had his first acceptance of an article in a refereed journal, and he was clearly ecstatic as he shared the information with one or two people in his department. The next day, when he arrived on campus, he found his office filled with balloons, which spilled out as he opened the door. The message he got was one of acceptance, genuine caring, and congratulations for an accomplishment the people in the department were proud of.

Encouraging the heart deals with the whole question of motivation. What motivates faculty members? A chance to feel intellectually and emotionally challenged by their work, to perceive opportunities for personal and professional growth, to participate in decisions affecting their own development, to feel that they are part of an important ongoing enterprise, to know that they make a difference, and to be given recognition and visibility—to the extent that these conditions are true in academe, faculty will be motivated. (Faculty motivation is also discussed in Chapters Four, Five, Six, and Seven.)

Some motivational and supportive activities require the chair to be a mentor, a role with which chairs are often uncomfortable, particularly when some faculty members are senior to them. Nevertheless, faculty need to grow professionally, and if a chair cannot take on this function for some individuals, senior faculty in the department can assume this responsibility. The chair simply needs to arrange it.

Conclusion

Transformational leaders are both desperately needed and more likely to emerge in periods of distress and rapid change. Because higher education is currently in the throes of such a period, this is the time for chairs and faculty to seek change, value it as healthy, respond to it, and fully exploit it as an opportunity. Some of the reasons why the need for leadership in higher education is so compelling have already been presented. But what can academic administrators do to develop the needed leaders, and how can chairs and deans manage their own professional development?

Kanter (1983, p. 209) has written that "what it takes to get the innovating organization up and running is essentially the same two things all vehicles need: a person in the driver's seat and a source of power." Explaining the sources of a leader's power, Kanter (1983, p. 159) states that "organizational power tools consist of supplies of three 'basic commodities' that can be invested in action: information (data, technical knowledge, political intelligence, expertise); resources (funds, materials, space, time); and support (endorsement, backing, approval, legitimacy)."

Department chairs cannot be effective unless they are empowered by administration and supplied with these three basic commodities. Relevant information and resources must be shared with them, and chairs must know that the dean or vice president stands behind them. On the administrative level, deans must not permit faculty members to complete end-runs around the chair to the dean. On the administrative level, if a faculty member is late in submitting a class roster or a book order, it is the chair, not the department secretary, who should be informed. Such failures to deal directly with the chair erode the chair's power, as do any instructions from a dean or vice president for academic affairs to a department secretary rather than to a chair. People in the institution should be knowledgeable about who is running the department. And, most importantly, chairs should not receive information about events from the secretarial grapevine or their own faculty before they are officially informed about those events.

An institutional supportive communication climate must be created so that deans' meetings for chairs can be problem-solving forums to which chairs can freely bring issues that concern them. When such meetings are regularly used by deans simply to provide information, input from chairs is cut off, and they leave feeling frustrated and disenfranchised. Institutional leaders must take an active part in informing department chairs about what the role of the chair entails. Although administrators may differ from faculty in their views of the chair's position, chairs, deans, and faculty all need to confront the issue of role and expectations. A chair needs to face any ambiguities from the outset, and since most chairs have little prior experience in administration, some mechanism must be put in place so that the chair can become effective quickly. There is a body of knowledge about chair leadership to be learned, from sources such as this book. Task and process functions (sometime called the structural and individual consideration) of leadership need to be developed. There are also skills to be acquired in communicating, team building, motivating faculty, enhancing the quality of teaching, problem solving, performance counseling, handling feedback interviews, resolving conflicts, third-party mediating, negotiating, and confronting dysfunctional behavior. As mentioned earlier, essential skills and concepts can be mastered through reading, attending conferences, talking to colleagues who are also chairs, role-playing or rehearsing behavior, and attending workshops and conferences. The latter also help chairs to create a support network.

Some chairs have benefited from having more experienced chairs as mentors, others from overlapping terms in which a new chair serves as deputy chair for one semester (or in a large department, for one year), still others from support groups of chairs within their institution.

The leadership matrix also provides an important approach to facilitating leadership development. The development of mutually agreed upon goals not only has the advantage of keeping dean, chair, and faculty focused on learning and problem solving but also increases all parties' awareness of the support system needed to make the institution operate effectively and to achieve maximum professional growth.

Finally, one of the important functions of leaders is to motivate others. Chapter Four discusses the factors that motivate faculty and what the department chair can do, based on motivational research, to encourage faculty to achieve departmental goals as they accomplish their own goals.

Chapter Four

Motivating, Evaluating, and Rewarding Faculty Members

When I have asked department chairs what it would take to create a quality department, the answers usually center around motivating faculty members to be more effective teachers; more productive scholars; more committed to departmental goals, including outreach activities; and more willing to accept their share of departmental work, that is, serve on committees or handle more student advising.

What does it take to motivate faculty? At a workshop I conducted recently, a dean stated, "Chairs don't have to be concerned about motivating faculty. Faculty motivate themselves." The dean's statement has a kernel of truth in it and may be believed by many; yet it is only part of the picture, for many factors external to individuals also affect their behavior.

Techniques That Increase Faculty Productivity and Prevent Alienation

In this chapter, a number of elements related to motivating faculty will be discussed. The overriding principle, however, is that individuals are motivated to do those things that are rewarded. Much of the controversy about why faculty in doctorate-granting and comprehensive institutions do not devote more time to teaching undergraduate students can be explained by the fact that research, not undergraduate teaching, has been the institutional basis for positive decisions about tenure, promotion, and merit. This principle is delightfully summarized in the title of an article written a number of years ago and called, "On the Folly of Rewarding A, While Hoping for B" (Kerr, 1975). Behavior that is rewarded is the behavior to which faculty will devote their time and effort.

As this chapter will show, many variables typically have formed, and continue currently to shape, faculty members' individual motivation, and faculty may be viewed as the center of an open-ended system that is influenced by a number of elements in their lives, including those factors responsible for their being attracted to and remaining in academe. Next, the discussion emphasizes the ways in which faculty in general, new faculty, and tenured faculty are motivated by the department and by the chair. The key approaches available to a chair to enhance faculty productivity are goal setting, evaluating performance, and rewarding performance. What are the steps in using goal setting both as a faculty development tool and as the basis for performance evaluation? How can the goal setting process prevent alienation? How can written annual faculty development goals reduce the need for disciplinary interviews? All of these questions will be discussed, and the chapter will close with some suggestions for motivating two special groups: midcareer faculty and difficult colleagues. (Motivating faculty in the specific areas of teaching, scholarship, and service will be discussed in Chapters Five, Six, and Seven.)

What Motivates Faculty?

Chairs can think about each faculty member as the center of an open system with semipermeable boundaries. Faculty are subjected to ever-widening circles of influence from within and outside of these borders. Beginning with individual faculty members themselves, chairs can observe that faculty members' abilities, knowledge, skills, values, interests, personal aspirations, age, health, financial concerns, and scholarly discipline all have an impact on their motivation. Family, friends, and former teachers have had a place in molding faculty members' values and aspirations and have influenced the effort faculty are willing to expend on their careers. And of course, a faculty member's performance in teaching, scholarship, and service is significantly affected by departmental culture, norms, and expectations. However, for some faculty, the scholarly discipline is a more potent motivational force than the department, and this is particularly true when individuals receive national recognition for achievement but no departmental or institutional recognition.

More remote as a stimulating force, yet still important, is the university climate, which is shaped by the degree of faculty involvement in governance, the economic conditions of the geographic region, the "market value" of a particular discipline, the national reputation of the university, the respect it has generated in the local or regional community, and the quality of students it attracts. The final factors that cross the boundaries of the open-ended system are the forces in the outside world that affect education: for example, the extensive criticism directed at higher education by the general public, education commissions, state departments of higher education, and the federal government; the reduced funding for higher education, which results in reductions in budgets, grants, and tuition assistance; and the legal climate, which affects academic job security, academic accountability, and litigation by faculty and students.

Because motivation is so complex, and there is great individual variability among people, a chair must discover what is particularly important to each faculty member. Is it recognition, status, visibility, challenging opportunities, or the knowledge that he or she makes a difference? Discovering what is important to individuals need not take a lot of time; many of a chair's ongoing discussions with faculty, both one to one and at departmental meetings, will yield information about the unique factors that motivate each person. But there are also motivational factors that many academics have in common in the form of career anchors.

Career Anchors

One way to look at commonalities is to view faculty motivation in terms of *career anchors,* a term coined by Schein (1978, p. 125) and defined as self-perceived motivational patterns or categories that include orientations toward work, motives, values, and talents. Schein finds that, typically, one or two of these career categories will be so important to a person that they cannot be given up easily and that is why they function as anchors, providing career stability for an individual. Schein (1987, 1990) has expanded his original list of five career anchors to eight: technical or functional competence, service and dedication, autonomy or independence, life-style integration, security and stability, managerial competence, entrepreneurship and creativity, and pure challenge; however, not all of these anchors apply generally to academics.

A study investigating career anchors as motivational forces for academics in higher education was recently reported by Little and Peter (1990). The findings were based on one hundred in-depth interviews with academics between the ages of forty-five and sixty at three different Australian universities, as well as a ranking of career anchors' importance to them as new academics and in their present lives. The study found that technical or functional competence, and service or dedication, both pivotal factors in professional values and ethics, were the two principal career anchors for faculty members. Autonomy or independence and life-style integration were the secondary career anchors, with life-style integration being valued more by academics in their later years than when they joined the profession. I will focus here on these four career anchors. Managerial competence, entrepreneurship and creativity, and pure challenge did not emerge as overriding issues, or factors that were so important to academics in general that they would not be willing to give them up. Security was ranked fifth in their current jobs, but fourth when they joined the profession. Presumably, since the academics in the Little and Peter study were midcareer and senior faculty, security was something they could now take for granted.

Technical and Functional Competence.   The Little and Peter research on the motivation of academics certainly suggests that faculty members want to be competent. Some individuals have their own internal measures of competence against which they compare their behavior and reinforce themselves for success. Others need external recognition and respect as an affirmation of their ability, and some, of course, want both. External recognition is especially meaningful when it comes from colleagues who are in a position to evaluate and thus appreciate the quality of work being accomplished.

The difficulty is that faculty members function in university bureaucracies, and bureaucracies are generally characterized by a vacuum of recognition and respect. However, this vacuum creates an opportunity for academic chairs to take a significant role in recognizing faculty accomplishments. A chair is one of the few university representatives who sees most department members at least two or three times a week and thus has a number of opportunities to talk with them about teaching, scholarship, their goals, and their work in the department, to celebrate their accomplishments, and to be supportive and a good listener when individuals fail. Most importantly, positive feedback from chairs who are respected, who are from the same discipline, who know what competent performance in the discipline is, and who have the weight of position power in the department is highly valued by faculty. Because competence is a major career anchor for faculty, department chairs' ability to reinforce it enables them to exert tremendous motivational leverage.

Chairs also use recognition as a motivational force when they publicize departmental accomplishments, thus creating visibility, an important currency for faculty. The department chair has a special responsibility to see that the department is acknowledged and recognized throughout the university as a group of successful, competent teachers and scholars. The following example illustrates the significance of recognition as a motivational force. I was consulting with a biology department that had just been transferred from a college of arts and sciences to a college of science and engineering, as part of a university restructuring effort. The biology faculty complained that they felt the engineering faculty treated them "like second-class citizens, not as equal members of the college." Further questioning uncovered the fact that this treatment was based on the engineering faculty's perception that biology faculty were not involved in scholarly research. When I asked about faculty accomplishments, however, it turned out that the biologists had done quite a good amount of research and publication, had obtained some grants, had a large percentage of graduates admitted to doctoral programs, and were doing an excellent job of teaching both in and out of the classroom. The interesting thing was that even individual biology faculty members did not know what others in their own department were doing. Moreover, they were not communicating their accomplishments to the rest of the university community. Faculty members did not bother sending items about their work to the university media because they felt this publicity would be too self-serving. When we worked together on team building and goal setting in terms of their new position in the university, two of the goals the biology faculty set were to increase their research output by a specific amount and to enhance their visibility. To increase attention to their achievements, they selected individuals who would rotate the responsibility of interviewing each faculty member to discover recent accomplishments and activities and publicize those events in the university press and the local community. Recognition as respected colleagues from other members of the university was not long in coming for the department.

Service and Dedication. The second highly motivating career anchor of faculty is service and dedication, or caring.

Although my personal observation suggests that this motivating force is fairly widely distributed in the academic community, individuals are not likely to articulate it in this language. Instead, people may complain about the hours they have just spent revising an article to meet the requirements of an editor; the time spent grading papers and giving students individual comments; the work involved in preparing a new course; or the work done on a faculty promotion and tenure committee, educational policy committee, or grievance committee, when they are simply looking for affirmation of their dedication and caring. In point of fact, it is probably because there are so many dedicated people in our university communities that we become so irritated with the notable few who shirk responsibilities.

Autonomy. Autonomy is a secondary, yet important, career anchor that motivates faculty. Most department chairs recognize the value academics place on setting their own hours, choosing the time and place in which they do much of their work, determining research topics and scholarly activities, and deciding what their contribution will be in achieving departmental goals. The desire for autonomy is also the reason why top-down planning and decision making, with no faculty participation or consultation, is not likely to be successful. However, because faculty members generally value their autonomy and independence, they can be highly creative when they are empowered to carry out their own ideas, provided, of course, that these ideas fit in with the mission of the department.

Life-Style Integration. The secondary career anchor of life-style integration emerges primarily among senior people and was ranked as less important to them when they were new faculty members. In particular, senior faculty in the Little and Peter (1990) study placed considerably more value now than when they were younger faculty members on being able to integrate their academic profession with the rest of their lives. Part of the explanation for this is undoubtedly that the amount of time new faculty spend in preparing courses and in beginning to establish themselves in a meaningful area of research is so great that they often feel they are neglecting both family and friends. Being able to allocate time in a reasonable manner, thus creating a balance among all facets of life, often comes only with experience.

Implications.　For leaders, the major implication of the existence of career anchors is that they make it possible to define, at least in part, what matters to people. Once chairs identify matters of importance to faculty, chairs are in a better position to meet the challenge of matching individual and organizational needs in order to maximize both organizational performance and individual satisfaction (Schein, 1992, p. 36).

New Faculty

Particularly at this time, when many colleges and universities have begun to hire new faculty once more, often for the first time in several years, finding a good match between individual and organizational requirements is crucial. Many departments have had the experience of successfully competing for an unusually good candidate only to have the individual leave the university after a year or two. Considering the time and money invested in recruiting and selecting a new faculty member, it is both wasteful and frustrating to have to start the process all over again so soon to fill the very same faculty slot. The chair of a marketing department, for example, was delighted to have hired an outstanding scholar who had a long list of publications and was also a very good teacher. The chair constantly bragged to other faculty how pleased he was to have hired this individual over the competition. However, at the end of the year, the faculty member with the outstanding potential left, because all his committee and service assignments left him no time to do the research he wanted to do. This is a good example of a chair's disregarding what a faculty member valued, something that should have been obvious during the selection interviews.

Chairs and faculty members must identify their organizational needs and discover what candidates want so that the department can learn whether there is a good fit. A department must take enough time during the interview process (as much as two days with a final candidate) to discover each candidate's goals and to consider whether these goals are likely to be satisfied in this particular institution.

Tenured Faculty

Matching organizational needs with what individuals value is also a pivotal ongoing task for chairs as they interact with tenured faculty. When chairs serve as respected arbiters of competent performance, their reinforcement of individuals for quality teaching and scholarship can be highly rewarding. If valuing competence, as Little and Peter (1990) have reported, is a primary reason many faculty members have chosen to be academics, recognition of their proficiency can motivate them to continue to perform high-quality work.

As suggested earlier, chairs also need to be sensitive to indications that tenured faculty are asking for acknowledgement of their dedication and caring when they seem to be complaining about the time they spend completing academic tasks related to teaching, scholarship, and service. The challenge for the chair is, first, to recognize what is behind the "complaint," and second, to be responsive to and support faculty's dedication. Moreover, chairs must be respectful of faculty's strong desire for autonomy. When faculty are elected or appointed to committees or given other assignments, they need to be informed about their responsibilities but not how to discharge those responsibilities. The following event illustrates the disastrous consequences that can occur when a chair disregards the high value faculty members place on autonomy. A chair who was unhappy with the work of a departmental promotion and tenure committee took committee members to task for not considering some elements important in personnel decision making. When he told them they had provided insufficient justification for their recommendations, discussion became heated and the entire committee threatened to resign. After a somewhat prolonged conflict, the chair agreed to accept the work of the committee but voted against their recommendations with respect to several faculty promotion and retention decisions. Although the issue was ultimately resolved at a higher administrative level, for a time, conflict in the department escalated, dividing the department as faculty supported either the chair or the committee.

The Little and Peter study, in emphasizing the importance of life-style integration, also offers a perspective on why faculty scheduling issues are so sensitive. The need to meet faculty's need for life-style integration in order to motivate them provides yet one more reason for chairs to consult with faculty about course preferences and hours for teaching (or to appoint an individual or committee who will not only handle scheduling equitably but whose work will also be perceived as fair). Faculty want to balance the elements of their lives in ways that reflect their own values, not values imposed by someone else.

Goal Setting for Faculty Development and Performance Evaluation

Before goal setting, performance appraisal, and rewards can be used to increase individual and departmental productivity, expectations of what constitutes acceptable faculty performance need to be clarified. In view of the new definitions of scholarship and service, it is important that departments take on this responsibility; otherwise, college promotion and tenure committees will lack guidelines about appropriate criteria for judging the value of scholarship and service in different disciplines. Moreover, such departmental discussions about performance expectations have the advantages of helping junior faculty discover what is required for tenure and promotion and encouraging tenured faculty to view their own performances from their colleagues' perspective.

In many colleges and universities, general information on performance expectations can be found in faculty handbooks, departmental governance documents, and collective bargaining agreements. However, chairs should not rely solely on these existing documents. Collective bargaining agreements often list minimally acceptable, rather than ideal, levels of faculty performance. Other documents may be deliberately written in vague language so that promotion and tenure committees have latitude for discretionary judgment. However, such language also renders these documents unhelpful to junior faculty who are looking for specific guidelines and to chairs who would like to communicate clear-cut expectations to the occasional faculty member whose professional life seems to be stagnating. It is only after defining performance expectations that chairs can take the next steps in motivating faculty, using individual goal setting and evaluating progress and outcome. The approach suggested here can be used both as a tool for facilitating professional development for faculty and for evaluating faculty. Moreover, research has clearly demonstrated that goal setting enhances productivity and is beneficial both to the individual and to the organization (Eden, 1988; Locke & Latham, 1990).

Goal Setting as a Faculty Development Tool

Motivating faculty whose performance is inadequate is a perennial source of concern to department chairs, and it is very difficult for a chair to conduct a disciplinary interview with a colleague in order to confront inadequate performance. Thus, generally, the best way to handle the problem of inadequate performance is to prevent it from happening. Chairs take an excellent approach to problem prevention when they conduct annual goal-setting interviews with faculty. In this process, every faculty member is asked to generate professional development goals at the beginning of the academic year and submit them in writing to the chair. Outcome is then reviewed at the end of the year.

Before chairs meet with individual members of the department, they must prepare the ground for the goal-setting process. First, chairs should discuss goal setting with informal leaders of the department and obtain their support. Once their support is ensured, a discussion of the goal-setting process should be placed on the agenda for the next departmental meeting. At that meeting, chairs should present goal setting to the faculty, describing its advantages for ongoing professional development and the achievement of department goals. If faculty agree to try the approach, chairs should summarize, in writing, what faculty are being asked to do, so that individual faculty members will have lists of their goals with them during their individual meetings with the chair.

Chairs should prepare for these individual meetings. They should be ready to reinforce all good ideas, and they should have formulated a few questions that will stimulate the thinking of mid-career faculty or others who may have gotten stuck when they tried to list some goals. Chairs must also be prepared to be facilitators, helping faculty reformulate abstract goals so that they become concrete and measurable, and helping change unrealistic goals to those that can be accomplished.

In this process, chairs must define the characteristics of acceptable goals. Like departmental goals, goals for individual faculty should be challenging, realistic, moderately difficult, behaviorally defined, and measurable, so that progress towards the goals can be monitored and outcome evaluated objectively. If goals are too difficult, the possibility of achieving them is reduced. If goals are too easy, they are not motivating. If goals include implementation steps and timelines, faculty are more likely to achieve them. Behaviorally defined goals are also more achievable and measurable. This example of a behaviorally defined goal shows the level of detail desired: "To help achieve the American Assembly of Collegiate Schools of Business recommendations for improving oral communication of students, I will require that all students in [a particular course] make one five-minute presentation (to reduce their anxiety before they make a longer presentation) and be part of a team that makes a one-hour presentation to the class. Immediately after each class, I will provide individual feedback interviews to all presenters. During the twelfth week of the semester, I will ask all students to write an anonymous statement concerning what they liked about this approach and what might make it even more effective, and collect the responses." Compare the specificity of the behavioral goal to this example of a nonbehavioral goal: "I will increase the effectiveness of oral communication among my students." In the goal-setting interview, chairs assist faculty members to formulate appropriate goals that also advance the mission of the department.

All goals must be written so that progress can be monitored and outcome can be evaluated when the chair and the faculty member meet at the end of the year. Chairs should ask if there are ways in which they can help faculty achieve the goals and they should reinforce faculty effort and involvement in the goal-setting process, being enthusiastic and empowering faculty while working with them. If necessary, a chair may also request a progress report from some individuals just before the beginning of the spring semester rather than waiting until the end of the year to evaluate the outcome. This opportunity for a midstream correction is particularly useful for new faculty members or those who may have set goals that are unrealistic. At midyear, goals can be adjusted or action steps planned to overcome any problems a faculty member may have in meeting the stated goals. Thereafter, the chair and individual faculty members hold annual meetings at which they review the completion of the goals for the past year before setting goals for the coming year. In many universities, departments already using this process find these meetings to be quite successful as formal occasions for giving positive feedback, jointly determining objectives faculty plan to achieve, and increasing productivity.

If goal setting as a tool for faculty development or performance evaluation has not been used in the department before, and if chairs do not feel they have much position power, it is worthwhile for deans to announce that annual goal setting is a process to which they are committed. Such a policy, stated in writing by the dean, empowers chairs to carry out goal setting. During the department's initial experience with this approach, deans may even choose to be present at the meetings between the chair and faculty members. A dean's presence may be singularly useful for chairs who anticipate resistance as they initiate a goal-setting process, particularly when they deal with difficult colleagues. This involvement also gives the dean an opportunity to become better acquainted with faculty members and their work. However, when relationships between the chair and the faculty are good, the goal-setting process is best done without including the dean in the process.

Although goal setting can be used solely for faculty development, some departments resist it for fear that it will become an instrument for performance evaluation. A large state system of higher education with a number of comprehensive universities provides a good example of this concern. The universities are unionized, and the chairs are part of the bargaining unit. Although the chairs saw an immediate value in introducing goal setting for many reasons related to developing faculty and accomplishing departmental goals, they felt faculty would be concerned about the possibility that their individual goals might be placed in their personnel files and that they might be held accountable for them and penalized if they did not achieve them. Even if the chairs did not place these goals in the personnel files, the chairs felt faculty would be suspicious that somehow, despite the chairs' best intentions, faculty would be held formally accountable. In other words, the chairs said that, since faculty do not currently feel accountable, they do not want a process initiated that might in some way work to their disadvantage. Interestingly enough, however, more protection is given to faculty if they know in advance what will be expected of them and if they participate in developing their own goals.

Goal Setting as a Tool in Performance Evaluation

When goal setting *is* used as an overarching process for faculty evaluation, it has many advantages over other forms of performance appraisal. Goal setting is a broader approach than the teaching portfolio in that it also includes scholarship and service activities. However, like the teaching portfolio, it helps faculty be reflective practitioners, allowing them to deliberate on what they are doing, where they are experiencing success, where they need to improve, and exactly what they can do to enhance their effectiveness. Although both approaches require generation of data, goal setting also demands specific goals stated objectively, so that progress can be monitored and final outcomes evaluated. Because goals are behaviorally defined, the goal-setting process makes it easier for faculty to collect relevant data to support their year-end statements about goal achievement. The goal-setting process also encourages faculty to determine their short- and long-term objectives in the areas of teaching, scholarship, and service and ask whether the ways they are spending their time will help them achieve their objectives.

Because goal setting emphasizes data collection, it also diminishes another problem that surfaces frequently in faculty performance evaluation, that of inflated self-perceptions of competence. Studies reviewed by Feldman (1989) indicate that faculty tend to rate their teaching higher than their students or colleagues do. Mediocre and poor teachers are even less accurate in their self-assessments than good teachers (Barber, 1990; Centra, 1993). Since self-perceptions, particularly of poor teachers, tend not to be accurate, Centra (1993) recommends that self-assessments not be included in performance evaluation reports. However, faculty did identify the same areas of strengths and weaknesses in their teaching as their students did, even though faculty gave themselves higher overall scores (Centra, 1973; Feldman, 1989). When chairs have access to data on faculty performance, the chair can confront inconsistencies between faculty self-perceptions and colleague and student reports.

Performance appraisal should include a dialogue between the chair and the faculty member who is being evaluated. Such a discussion may inform the chair about problems a faculty member is having, shedding a new light on "objective" data. Reflect on the chair who had hired an Indian faculty member with high potential but had not taken the time to orient him to the department or provide any mentoring for him. Student evaluations taken in the fall of his first year were poor, and the problem was brought to the attention of a senior faculty member when several excellent students complained about the new instructor, saying that he did not assign any papers or give exams. Instead, he had students make team presentations to the class but did not give them any feedback afterward. Moreover, though the class had only twenty students, he did not know any of their names. When a student asked him how he could grade them when he did not know their names, he simply laughed. The week before student evaluations were distributed, the professor asked students, in class, "How does the grading system work in this university?" The students were angry, and the high achievers were concerned that their grades would suffer because he did not know them by name. And there were several other problems related to his lack of familiarity with U.S. culture.

These issues were resolved when the senior faculty member informed the chair of the problem. She volunteered to review the new faculty member's student evaluations with him and to discuss grading procedures and answer questions about his teaching. The chair was very willing to have her do this. However, since it was his custom to simply write a one-line memo to faculty members informing them whether he had recommended continuation or termination, a faculty member with good potential could have been lost if the chair had not been informed about the senior faculty member's actions ahead of time. Obviously, in this department, the chair was remiss in that there was customarily no dialogue or feedback during the performance evaluation process. Neither was there any orientation or mentoring for new faculty members that could have prevented the behavior that triggered poor student evaluations. And in addition, the chair was poorly informed.

It is difficult in any organization for people to conduct performance evaluation interviews. However, individuals want to know how they are doing; they need and want feedback. Feedback interviews create an opportunity for faculty members to develop more realistic insights about their level of performance. When performance evaluation involves a dialogue between chair and faculty member, objective information from a variety of sources can be put in perspective, effective performance can be celebrated, and goals set for the next year indicating exactly what will be done in the areas of teaching, scholarship, and service.

Since the primary focus of this book is the leadership and faculty development responsibilities of chairs, I have not included a comprehensive report on performance evaluation systems. However, chairs will find the following two excellent books helpful: John Centra's *Reflective Faculty Evaluation* (1993) offers a useful guide through the many complicated issues of evaluation and provides helpful strategies for improving faculty effectiveness; Larry A. Braskamp and John C. Ory's *Assessing Faculty Work* (1994) describes a comprehensive and human approach to the evaluation process.

Goal Setting from the Faculty Viewpoint

While I have been looking at goal setting primarily from the point of view of the chair and the department as a whole, goal setting is also highly beneficial for faculty, whether it is used for performance evaluation or professional development.

Since most faculty members get relatively little feedback about their work, goal setting provides an opportunity for them to share their goals, celebrate their accomplishments, and share their failures with a supportive listener. Faculty can learn to profit from their mistakes, viewing them simply as experiences from which they can learn. While some faculty members can do this for themselves, others need to have a chair who will support them in their risk taking, increase their tolerance for mistakes, and help them discover what they have learned from the experience. The annual goal-setting process can assist faculty in reviewing their personal progress, sustain them because their efforts are recognized, and provide the stimulation they need to continue personal and professional growth.

In order to develop goals and action steps, individuals become reflective practitioners and devote energy to thinking about a direction for their lives. A faculty development process empowers people to decide where they want to go professionally and how they are going to get there. When goals are clearly stated, and followed by implementation steps and timelines, individuals develop a clearer sense of what steps they will have to take to get from here to there. I once spoke with a faculty member who described himself as a very creative individual. He said he could not set goals because he never knew what would come out of his computer once he sat down to work. But as a result, he published nothing year after year. Goals set directions and the sequence of activities necessary to achieve the goals.

The research evidence is clear: goals enhance productivity. When faculty are assisted to state goals that are specific, measurable, realistic, time related, challenging, and moderately difficult, they can enjoy a higher level of achievement and the rewards that achievement may bring.

Goal setting enhances faculty accountability. The process of matching individual with departmental goals can be conducted so that it is a good experience for faculty. The chair makes goal-setting meetings positive by using them as a specific time to give positive feed-back for accomplishments. And because goal setting requires that faculty plan the direction for their professional development, it also prevents individual stagnation, a condition that is dysfunctional for both the faculty member and the department.

The chair's contribution to faculty goal setting is to be sup-portive, to help faculty concretize goals, to ensure that goals and timelines are realistic, and to confirm the measurability of faculty progress. Chairs can recommend that behaviors on which an indi-vidual falls short be included as goals: for example, serving on a committee that will help the department reach departmental goals. When goal setting is used as a tool in performance evaluation, there will certainly be times when a faculty member sets goals that are too easy or does little to achieve goals once they are set. On these occasions, the chair must confront the difficulties. Untenured faculty should be told what is required in order to become tenured. Tenured faculty and the chair should examine the way implemen-tation steps and timelines were written to discover what barriers prevented achievement of the goals.

Antidote to Alienation

In one of the small-group discussions at the July 1993 Conference on Institutional Priorities and Faculty Rewards, organized by Syra-cuse University, R. Eugene Rice made an observation about "fac-ulty disconnectedness," saying that faculty often find satisfaction in doing work that, though scholarly in nature, is not related to their university work and is not acknowledged by the university. As a result, meaningful areas of a faculty member's work may no longer be connected with the university. In a presentation at the same conference, Phyllis Franklin, Executive Director of the Mod-ern Language Association of America, after discussing "persistent, normal pressures" on academics, spoke about the "recent, abnor-mal pressures of the 1970s and 1980s, when institutions began to

impose increased demands for publication on faculty members,"
observing that

> There have been real consequences for the generations receiving
> Ph.D.'s in the 1970s and '80s. On their personal lives, which were
> often sacrificed in order to publish early; on their attitudes towards
> senior colleagues, which are not warm; on their attitudes towards
> their institutions, which are often hostile; and on their sense of
> themselves as professionals. No studies of these attitudes have been
> done as far as I know, but there are many anecdotes.
>
> My own sense is that these faculty members have been forced
> to walk a treadmill, to function in a seemingly inflexible system.
> Some dislike the system, and others support it. But many object to
> its rigidity. I see an important point of leverage here. What is likely
> to tempt people who have been inducted into the academy during
> these pressured times is greater flexibility in shaping the rest of their
> careers. I believe they would welcome the opportunity to focus their
> energies on different kinds of projects at different points in their
> careers—now on scholarship, now on curricular and teaching
> improvements, and now on work outside the academy that utilizes
> their expertise—and receive credit for these efforts [Franklin, 1993,
> pp. 4–5].

The goal-setting process is one of the places in which chairs
can address the issue of faculty disconnectedness and the questions
of providing the flexibility that faculty need and giving credit to
faculty for work done outside the academy. Obviously, if faculty
goals are to be considered legitimate, they must fall within the
purview of the departmental mission. However, mission statements
should be reviewed every three or four years to explore their rele-
vance to the needs of a changing society. It is probable that much
of the scholarly work that faculty are doing could be done within
the scope of a departmental mission, particularly since the definition of scholarship has been broadened. However, there are chairs

who interpret departmental goals in an uncompromising fashion. I am aware, for example, of a chair of a management and marketing department who refused to grant release time for research to a faculty member with an excellent publication record, because the research applied management concepts to higher education instead of industry. In this rejection, the chair neglected the fact that management concepts can be adapted and applied to any organization. Using more realistic, less rigid criteria, in tune with the changing concepts of scholarship, to examine faculty work is an effective approach to valuing the work in which faculty are engaged. Acceptance of scholarly work as a legitimate part of faculty goals, and reinforcement for such accomplishments at an annual performance review, can make it possible for faculty to reconnect with academe.

Motivating Special Groups of Faculty

In addition to addressing general motivation for faculty, academic chairs must face problems of motivating, and even simply dealing with, particular groups of individuals. During the past twelve years, prior to my conducting on-campus workshops, I have asked several thousand chairs to complete questionnaires focused on, among other issues, the degree of success they have had in motivating faculty. Fairly typical in terms of results is the survey I mailed to all 363 participants of the 1991 Kansas State University National Conference for Academic Chairpersons. Participants included academic administrators, chairs, and faculty leaders. From the 201 chairs at the conference, 153 questionnaires were returned (a 76 percent response rate). Chairs were asked to rate, on a scale of one to five, how successful they were in motivating faculty in a number of areas. One was very successful; five was very unsuccessful. Only one-third of the responding chairs reported any degree of success in motivating faculty members in three categories: midcareer faculty, alienated tenured faculty, and poor teachers (see Chapter Three for similar results from another study). The first two problems will be examined here; motivating poor teachers will be considered in Chapter Five.

Midcareer Faculty

When people reach midcareer in academe, unless they have achieved some prominence in the field or feel content because they are respected and given some recognition in the department and in the university, life can become terribly dull and repetitious. Burnout among faculty members seems to be greatest when they teach the same courses again and again, particularly introductory courses, and serve on the same committees year after year. Given those conditions, an important intervention can be made when annual goal setting is used for faculty development. A faculty development plan can stimulate midcareer individuals to think about what they could do that would challenge them. When individuals do not spontaneously create goals about which they are enthusiastic, it is helpful if the chair asks questions regarding activities that might arouse some excitement: When you first came into academe, what were your goals? Which of those objectives have you achieved? Are there one or two you would like to accomplish during the next two or three years? After those questions have been answered, the chair can perform a gap analysis, asking, What would it take to get you from here to there? And, What can I do to help you? The chair's goal is to unleash creativity, jolting faculty out of looking at life in a routine fashion by asking questions that faculty do not regularly ask themselves. Often, with just a bit of brainstorming, some goals will emerge along with some activities that spark interest. As chairs empower faculty in need of revitalization, these individuals become free to generate goals representing challenging but realistic new directions. Then the chair's task is to be sure the usual goal guidelines are met so that the proposed goals can be achieved.

Other suggestions culled from chairs who completed the questionnaire and reported success in motivating burned-out faculty included mentoring a new faculty member or starting activities that involve faculty in altering their lives' routines: for example, a faculty exchange program with another university in which a faculty member could go to teach and perhaps audit some cutting-edge courses in the discipline. Chairs also suggested that burned-out faculty could team teach a course; attend workshops to develop new interests; learn more about instructional developments; write an article about something in which they have expertise; get involved in some personal development activities; or even learn a new sport. Basically, the chair must become the catalyst that causes a mid-career faculty member to develop talents and skills that have not been explored earlier, or to make contributions that integrate mature wisdom with experience in the discipline.

Difficult Colleagues

Another area that plagues department chairs is dealing with difficult colleagues. Chairs tell many war stories about not knowing how to handle people who behave in unacceptable ways. For example, one chair asked how he should handle a faculty member who always sat looking out the window at department meetings, with his back to the rest of the group. The chair had done nothing because he had not known what to do, and when I asked how long this had been going on, the chair's response was, "Four years." Often, it seems to chairs that doing nothing is better than antagonizing difficult colleagues further, particularly if a colleague has shown abrasiveness in interpersonal interactions.

When I asked 100 chairs to identify what characterizes difficult colleagues, or alienated tenured individuals as they are sometimes called, they described the following behaviors as typical:

Their performance was minimal; they attended their classes and went home.

They were loners and had limited interaction with others in
the department.

They made frequent sarcastic comments at department
meetings.

They assumed very limited responsibilities in the department.

They alienated students by making denigrating remarks about
them in class.

They had done little scholarly work in over a decade.

About 80 percent of these difficult individuals were male; about 20
percent were former chairs, deans, or directors of programs. After
these difficult people had been identified by their chairs, I interviewed twenty-five of them. The most frequent explanation they
offered for their current feelings and behaviors was that they had
been treated unjustly by chairs and administrators. The incidents
they mentioned included not getting a promotion; being regularly
assigned four different preparations in a semester while others
taught no more than three different courses; being passed over for
a merit increase; not getting release time for research; and never
getting a graduate research assistant (nor an explanation for this
treatment).

The second most frequently given reason was a lack of appreciation, not "even a thank-you," for labor-intensive work they had
completed. The examples they furnished were devoting long
painful hours to work on a grievance committee, often during vacation periods, with no thanks from anyone; developing a proposal
for a new program that involved surveying many other universities
currently offering such programs, with no response from the person to whom it was submitted; and spending hundreds of hours
working on and writing a report for a committee but having the
senior academician who chaired the committee take all the credit.
The third most frequent reason for feeling alienated was that the
difficult individual had once had considerable power in the depart-

ment but had lost influence when the department made a decision opposite to one the individual espoused. The individual and the other departmental members then gradually pushed each other into adversarial positions, behaving more and more abrasively, and finally, the difficult person began to be ignored by the rest of the department.

A final reason given was the lack of sensitivity of department members to painful life circumstances—a bitter divorce, children addicted to alcohol or drugs, the death of a child while under the influence, a prolonged illness of a close family member, a personal illness, or personal alcohol addiction—that were felt to have contributed to the individual's demoralization. In addition, Bergquist (1992, pp. 49–56) presents a detailed case study of a faculty member who is angry and alienated because he receives contradictory messages about the value of what he is doing, as his university changes its emphasis from teaching to research. In this case too, the managerial culture is perceived as alien and unresponsive to the faculty member's real needs.

When interviewed as part of my research, these alienated faculty were usually very willing to talk about their own plight. They generally felt very isolated in the department. There was no one with whom they could even have a cup of coffee or go to lunch. One individual described a chance meeting with a colleague from another department on a night when both taught evening courses. The colleague suggested they meet early the next week to have a cup of coffee together, but the next week, the colleague did not come to the cafeteria. The faculty member described his disappointment, saying that this was the first time in fifteen years anyone had invited him to have a cup of coffee.

The alienated faculty members said they often closed their office doors because they felt no one in the department spoke to them anyway, and they did not like being blatantly ignored. By the time of the interview, they had often invested themselves heavily in activities outside of the university. A few were involved in consulting activities that were more satisfying to them than what they were currently doing in the department. Surprisingly, however, most were engaged in activities far removed from academe. Typical examples were operating a small business that they owned, such as an antique, stationery, or motorcycle shop; several had invested heavily in real estate that they spent time managing; a few had started companies, such as painting and wallpapering businesses, doing the work themselves. Their comments could be summed up as, "Well, if those donkeys back there don't appreciate me, at least I can earn extra money, or get the feeling that what I am doing is valued by someone."

While almost all the chairs in my study expressed discomfort about their difficult colleagues, they seemed to have little idea of how to handle the situation. The suggestions that follow are based on my interviews with both the chairs and the alienated individuals as well as the research on what motivates people. The first suggestion is simply to reach out to alienated faculty members on a human level. Acknowledge their presence when they come into the department. This is important because many of their colleagues will have gotten into the habit of not talking to them, not even saying hello. After doing this several times, so that the alienated person starts to expect a greeting, the chair can stop at the door of the individual's office and engage in small talk for a minute or two. Next, the chair can then raise the level of interaction by bringing a cup of coffee or tea into the office, sitting down for several minutes, and engaging the individual in conversation about something of interest: politics, sports, or some university event.

When these interactions have been going on several weeks, the chair might request assistance about some departmental matter, saying something along these lines: "I have a problem I wonder if you could help me with. Do you have any ideas about . . . ?" The problem could be any issue that is of genuine concern to the chair, such as orienting or evaluating adjunct faculty, creating more internships for graduate students, creating a liaison with an external organization, or collaborating more effectively with another department. The question should be one about which another perspective is in fact desired and about which this individual is likely to be informed and interested. The chair should thank the individual for whatever suggestions are made. This provides an opening for the chair to say, "I have missed your active involvement in the department. What would it take to bring you back into the mainstream?"

For this interaction to work well, it is important that chairs prepare themselves for a possible tirade. If the difficult colleague has not spoken to anyone about his or her being unappreciated or about the injustice he or she feels has been suffered, the colleague may vent that anger on the chair, even when the current chair is not the source of the difficult person's wrath. In this situation, the chair must not defend the system or the previous chair. Further, the chair must not judge, evaluate, or disagree with what is being said, no matter how strongly it is verbalized. All that is necessary is to use active listening, that is, paraphrase what the alienated faculty member says and the emotions expressed to show that they have been heard correctly: for example, "I understand that you postponed your vacation to attend all those grievance meetings and people just seemed to take it for granted that it was all right to inconvenience you. And then most other committee members voted against your position, so you felt as if your being there was a waste of time." Having someone listen to you and understand your point of view is very affirming, and difficult or abrasive colleagues get little affirmation. However, the chair should not agree with the faculty member just to win his or her confidence, particularly if he or she feels the individual is wrong. Active listening is simply summarizing what is heard. It requires no agreement or disagreement. Also, it is important that chairs remain detached and not allow themselves to be pulled into an argument. At the end, the chair can still say, "I am glad we talked. I have a much better understanding now of your position. However, I would still like to have you become more involved in the department again."

I made these same suggestions to the chairs whom I had interviewed about their difficult faculty, and a number of them have reported that, after they tried this approach, their difficult colleagues had come to them after a few days with an idea of some way in which they could contribute to the department. If this does not happen, the chair can suggest some meaningful work that the individual can take on. It is useful if such work involves a meeting with each member of the department to ask for some information or an opinion about something that cannot be obtained in writing. This work will provide a reason for the faculty member to visit the office of each faculty member on a meaningful errand. Sometimes, it will be necessary for chairs to discuss this approach ahead of time with the dean, so that, if the previously uninvolved faculty member makes a meaningful contribution, the dean can support it in whatever way is necessary.

In my research, when chairs have tried this approach, there has been a 92 percent success rate, defined as the chair's having a better relationship with the difficult faculty member, the individual's getting more involved or accepting more responsibility in the department, and the individual's making fewer abrasive comments at meetings. Using a similar approach to dealing with difficult colleagues, Boice (1990a) reported a chair success rate of 84 percent, defined as restored communication with other faculty members and involvement in departmental affairs. Since this approach has such a high success rate, it is clearly worth trying. Otherwise, difficult colleagues will continue to be a constant source of frustration and tension in a department. Additional ongoing improvement in their behavior should come about when the goal-setting approach to faculty development is used.

Lastly, some of the reasons that emerged when difficult colleagues were interviewed point to methods chairs can use to prevent alienation. For example, the injustices described may seem to reflect no more than a biased perspective, and in fact, those who did not get promotions or merit increases may not have been entirely justified in feeling that discrimination was operating. However, in no case did the individual who was chair at the time discuss with the faculty member the reason he or she was passed over or describe what had to be done to earn a promotion or merit increase in the future. Sometimes, criteria seemed to have been ambiguous, subjective, or in the process of changing. Most importantly, when former chairs of difficult colleagues were interviewed, they reported that they felt no need to discuss the incident with the faculty member. Former chairs usually remembered the incident when it was described to them, but they seemed to feel that, if the faculty member had a problem, it was up to him or her to take the initiative to approach the chair.

The principle that emerges is the need for a chair to keep open the lines of communication between faculty members and the chair and, when appropriate, to recommend to deans or chairs of important committees in the university that they take the time to thank faculty who have served with them on significant university committee work.

A final, fairly simple recommendation for motivating faculty is that the chair visit all faculty members, in their own offices, several times each semester. These visits do not have to be formally scheduled interviews. They are simply informal visits, lasting only a few minutes, but creating an occasion for the chair to discuss with faculty members whatever they want to talk about. Chairs sometimes feel they make themselves accessible by maintaining an open-door policy. This is not enough. When faculty members complain about chairs, a frequent comment is, "My chair has not even dropped into my office to find out what I have been doing this year." Faculty members feel such visits are a demonstration of interest and respond positively. Also, as has just been demonstrated, visiting faculty members in their offices is a positive step in dealing with difficult colleagues.

Conclusion

In conclusion, chairs should remember that the most basic principle in motivation is that faculty will engage in those activities that are rewarded, and that reward does not have to be economic. Acknowledgement of effort, accomplishment, and contribution to the discipline and to the department are highly rewarding. Goal setting is the key process in motivating faculty, helping them continue their professional development, helping chairs evaluate performance, and helping the department to reach its goals.

I recommend that chairs establish two goals for themselves from this and each subsequent chapter. One suggested goal for chairs from this chapter is to begin the goal-setting process with department faculty, starting with a discussion with the informal leaders in the department and continuing through the process of discussing goal setting with faculty at a departmental meeting and then getting together with individual faculty members to assist them to formulate appropriate goals for themselves. A second suggested goal is to bring a difficult colleague back into the departmental mainstream, remembering to reach out to your colleague as one human being to another, following the suggested steps for moving gradually toward your goal of ending this colleague's isolation and helping him or her to contribute to the department once again.

Chapter Five

Supporting Effective Teaching in the Department

Today, many universities, even the prestigious research universities, are advocating that teaching effectiveness become a high priority in their institutions. Since the mid 1980s, compelling recommendations that more attention be given to college teaching and the development of a cohesive curriculum have been issued by the National Endowment for the Humanities (Bennett, 1984), the National Institute of Education (1984), the Association of American Colleges (1985), the Carnegie Foundation for the Advancement of Teaching (Boyer, 1987), and the Wingspread Group on Higher Education (1993). Teaching was also given new importance when Boyer, in his *Scholarship Reconsidered* (1990), expanded the concept of scholarship to include the scholarship of teaching. Adding to this groundswell, which may create a true paradigm shift, Rice (1991) has discussed the transformation of knowledge as the scholarly work of teaching in his significant article "The New American Scholar."

Working along an independent, yet parallel track, the Center for Instructional Development at the University of Syracuse, under the creative leadership of Robert Diamond (1993), has assessed the relative importance of research and undergraduate teaching at forty-seven universities across the country, tapping the perspectives of more than 23,302 deans, unit heads, and faculty. The results (Gray, Froh, & Diamond, 1992) show a clear tendency of all respondents "to favor balance between research and undergraduate teaching" (p. 5). However, survey participants also indicated that universities are moving in the direction of valuing research, whereas the participants think universities should move in the direction of valuing teaching. Thus, the assessment concluded that "there is a serious conflict between the culture of the university and the values of individuals" (p. 9). In a follow-up effort that may have a major influence, Diamond has also involved the major scholarly and national accrediting organizations in translating what an expanded view of scholarship, teaching, and service will mean to each of the different disciplines. In an attempt to secure input from all segments of the academic community, Diamond has been consulting with the national educational organizations, as well as with leaders in the movement to reconsider faculty reward systems in light of changing institutional priorities. As a way of encouraging dialogue to reexamine faculty priorities, the American Association of Higher Education secured support from the Fund for the Improvement of Post-Secondary Education (FIPSE) for a three-year project, the Forum on Faculty Roles and Rewards, which, under the direction of Clara M. Lovett, has now sponsored two national conferences on the topic of faculty roles and rewards (in San Antonio in 1993 and in New Orleans in 1994). Ongoing work of this impressive proportion seems certain to have a critical impact on the way that teaching is viewed in higher education.

While some groups and individuals have looked at faculty priorities and rewards for teaching, others have looked at the university culture that has kept teaching from being discussed. On this topic, Lee Shulman (1993, p. 1) has written, "We close the classroom door and experience pedagogical solitude, whereas in our life as scholars we are members of active communities: communities of conversation, communities of evaluation, communities in which we gather with others in our invisible colleges to exchange our findings, our methods, and our excuses. I believe that the reason teaching is not more valued in the academy is because the way we treat teaching removes it from the community of scholars."

Yet another scholar, Parker J. Palmer (1993, p. 11), adds weight to this view when he focuses on the kinds of conversations that can deal with critical moments in teaching and learning for faculty and students. According to Palmer, diagnosing students as "brain-dead," and therefore incapable of learning what we have to teach them hides fear—theirs and our own. For students, it is "fear that their lives have little meaning, that their futures are dim, and that their elders do not care about their plight. . . . This fear leads them to hide behind masks of silence and indifference in the classroom—the same silence that marginalized people have always practiced in the presence of people with power." But faculty also have fears, Palmer says, fears of being rejected by students: "One of the occupational hazards of college teaching is to walk into classroom after classroom, year after year, and look out upon a sea of faces that seems to be saying, 'You're out of it.' We take this silence and apparent indifference personally, and we defend ourselves against the implicit judgment on our lives by declaring our judges intellectually and morally bankrupt." Understanding and overcoming these fearful conditions in the classroom, Palmer suggests, requires that each teacher "have a community of honest and open colleagues with whom to explore [his or her] struggles as a teacher."

But Palmer also says that little talk about teaching will take place if presidents and provosts, deans and department chairs do not invite these conversations regularly. If effective teaching is to become more important in higher education, leadership of department chairs will be crucial in improving the overall quality of instruction in every department. Yet, many chairs do not currently have the knowledge, skills, and confidence required to make this happen. As I mentioned in Chapter Four, only one-third of the chairs who attended the 1991 Kansas State University National Conference for Academic Chairpersons indicated that they had experienced any degree of success in motivating poor teachers to improve the quality of their teaching. Academic chairs will have to become better informed about pedagogy, learning theory, and motivation. This chapter is intended to help chairs create a departmental climate that makes effective teaching an ongoing professional development activity and to use classroom observation as one tool in enhancing teaching competence.

A Reason for Poor Teaching

Why do we have so many poor teachers in college classrooms? There are several reasons, but one is probably related to the enormous number of people hired for faculty positions in the 1960s and early 1970s. Colleges and universities gave these new faculty members no help in becoming competent teachers. The myth was strong then that, if you know your subject, you can teach it. There was also not much practical information in the literature on pedagogy, learning, and motivation that could be immediately applied to the college classroom. So, thousands of faculty members began their first teaching experiences with little or no assistance. If their experience was not very satisfying, they undoubtedly developed defenses to deal with their discomfort. The most common defense, as Palmer suggests, was probably to blame the students: I am here to teach. Students are here to learn. If they are not motivated, there is nothing I can do about it.

There is little empirical evidence from those times to indicate whether this was in fact the most common defense; however, a recent study indicates that this is the way new faculty currently defend teaching that falls short of expectations. In his longitudinal study of 185 new faculty members at several comprehensive institutions, Boice (1992, p. 77) found that when student evaluations were disappointing, faculty explained the fact by externalizing blame. Poor ratings were seen to be the fault of unmotivated students, heavy teaching loads, and invalid rating systems.

K. Patricia Cross (1977, p. 10), drawing on her survey of self-report data from college teachers, found that "an amazing 94 per cent rate themselves as above-average teachers, and 68 per cent rank themselves in the top quarter in teaching performance." If the perception of a large percentage of college faculty is that they are quite good as teachers, that defense mechanism enables faculty members to maintain a reasonably high level of self-esteem. But what happens when faculty members receive the printouts of student evaluations and find a considerable gap between how they think they are doing and how students think they are doing? The dissonance has to be dealt with in some way and what many faculty members did and still do, I hypothesize, is pretty much what the new faculty members in Boice's study did, externalize the blame.

Boice's study also found that the primary pedagogical approach of new faculty members was "a facts-and principles style of teaching" (p. 68). Discomfort in the classroom was a chief problem for new faculty; yet they resisted change and dealt with low student evaluations, first defensively, and then by working hard at improving their lecture notes to get all their facts straight.

Based on Boice's findings about the teaching style of new faculty in the late 1980s, some inferences can be made about the teaching methods of new faculty hired in the 1960s and early 1970s. It is probable that, lacking guidance, large numbers of the new faculty taught as they had been taught and settled into an approach that depended heavily upon lecture as the only way to teach. After becoming accustomed to this "content-only" approach, most faculty found it comfortable, and the style conformed to students' expectations, if not their preferences. While these poor teachers have built up defenses that help them maintain their self-esteem, they do not want to talk about teaching, except in the most cursory fashion, because such discussion might force them to examine their teaching in ways that would create discomfort.

It is likely that these assumptions are true; otherwise, why is it that so few faculty members talk about their teaching? Individuals in other professions certainly talk about what they do and how they might do it better. Why is it that when workshops on teaching are given at universities, most of the people who sign up are already good teachers, although there are always a few in attendance who have been told by their chairs that if their teaching does not improve they may not get tenure.

Therefore, as chairs attempt to change the climate in their departments with respect to teaching, they can expect to encounter considerable defensiveness. When the topic of teaching effectiveness is introduced at a departmental meeting, it is unlikely that the faculty will immediately respond with enthusiasm. It is more likely that they will be thinking, I have been teaching for a long time. Therefore, since I know I am above average in my teaching, it would be a waste of time to discuss teaching. In other words, what is there to discuss?

Through the work of such instructional developers as Weimer (1990), we now know that most faculty can benefit from reflection on how they teach as a beginning step in becoming better teachers. Integrating observer feedback with an increased understanding of how learning takes place is the next step. Faculty can learn that, although the use of lectures is highly defensible, a series of other pedagogical approaches can also be used, depending upon the goals for a program, course, or particular class. This learning constitutes what Weimer has called instructional awareness. The question is how to bring this awareness to the department.

Myths that Prevent Chairs from Discussing or Evaluating Teaching

Since it is the chair's task to initiate this awareness, the myths that prevent chairs from initiating discussion about teaching, or sponsoring colleague or chair observation of classroom teaching must be confronted before the process can start. Such myths may be verbalized with such conviction by faculty members that chairs may find themselves reluctant to attempt to change the culture.

Myth 1. If I know the discipline, I know how to teach it.
Rebuttal. This myth is a rationalization used by numerous fac-

ulty members who have been teaching for many years. They feel they will appear foolish if they now admit they have something to learn about teaching. But learning a discipline and learning to teach are two separate sets of concepts and skills. Of course individuals cannot teach an academic discipline such as chemistry or philosophy if they do not know the discipline. But faculty members' knowledge of the discipline does not mean they can teach it.

Myth 2. Teaching is a mystical experience. Sometimes a faculty member teaches two sections of the same course in one semester. One section goes very well; the other miserably. This proves that there are no right answers about what makes teaching effective. Instructors cannot predict how students will respond to what they do in the classroom.

Rebuttal. The myth that teaching is a mystical experience is belied by what we now know about small-group process and the effect a group leader's behavior has on others. What is required to understand teaching is a focus on behavior, both the instructor's and the students'. An observer who looks at the classroom dynamics in each of the two sections can help a faculty member to understand what he or she is doing well in one section and what has been dysfunctional in the second. Then recommendations about useful interventions in the section that is not going well can be tried.

Myth 3. There is no legitimate knowledge out there about effective teaching. When someone can prove to me that hard data exist and that the methodology used in such research is sound, I will read the findings.

Rebuttal. This myth must obviously be uttered by someone who has never read an article about pedagogy. It is all the more devastating because individuals who believe it have a closed mind on the subject of teaching and learning. Yet a great deal is known about effective teaching and what constitutes a good teaching-learning process. Chairs need to stimulate faculty members' thinking through discussion and reading materials, rather than attack, which will only make faculty more defensive.

Myth 4. Individuals who initiate discussions and give feedback on teaching need first to be excellent teachers themselves. Moreover, people who give others feedback on teaching create the impression that they are presenting themselves as model teachers, and that makes them vulnerable to criticism.

Rebuttal. Conducting good classroom observations requires an individual to be a good observer and record objectively what occurs, thus separating interpretation from behavior. Giving feedback requires that a chair be able to discuss what was observed, emphasize what was successful, thoroughly understand problem behaviors that interfere with effective teaching, and assist the person observed in identifying problems and generating solutions.

Chairs can demonstrate that they are not creating an unequal relationship—that of an expert teacher speaking to an incompetent instructor—by placing colleague observation in the following context: becoming an effective teacher is a life-long experience and discussion about teaching between colleagues is beneficial to both parties. Chairs need to show that they are working on improving their own teaching. This sends the message that all faculty are expected to continue to enhance their teaching, as part of their professional development.

Myth 5. Because I have not kept up with the literature on teaching, I will only expose my ignorance if we talk about teaching. I do not know all the new buzz words in higher education. Moreover, my time is so limited I can barely keep up with the literature in my own discipline.

Rebuttal. It is true that in my surveys of chairs, less than 10 percent indicate that they have had any degree of success in keeping up with the literature on pedagogy, learning, and motivation. However, instructional development staff are very willing to make short articles on relevant topics available to department chairs. Development professionals will also conduct workshops in a department, some of them in collaboration with faculty members if that approach is preferred. (A list of references on different aspects of teaching and learning that chairs and department members can read and share with each other is supplied later in the chapter.)

Myth 6. If I, as chair, observe a class, my ignorance about the teaching-learning process will be exposed. Also, handling feedback interviews is a mystery to me and to most chairs. My colleagues will resent me if I observe them and tell them they are doing something wrong.

Rebuttal. Many chairs have never had their teaching observed by a colleague, and it is true that sometimes they are not certain that they are knowledgeable about the process of observing and talking about what they have observed. However, when feedback is handled well, it is valued. Feedback is a gift that increases teaching effectiveness. Chairs may need some training in observing classroom teaching and handling feedback interviews, and this need can be communicated to the dean. (Chapter Six offers many helpful suggestions about classroom observation and feedback.)

Myth 7. Students are not only illiterate, they are unmotivated. It is my job to teach. It is their job to come to class to learn. There is nothing about what I do that needs to be changed.

Rebuttal. It is true that many students lack the academic skills necessary for success in college. However, if they have been accepted by the university, part of faculty responsibility, particularly in introductory courses, is to engage in triage, that is, to sort needs and allocate treatment in a way that maximizes the number of survivors. Some students can be taken as they are and motivated to learn what faculty are teaching. Others may require referrals to the institution's learning center early enough in the semester that, with help in developing better approaches to learning, they have a chance of passing the course. Still others may need to receive recommendations to complete remedial courses before taking certain regular courses. What may be required for many others is a faculty member who is willing to spend an entire class period or two showing students how to learn a specific discipline, because academic areas differ in what is important and how one learns the important things. Even with triage, not everyone can be saved, and faculty will not always be successful. But the teaching-learning process is a two-way venture. Instructors have some of the responsibility and cannot place all of the burden on the students.

These myths help to create the strong faculty resistance a chair is likely to encounter in the process of trying to make quality teaching a high priority in the department. Although barriers to change sometimes appear to be insurmountable, a chair can have available a number of strategies to change the departmental climate to one in which teaching effectiveness becomes an ongoing professional development activity for every faculty member.

Strategies for Improving Teaching Effectiveness

The following two dozen strategies form an expanded list of workable interventions first listed in Lucas, 1990a, pp. 68–71.

Make teaching effectiveness a high-priority goal of the department. Chairs must talk about teaching. They need to discuss their own classes and what new things they are attempting to do in the present semester, based on how the same class went last term. Chairs can then inquire about innovations faculty are using in their classes and strategies faculty have used in teaching particular topics. A chair can try what a faculty member suggests and report back to that individual. It is vital that chairs talk about teaching!

Let faculty know that teaching effectiveness, like learning, is a lifelong process. Chairs must set the goal of ongoing professional development in teaching. One concept chairs need to share with faculty members is that teaching effectiveness, like building a relationship or managing anger, is not a goal that once reached can be taken for granted forever after. Teaching effectiveness must be an enterprise that continues to engage faculty, one that requires that a faculty member be, in Schön's term (1987), a reflective practitioner. When most of the department faculty begin to view teaching as a process that requires continued reflection and discussion, the potential for learning is great. Excitement is contagious, and some of the less able teachers are influenced to become better teachers.

Create a climate of trust and support so that faculty's visits to each other's classrooms are acceptable and nonthreatening. The goal of ongoing professional development in teaching can make observation possible. Chairs can emphasize classroom observation as positive feedback and an opportunity to receive additional perspectives on teaching. Although chairs still need to evaluate faculty for purposes of personnel decision making, they can accentuate observation as a chance for useful feedback and positive growth.

A personal example may be helpful here. When I became chair of one department, several faculty members indicated to me privately that something should be done about several untenured faculty who were very poor teachers. Since I had come from a department where peer observation was done routinely, I assumed that was the way my new department functioned as well. However, when I checked with the two of the senior tenured faculty who had told me about the poor quality of instruction, one of them said, "We don't do colleague observation in this department, but if Harry and I volunteer to have you visit our classes, then it won't seem as if you are just observing the worst people in the department." I accepted their advice, and when I said at a departmental meeting that I would be observing classroom teaching, the two senior tenured faculty, who had the reputation of being excellent teachers, volunteered to be the first two to be visited. Beginning my observation with these highly regarded instructors really worked well to modify the norms in that department.

Invite a few faculty members to observe one of your classes. To emphasize the value of feedback, a chair can announce his or her own intention to be evaluated. At a departmental meeting, the chair might say, "I have not had any feedback on my teaching for a long time. I'm going to ask a couple of people if they will give me feedback on my teaching, and I will let you know how I make out." If even the thought of doing this is disquieting, a chair can begin by inviting two kindly senior colleagues, or two of the least critical people in the department, to observe a class. Then, chairs can manage the feedback so that they receive favorable comments about what they are doing well while also getting suggestions about what they might work on improving. To ensure constructive feedback, a chair might say, "Bob, I would love to have you observe my class and give me some feedback. What I would like to know particularly is, when are my students most engaged in learning? When are they most involved? What did I do, or what happened to create that? When were they least engaged, and what did I do to create that situation?" Chairs may suggest any questions that will give them meaningful, affirming feedback. Notice that, with such questions to answer, it is almost impossible for the observer not to give the instructor some positive feedback.

If individuals are going to accept criticism, they also need to know that their colleagues saw some effective teaching behaviors. Once they have heard what they are doing effectively, they can tolerate some negative feedback and will listen when they are told what they did that turned students off. After chairs have been observed and have received some suggestions, they should try one or two of the recommendations so they can report on the results at the next departmental meeting. A chair might announce, for example, that "Bob and Doug each observed one of my classes, and I found it to be very useful. First, it felt good to get some positive feedback. Then, we talked about some approaches I might use that I haven't attempted before. In my next class, I tried a new way of involving students, and it really worked." Chairs can go into as much or as little detail about the experience as they wish, but the goal is to build an open climate that makes it easier for a chair to conduct teaching evaluations. When the chair next points out an area in which improvement is necessary, it will be in the context of ongoing professional development for everyone.

When advertising for new faculty, include the potential for effective teaching as one of the requirements for the position. If departmental travel funds are limited, a search and screen committee can request videotapes of a teaching module (a lecture or a discussion led by the applicant) from candidates who live at a distance. This will let candidates know from the outset that the committee is serious about effective teaching and gives the department a position to build on after a candidate is invited to join the faculty. *The Role of the Department Chair*, a document distributed by the American Sociological Association, makes a strong recommendation that considerable effort be devoted to assessing candidate's teaching ability (Bowker, Mauksch, Keating, & McSeveney, 1992), advising that "documentation of teaching abilities should precede the campus interview. Candidates who reach the semi-final stage in the search process should be asked to submit sets of teaching evaluations, course syllabi, statements of teaching philosophy, and any other available written evidence that bears on their teaching ability" (p. 20). When the time and expense devoted to recruitment and selection of faculty are considered, creating opportunities to observe candidates doing what they are being hired to do is certainly warranted.

Require all applicants for faculty positions to make a presentation to faculty and students before receiving a faculty appointment. The document quoted in the preceding paragraph also recommends that "candidates for teaching positions should be kept on campus for at least two full days, during which they teach three or more regular classes in addition to the scholarly lecture often delivered to an audience of faculty members. Bring them in as guest lecturers to a regularly scheduled class."

Candidates' attitudes toward students, their ability to answer questions, their facility to adjust their language level and presentation of a topic to graduate or undergraduate students, and their capability for involving students are all significant attributes to consider in the screening process. After a candidate's visit, discussion between faculty and students about the candidate should be encouraged. Faculty can learn a great deal about what students value in a teacher from such an experience while students enjoy this level of participation, and their sense of community is increased when they recognize that the department values their input and they begin to realize how much care goes into selecting faculty.

Of course, before chairs implement these hiring procedures, they should discuss them with the informal leaders in the department and obtain their support. Then, the procedures for evaluating teaching effectiveness of future candidates should be discussed at a departmental meeting.

Reward good teaching. Be creative. Money is not the only reward. Chairs should brainstorm with faculty to come up with a list of items faculty find reinforcing. For example, fund teaching activities, not just research projects, using funds from the departmental budget to purchase experiential materials to enhance classroom teaching; fund classroom research; provide travel money for attending faculty development workshops; institute departmental awards for excellent teaching. A few departments have picked up the lunch tab for an excellent teacher and two student guests. Others have set up small accounts in the bookstore to reward good teachers.

Sponsor departmental workshops on different aspects of teaching. Teaching workshops can be conducted by a few of the faculty, who can integrate their experience with an article or a section of a book that they read for this purpose. Occasionally, chairs or teaching committees can invite staff from the institution's instructional development center to present a departmental workshop on a relevant topic.

Share course syllabi with all department members. Trask (1989), a chair of a history department in the Wisconsin system, points out that nothing makes faculty members more thoughtful about preparing a syllabus than knowing their colleagues will be reading it.

Provide feedback to department members by circulating an anonymous list of grade distributions for all courses offered by the department.

Each copy of this list identifies by name only the grades given by the particular faculty member who receives that copy. No names of courses are listed; however, graduate courses are distinguished from undergraduate courses. This intervention is useful when there are several individuals whose grades are excessively high or low. Often, when they see how different their grading is from the rest of the department, they adjust to a more realistic distribution without the chair's having to speak to them. At the very least, faculty's bases for grading and their individual expectations can more easily become a topic at a departmental meeting.

Begin a teaching committee. This group can work with new faculty and share relevant issues about teaching with the rest of the department. Subcommittees can deal with curriculum revision, classroom instruction, and colleague observation. Faculty are sometimes more responsive to workshops on teaching planned by colleagues but clearly supported by the chair than to workshops to which only the chair seems committed.

Build a departmental library on teaching. The literature on pedagogy, learning, and motivation is becoming very rich and comprehensive. Selected items from the suggestions later in this chapter and from the references for this book and other sources could be purchased to start a departmental library; material could be borrowed from the instructional development center or university library.

Use student and colleague evaluations as feedback to celebrate good teaching. Do not take good teaching for granted. Give good or improved teachers a chance to savor their success on evaluations. When faculty need improvement in particular areas, develop a specific plan and a follow-up to improve their teaching techniques. (Handling a feedback interview is addressed in Chapter Six.)

Develop a mentoring system. Ask two faculty members to work together as a teacher-observer team. Once a week during the semester, both of them interview approximately three students from one of the teacher's classes. These interviews focus not on the teacher but on the students and their ways of learning, how they read assignments and prepare for class, and the student-teacher interactions during class periods. The teacher and observer then meet for about one hour once a week to discuss the implications of these interviews with respect to how the course is taught. Faculty involved in such a program are usually extremely enthusiastic about the ways in which this mentoring process benefits their teaching (Katz, 1985; Katz & Henry, 1988; Wunsch, 1994).

Introduce classroom research techniques for evaluating the effectiveness of teaching strategies and aiding understanding of what is going on in the classroom. A variety of simple research tools can be used to discover what topics and approaches students are most enthusiastic about, what faculty members were doing at the time in the semester when a number of students stopped attending class, what student expectations are, and generally what works and does not work in the classroom. One quick and easy but very useful research approach is the two-minute quiz (Angelo & Cross, 1993). At the end of a class, students are asked to write an anonymous answer to a question such as, What topic presented today was most interesting to you? or, What issue in today's class left you feeling confused?

Send interested faculty to workshops on teaching and have them run a workshop when they return. One way to get the most from travel money is to have a funded faculty member present a workshop so that everyone can benefit from what one person learned.

Invite faculty and students to brown-bag lunches, so that students can share what classroom experiences are meaningful to them. Some preparation of faculty ahead of time, so that they do not become defensive, and some instruction to students to focus on issues, not professors by name, are useful. Even faculty who feel tuned in to student issues find such informal meetings can give them a whole new perspective on how students view academic experiences.

Pass on the good news whenever you hear students commenting about exciting classes or interesting projects. This not only reinforces good teaching, but also creates the norm that good teaching is a topic worthy of discussion.

Create a tolerance for risk taking, so that individuals are willing to try new things in their classrooms. Innovations are not failures if faculty learn something from them. For example, the first time an instructor attempts small-group discussions, he or she may become disenchanted with the method because one or two groups in the back of the room discuss sports instead of the assigned topic. If as a result of the attempt, however, a faculty member learns that questions must be structured more carefully or that it is useful to walk around the room to listen in on what each group is doing or that groups can be kept on track by requiring that someone from each group give a short report on the outcome of the discussion, faculty can revise the approach and try it again in the next class.

Experiment with the teaching portfolio. This instrument is particularly useful for new faculty and for those preparing for promotion and tenure. One of this device's great advantages is the amount of introspection and analysis involved in the process of compiling the portfolio. Also, because the teaching portfolio involves working with a colleague as mentor, many of the advantages of thinking through the process of teaching occur, to the benefit of the individual, the mentor, and the department.

Use team teaching. Although difficulties often surround assigning credit to individuals when two people teach the same course in alternate semesters, what faculty learn from team teaching can be well worth the extra effort. However, in order for team teaching to be a learning experience, both teachers must attend all classes. If each simply teaches half the course, there are no benefits gained from observing another faculty member teach, handle questions, and involve students.

Encourage faculty to make videotapes of their teaching. These tapes can be viewed in private, with an instructor measuring his or her performance against a list of statements that relate to a variety of teaching skills, such as the list in Erickson's *Teaching Analysis by Students* (1974) or Centra's sample student and classroom observation forms (1993, pp. 179–215). If an instructor wishes, he or she can invite someone to act as a consultant, making recommendations about areas where improvement is needed.

Recommend that faculty collect their own student evaluations early in the semester, while there is still time to make adjustments in the course. This technique lets students know that the instructor cares about students' response to the teaching approaches employed. It can also initiate a dialogue about what is and is not working. (These early student evaluations do not replace those normally used by universities in the last third of the semester.)

Have faculty who teach related courses meet informally on a regular basis to talk about common problems and strategies. In these support groups, faculty might offer mutual help to each other by offering to observe each other's classrooms. Other ideas a chair can use to enhance teaching effectiveness can be found in an earlier book of mine (Lucas, 1989a).

Teaching Topics Worth Talking About

Once the department chair legitimizes the subject of teaching as a topic worthy of attention, there are many teaching topics to be explored. Although some may have surfaced in connection with other subjects at department meetings, the topics listed here in the form of questions to be regularly discussed are all worth consideration by faculty who have made a commitment to instructional effectiveness. When teaching topics are discussed in the department, the chair should guard against allowing conversations to become generalizations about pedagogical theory. The primary purpose of such discussions is to stimulate faculty reflection about their own teaching, to share success stories with colleagues, to generate interest in looking at teaching from different perspectives, and to learn methods of teaching difficult topics that have already worked for others in the department. Such conversations, which

Parker J. Palmer (1993) says faculty need in order to keep up their courage, provide an opportunity that faculty might not otherwise have to engage in conversations about teaching—and in the action-oriented support groups that encourage the heart. (An earlier version of this list appears in Lucas, 1990a). References are provided so that faculty can integrate outside readings with their classroom experience.

What constitutes effective teaching? What can faculty do to enhance their own teaching effectiveness? (See Bateman, 1990; Brookfield, 1990; Daloz, 1986; Lowman, 1990; Schön, 1987; Svinicki, 1990; Weimer, 1990.)

How do we motivate students? (See Guskey, 1988; Katz & Henry, 1988; Lucas, 1990b.)

How can we reinforce students' efforts and improvement without creating grade inflation? What is the purpose of feedback? (See Janzow & Eison, 1990; Milton, Pollio, & Eison, 1986.)

What makes a lecture good? (See Eble, 1994; Erickson & Strommer, 1991; Frederick, 1986.)

What are some alternatives to lecturing? What are some useful strategies for leading a discussion? (See Clark, 1988; Davis, 1993; Frederick, 1989.)

How can we involve students more actively in learning? (See Davis, 1993; Meyers & Jones, 1993; Neff & Weimer, 1989; Wilkerson & Feletti, 1989.)

How can the first day of class be used to create positive student norms and expectations for the rest of the semester? (See Davis, 1993; Erickson & Strommer, 1991.)

What is collaborative learning? How can it be used as an alternative to traditional classroom learning? (See Bruffee, 1984; Gabelnick, MacGregor, Matthews, & Smith, 1990; Goodsell, Maher, & Tinto, 1992; MacGregor, 1990.)

How can our discipline be used to teach critical thinking?

(See Browne, 1986; King & Kitchener, 1994; Kurfiss, 1988, 1989.)

How do students' levels of cognitive development affect what and how they learn, and what are the implications for teaching? (See Perry, 1970, 1981.)

How does one assess institutional, program, and instructional outcomes? (See Angelo, 1991; Banta, 1993; Erwin, 1991; Gardiner, 1989.)

How can valid examinations be constructed so that they accurately assess learning outcomes? (See Bloom, 1956; Bloom, Madaus, & Hastings, 1981; Jacobs & Chase, 1992.)

What are some classroom factors related to increasing student retention? (See Noel, Levitz, Saluri, & Associates, 1985; Tinto, 1987, 1988.)

How can classroom management issues (for example, students who dominate discussions, are disruptive, or shy) be handled? (See Eble, 1994; McKeachie, 1994.)

How do we prevent cheating and plagiarism? (See Center for Teaching Effectiveness Staff, 1985; Haines, Diekhoff, LaBeff, & Clark, 1986.)

How can adult motivation to learn be enhanced? (See Marienan & Chickering, 1982; Wlodkowski, 1993.)

What are some of the better ways of handling students who come to class unprepared? (See Eble, 1994; Lawrence, 1989.)

What are the essential ingredients in a course syllabus? (See Altman, 1989; Mager, 1984.)

How can student and colleague evaluations be used to improve teaching effectiveness? (See Lucas, 1989b.)

Are there special approaches to teaching college freshmen? (See Erickson & Strommer, 1991.)

How can we develop and use tests effectively? (See Jacobs & Chase, 1992.)

What different levels of educational goals are tapped by the different kinds of questions that can be asked in class or on examinations? (See Bloom, 1956; Bloom, Madaus, & Hastings, 1981.)

How can large sections be taught most effectively? (See Davis, 1993; Holmes, 1985; Lewis, 1987; Weimer, 1987.)

How can we deal with classes that vary markedly in terms of such student characteristics as intelligence, prior knowledge, cognitive stage, and gender? (See Belenky, Clinchy, Goldberger, & Tarule, 1986; Hall & Sandler, 1982; Magolda, 1992; McKeachie, 1994; Pearson, Shavlik, & Touchton, 1989; Perry, 1970, 1981.)

What special considerations and practices are useful in teaching classes in which there is cultural diversity? (See Anderson, 1988; Banks, 1988; Border & Chism, 1992; Green, 1988b; Halpern, 1994; Hilliard, 1989; Pemberton, 1988; Sedlacek, 1983; Smith, 1989.)

What classroom research techniques will provide information on the relationship in a given course between specific teaching techniques and student learning? (See Angelo & Cross, 1993.)

How does one go about planning a new course, curriculum, or program? (See Diamond, 1989.)

How can minority retention be improved? (See Carter & Wilson, 1993; Clewell & Ficklen, 1986.)

How can the case study approach be used to enhance teaching? (See Boehrer & Linsky, 1990; Christensen & Hansen, 1987; Lang, 1987.)

What is writing across the curriculum? (See Tomlinson, 1990.)

How can we help students improve their learning effectiveness? (See Angelo, 1991; Pintrich & Johnson, 1990.)

What are the important elements in creating a mentoring relationship for faculty? (See Katz & Henry, 1988; Sorcinelli & Austin, 1992; Wunsch, 1994.)

How can we build a diverse faculty in our department? (See Gainen & Boice, 1993.)

What is cooperative learning? (See Cooper et al., 1990; Johnson, Johnson, & Smith, 1991; Millis, 1991.)

In departments where talking about teaching is resisted by the departmental culture, particularly in those departments where a large percentage of the faculty have been teaching for many years but have not done any serious reflection, as a group, about their teaching, the topics just listed should pique faculty curiosity. A chair can distribute this list and ask faculty which topics they would like to discuss or which topics might provide interesting content for a workshop. A chair can also take a more formal approach, discussing the idea with informal leaders of the department, listening to their ideas, incorporating their suggestions, and obtaining their support, and then presenting the activity, along with a set of procedures, for discussion at a departmental meeting—calling the meeting, perhaps, New Ideas about Teaching in Higher Education, or Experiential Learning Strategies in the Classroom.

At this meeting, the chair tells faculty the department has not talked much about teaching lately and asks them to select, from the list in this chapter, some topics that can be discussed by two or three faculty members at the next meeting. The chair can mention five or six potential topics if necessary; the informal leaders can add a few more. The chair also asks for volunteers, either to organize the next meeting or to serve as discussion leaders. Discussion leaders are asked to read material from the references included with the topic list and to integrate what they read with their teaching experience. Acquainting faculty with some of the recent research and ideas about teaching and learning should provoke some stimulating discussions and start them thinking about teaching in a different way. If this discussion on a teaching topic goes well, the chair can then ask if a few people will volunteer to become a teaching committee to organize future discussions, panels, or workshops.

If some faculty seem not at all receptive, the chair might organize brown-bag lunches with the most effective teachers and anyone else who is interested. One of this group can give regular reports at subsequent faculty meetings on new ideas about teaching that are generated in the lunchtime discussions, and after a time, the lunchtime participants can evaluate the discussion program and decide on the next steps they will recommend to the rest of the department. One of the most enthusiastic participants should be asked to make this report.

In addition, the chair can distribute short articles on some aspect of teaching at intervals during the semester.

Making Competent Teachers of New Faculty

Since it is so difficult to reverse the process of ineffective teaching, preventing dysfunctional approaches from becoming deeply ingrained is clearly a better alternative. As vast numbers of new faculty are hired in the next decade, higher education has a special chance to improve the quality of its teaching. Instead of allowing this new generation of faculty to struggle in isolation, teaching by trial and error or simply in the way they were taught, chairs can use the knowledge from research on effective teaching to help them.

Some of the most useful research about the needs of new faculty and how individuals become proficient in teaching is Boice's comprehensive longitudinal study (1992) of 185 new faculty members. Results of this research have replaced a number of incorrect assumptions of the kind I frequently encounter when I am invited to lead a faculty development workshop for chairs. I ask whether the institution would like some attention given to the motivation of new faculty, and the response is usually, "No, the academic vice president's office already sponsors an orientation day that helps them learn all they need to know about the way the university operates. They are taken on a tour of the library, the computer labs, and other campus facilities. A luncheon is also included so the new faculty can get to know one another." Such orientation days are nice arrangements that undoubtedly make new faculty feel welcome, but they do not begin to address the information new faculty members need.

According to Boice's study, despite orientation days, the first three years of a new faculty member's life seemed permeated by feelings of isolation and loneliness, a perception of lack of collegial support, and lack of intellectual stimulation (1992, pp. 22–39). In addition, new faculty felt resentful that the feedback they did receive emphasized criticism, that the standards enforced for new faculty could not be met by the evaluators, and that the criteria for tenure were unspecified. Further, they felt there was no discussion of how to teach. Spending three to four hours a week preparing for each hour of classroom presentation, new faculty overprepared for their classes and felt underappreciated, for despite all of their preparation, the teaching of new faculty was rated as mediocre by their students (Boice, 1992, pp. 62–72).

What did new faculty members need from their institutions? Some direction emerges from the twenty-three new faculty members Boice identified as quick starters, those rated by students and expert-observers among the top quarter of their group of cohorts in teaching excellence by their second or third semester. When interviewed, all the excellent teachers were willing to offer advice to those working with new faculty. The most important factor in their success was achieving balance among preparing for teaching, performing scholarly activities, and social networking. Achieving this balance required a certain amount of self-management. The excellent teachers spent no more than two hours of preparation for one class hour, spent four to five hours a week on scholarly writing, and about the same amount of time on networking. These quick starters took the initiative in getting involved socially with colleagues in order to obtain the support they needed from experienced teachers and researchers.

Boice also offers important advice, based on his own intervention, about increasing the comfort level for new faculty in the classroom. This was accomplished through having new faculty engage in self-monitoring to pinpoint anxiety levels related to specific aspects of teaching. Faculty then participated in relaxation workshops conducted by Boice, which were followed by continued monitoring of anxiety to discover improvement. Finally, individuals were encouraged to initiate informal communication with students before class, and then to obtain early informal student evaluations so problems could be detected and solved (Boice, 1992, pp. 135–136, 141–146). To these highly useful interventions, I would add cognitive restructuring, a strategy demonstrated to have a significant impact on reducing anxiety. Cognitive restructuring asks new faculty members to examine their self-messages about teaching and to replace negative irrational thinking with positive rational thoughts. For example, if an instructor thinks, Perhaps my students will know more about this subject than I do, the instructor can replace this anxious thought with a positive message: If this happens, I will ask them to share what they know with the class. By sharing the spotlight I can make them my allies.

A new teacher might think, What if I don't know the answers to the questions students ask? For this anxiety-provoking thought, the teacher can substitute the thought, No one can possibly know everything there is to know. I will compliment the student for asking such a thought-provoking question. I will ask if anyone else can answer the question. If not, I will tell the student what I know about the subject, promise to look up additional information, and suggest that he or she do the same so we can compare notes at the next class meeting.

Unchecked negative thoughts raise anxiety levels and are, therefore, dysfunctional. When internal dialogue provokes excessive anxiety, teaching effectiveness is diminished. Therefore, chairs should plan on ways to reduce new faculty's anxiety.

Studies on new faculty are in strong agreement about the significance of the chair's role in these instructors' professional development. "Chairs cited as particularly helpful took time to assign courses that fit faculty interests, negotiated minimal new course preparations or reduced loads, secured internal funds for travel or resources, and provided guidance for annual reviews. In contrast, chairs who assigned excessive workloads and provided little mentoring to new faculty were a dominant source of stress" (Sorcinelli, 1992, p. 31).

Another approach that can be very effective with new faculty is a mentoring system, provided the mentors are supportive and able to form relationships with the new people as equals. Only in such circumstances will a new faculty member feel free to discuss difficulties and solicit help. It is also useful if mentors become familiar with the literature that identifies new faculty members' concerns, so the mentors can be sensitive to issues such as those just raised. During a new faculty member's first two years, some universities have found it productive to use colleague observations that are strictly formative and do not become part of the personnel records. The essential focus of these observations is instructional development. New faculty members might also visit the classrooms of experienced faculty and discuss with them what was observed and why one pedagogy rather than another was used. If chairs employ such approaches as these, the new faculty members added in the coming years will become a strong coterie of effective teachers in higher education. They will continue to discuss teaching as ongoing professional development, welcome colleague visits to their classrooms as a source of meaningful feedback, and find the teaching-learning process to be a valued activity that constantly generates new insights.

Conclusion

Chairs can motivate faculty to teach effectively by instituting colleague observation of classes and by asking to have their own classes observed first. Chairs must also recognize the myths that prevent discussion of teaching in the department and create a supportive environment in which faculty accept that pedagogy is an area in which they can all help each other learn. In addition, chairs can improve departmental teaching by making teaching ability a priority when new faculty are hired.

I suggest that chairs set these two goals for themselves after reading this chapter. First, they can ensure that the next person they hire for a teaching position will be an effective teacher. Reaching this goal will require obtaining the cooperation of other faculty to support new hiring procedures that follow the steps outlined in this chapter and to meet with students to discuss the candidates' teaching abilities. Chairs must also include steps for following up with a new instructor by giving him or her feedback and mentoring from effective teachers. Second, chairs can set a goal of increasing faculty's knowledge of topics important to teaching. Chairs can start the process informally before presenting it at a department meeting, and they can work primarily with those who are interested at first, letting interest build as faculty gradually get involved in workshops and discussions and readings on the topic through the steps described earlier. Again, for faculty to talk about teaching, chairs must talk about teaching.

Chapter Six

Providing Feedback on Classroom Teaching

Classroom observation of teaching is not done in a number of universities. Based on his 1993 survey of 658 undergraduate deans of liberal arts colleges, Seldin (1993a) reported that only 33 percent always used classroom observations as a source of information in evaluating teaching performance—an increase, however, over the 19.8 percent reported in 1983. In those institutions in which classroom observation is not used, it is probable that the departmental culture supports the beliefs expressed in these statements: "I am a tenured faculty member who has been teaching for a long time. There is certainly no question about my competence"; or, "I will not submit to colleague or chair observation of my classroom because that would be a violation of my academic freedom." These assertions reflect several difficulties that chairs need to recognize and deal with. First, length of time in the classroom is no guarantee of competence, particularly when an instructor does not engage in ongoing discussion of teaching. And there is evidence that, although teaching is evaluated with great frequency, faculty conversations about effective and ineffective teaching behaviors are not widespread. Based on his survey of 1,680 faculty members from fourteen institutions, Gaff (1978, p. 53) reported that 42 percent said that, during their entire academic careers, no one had ever discussed their teaching with them in any detail.

Second, the statement that equates colleague observation with infringement of academic freedom is not accurate because academic freedom does not protect faculty from accountability. Colleges hire faculty members to teach. Moreover, even at the most prestigious universities, where individuals may be selected purely because of their reputation as researchers, the teaching-learning process is usually emphasized as a value of the institution, and faculty members are expected to be at least adequate as teachers.

Finally, when neither colleague nor chair visits the classroom, teacher evaluation still occurs, but with other tools, ones that may not be as reliable as observation. For example, at one large university I visited in Australia, where colleague observations were rarely conducted, student evaluations formed the primary basis of judgments made about faculty teaching.

What Student Evaluations Can—and Cannot— Contribute to Evaluation

Student evaluations have been used for more than thirty years in higher education, and by the late 1970s, a majority of institutions reported using them for tenure and promotion decisions (Centra, 1993). Expanding use of student evaluations was also found in Seldin's longitudinal survey at ten-year intervals of 600 liberal arts colleges. Seldin (1993b, p. A40) reported that "the number of institutions using student ratings to evaluate teachers had climbed from 29 percent [in 1973] to 68 percent [in 1983] to 86 percent [in 1993]. No other method of evaluation approached that degree of usage, and other studies have found similar results." Seldin has also noted (1993a) that in these 600 liberal arts colleges, student evaluations of teaching are reported to be "always used" three times as frequently as colleague observation of classroom teaching.

Using Student Evaluations for Personnel Decision Making

Student evaluations are used to determine teaching effectiveness for purposes of making promotion, tenure, and merit decisions and for purposes of guiding faculty development efforts. The increase in the use of student evaluations as the primary method for determining teaching effectiveness for personnel decision making is due to several factors, the most important of which is that student evaluations do provide a valid measure of classroom teaching. As one measure of their validity, Cohen (1981) conducted a large study on the relationship between student evaluations of instructors and what students have learned. Using a meta-analysis of forty-one studies of multisection courses taught by different instructors but having common final exams, Cohen found a correlation of .43 between the mean of student ratings of the instructor and mean final exam performance. As a frame of reference for understanding the significance of a correlation of .43, consider the prediction of college students' freshman year grades based on their high school grades, a procedure that has a correlation of about .45 (Donlon, 1984). The comparison of these two correlations makes it clear that, in both cases, while the measures are helpful, additional measures are needed in order to produce truly accurate judgments about performance.

While research indicates that student evaluations can make a valid and reliable contribution to the evaluation of teaching, there are also other reasons for the escalation in their use. They are relatively easy to administer and score, they are the least costly and time-consuming method of evaluating teaching, and they produce easily reported statistical results. It is important to recognize, however, that results of student evaluations—means, histograms, and comparison data—can be misinterpreted to be purely objective data by those responsible for making personnel decisions. But statistical data from such evaluations are merely summations of very subjective judgments, influenced by the wide range of motivations found among students.

The literature on performance evaluation as it is used in a variety of organizations (for example, Carrell, Kuzmits, & Elbert, 1992, pp. 237–239) cautions about such rating errors as conscious or unconscious rater bias, the halo effect (generalizing from one aspect of a person to all aspects of performance), leniency (consistently high ratings), strictness (consistently low ratings), errors of central tendency (evaluating everyone as average), and recency (ratings based on the rater's remembering more about what someone did just before the appraisal than about actions in prior weeks or months). In many organizations in which evaluation of individuals is taken seriously, considerable time and money are devoted to training users of appraisal instruments. In academe, when ratings are done anonymously by students, who have no training in evaluation, who have no need to justify or explain judgments, and who can use evaluations to rationalize inadequate performance of their own, the possibility of error is great. The existence of such errors in the evaluation process is sometimes forgotten by chairs and members of promotion and tenure committees. But it is important for all concerned to remember that student ratings are at best rough approximations of those selected teaching characteristics that students are capable of evaluating, that small differences between faculty members' evaluations are often due to chance, and that course variables (such as class size; whether a course is required, an elective, or part of a major; and whether a course is for graduate or undergraduate students) are all factors that affect evaluations.

On the one hand, students are in an excellent position to form judgments about some behaviors. Does the faculty member come regularly to class and on time? Is there evidence of preparation for class? Is the material well organized as it is presented? Does the instructor provide a handle for difficult material, so that students are able to relate what is being taught to something with which they are already familiar? Are students treated with respect? Are questions answered in ways that increase students' understanding? Are assignments and their purposes clear, and are they directly related to what is being taught? Do the assessment measures used reflect the goals of the course? In all of these areas, students are in a good position to contribute a particular perspective that no one else can depict.

On the other hand, there are critical aspects of teaching about which students are not able to make valid judgments. Are faculty members knowledgeable or is misinformation given with some frequency? Are instructors up to date in the discipline? Are they devoting a sufficient amount of time to topics that are significant in a rapidly developing field? Are goals for a particular class or course clear? Is there evidence that instructors are using appropriate methods to achieve the goals of a course? Only an expert in the discipline can make informed judgments about these questions, and collecting student evaluations provides only part of the information needed to accurately assess teaching.

Higher education's current massive reliance on student evaluations as a single measure of teaching effectiveness, a reliance prompted by faculty resistance to colleague observation and to the time commitment that this observation requires, is a reason why the teaching portfolio has caught on so in the last few years. Faculty, particularly those seeking tenure or promotion, correctly feel that a teaching portfolio gives them some input into the judgments made of their teaching ability. Faculty are able to include in these portfolios such documents as course syllabi, reading lists, typical assignments, the kind of feedback they give on papers, and sometimes videotapes of their teaching and portfolios of students' work. The use of a teaching portfolio, particularly when it is developed with a mentor, can have a strong effect on faculty members because it prods them to be introspective about their educational philosophy and pedagogy, the relationship they see between course goals and the teaching methodology chosen to meet those goals, and the risks they took, the failures they experienced, and what they learned when classes did not go as planned. Seldin (1991, 1993c) offers a guide for what materials should be included in teaching portfolios and how different universities have used them.

Using Student Evaluations to Improve Teaching

The improvement of teaching is sometimes viewed as an automatic by-product of student evaluations. However, the way in which student evaluations are typically used may decrease their effectiveness in enhancing teaching. Leading experts in the field of appraising faculty performance (Centra, 1993; Miller, 1987; Seldin, 1985) recommend that student evaluations be completed during the last few weeks of the semester but before final exam week. This means that, if student evaluations are collected between mid-November and mid-December, and the semester break occurs during the month of January, the computer printouts will not be placed in faculty mailboxes until late February or early March. (Typically, these printouts include means and frequency distributions, plotted as histograms, for each class in which student ratings have been collected, along with comparison data reporting means for the rest of the department and the college.) This means that feedback is typically delayed by about three months, and the printouts are distributed the semester after the evaluated courses have been completed. Such a lengthy interval between performance and reaction greatly diminishes the effectiveness of feedback, which is most useful when given as soon as possible after behavior occurs (Bergquist & Phillips, 1975; Gordon, 1993; Ilgen, Fisher, & Taylor, 1979). Therefore, although the timing is intended to ensure that student grades are not influenced by student evaluations of the instructor, faculty members, already in the midst of working with a new group of students, can barely remember what they did to earn last semester's evaluations.

Moreover, since instructors tend to rate themselves higher than their students or colleagues do (Feldman, 1989), and since mediocre and poor teachers are even less accurate in their self-assessments than good teachers (Barber, 1990; Centra, 1993), many faculty members experience consternation when they look at their student evaluations. Although this consternation might be viewed as a catalyst or motivator for improvement, faculty who have been judged below average on some categories often have no clear idea about what they could do to improve. Unless they have an opportunity to discuss their student evaluations with an individual skilled in teaching consultation, and knowledgeable about managing feedback, it is unlikely that faculty members will know how to use this student-generated information to improve their teaching.

In a comprehensive paper on giving feedback to improve teaching, Brinko (1993, p. 577) concludes from her research that, "feedback is more effective when the source of information is perceived as credible, knowledgeable, and well-intentioned." In my work with faculty and chairs during the past twenty-five years, there have been a number of individuals who vehemently insist that student evaluations do not fit any of these criteria. It may be, as Centra (1993) suggests, basing his opinion on his review of Franklin and Theall's study (1989), that faculty who know more about the research on student evaluations have more positive attitudes about their use. However, many faculty members, uninformed about the research on student evaluation, often deal with the disappointment they feel through such rationalizations as, "Students just don't want to work as hard as I make them work in my class," or, "Students are not equipped to make a judgment about my competence." Such rationalizations as these are congruent with Boice's findings (1992), reported in Chapter Five, that faculty tend to externalize blame when student evaluations are poor.

However, even when some faculty members have made clear their negative feelings towards student evaluation, chairs can do several things to make student evaluations more effective tools for improving teaching. First, as suggested once before, chairs can encourage faculty to obtain their own student evaluations during the first third of the semester, when there is still time to change teaching practices that are not working. Since these evaluations should provide immediate information to the instructor about student reactions, the evaluation forms should include lists of concrete instructional behaviors to be rated, so faculty can learn, specifically, which behaviors work and which ones need to be changed. Excellent lists of teaching behaviors can be found in Centra's sample student and classroom observation forms (1993, pp. 179–215) or in Erickson's *Teaching Analysis by Students* (1974). Faculty can be encouraged to select items from these or similar lists for inclusion in early student evaluation forms, to use the feedback they get from the forms to guide personal experiments with different classroom approaches, and to administer the same form again around the twelfth week of class to discover the effect of the new approaches. Faculty who want concrete information about the effects of their teaching behaviors will find this method very useful.

Second, chairs can bring Weimer's checklist (1990, pp. 207–208) for developing instructional awareness to the attention of faculty. This series of questions about key classroom behaviors does not specify right or wrong answers but guides faculty introspection, so that a teacher can answer the questions: What am I doing? and, Is this what I want to be doing? This exercise allows faculty to detach themselves from their teaching to look at their own behaviors. Faculty can then videotape segments of their own classes to verify their perceptions of the impact of their behavior on students.

Third, chairs can arrange for faculty to receive consultation on improving problem areas when student ratings are distributed. Instructional development offices, which exist on at least one-third of college campuses, are usually able to provide this service. Alternatively, an external consultant can conduct a workshop for department chairs on how to teach faculty skills in conducting feedback interviews for both student and colleague evaluations. Research reported by Menges and Brinko (1986) provides evidence that investing in teaching consultation will pay off in improved instruction. Based on a meta-analysis of thirty studies on the effects of student ratings at midsemester on the student ratings at the end of the term, the researchers found that teachers who had received early student feedback were rated in the 59th percentile at the end of the semester, as contrasted with those who received no feedback, who were rated in the 50th percentile. However, when student evaluations were accompanied by consultation, teaching effectiveness increased to the 85th percentile. Since faculty in these studies had only half a semester to make changes, it can be expected that significantly greater improvement will occur over a longer period of time.

A final implication of the growing use of student ratings as a basis for major decisions is that chairs should periodically initiate discussions with faculty members on what student ratings can contribute to the evaluation process and on their limitations as a solitary measure of teaching effectiveness. As a first step for chairs wishing to make some sense of the large research literature on student evaluation, I recommend John A. Centra's *Reflective Faculty Evaluation* (1993).

Methods of Corporate Educators

As I have demonstrated in the last two chapters, many faculty members resist attempts at improving their instruction, so chairs need to address this culture of resistance, selecting methods from the variety of strategies included in this and the previous chapter. However, it is also instructive for chairs to examine briefly how approaches used in the corporate classroom differ from those of academe and whether there is something academicians might learn from corporate educators.

In contrast to most colleges and universities, corporate education centers are dedicated to increasing instructional effectiveness with a seriousness of purpose worth imitating. Industry educates employees on a scale that usually surprises academicians, who believe that higher education is their sole domain. In 1992, the total money budgeted by U.S. organizations with more than 100 employees for direct training expenses was $45 billion (Lee, 1992, pp. 32–33). This figure does *not* include the cost to employers of the time workers spend in the classroom instead of the workplace. In addition to this $45 billion investment, the development of corporate classrooms that offer academic degrees ranging from the associate's degree through the B.S., M.S. and M.B.A., J.D., and

Ph.D. degrees is another indication of the extent to which industry has become actively involved in higher education. Moreover, there are now more than twenty corporate colleges and universities that are sponsored by individual business organizations, industrywide interests, and professional, research, and consulting organizations. These twenty-plus corporate colleges, some with a number of campuses, are approved by state departments of higher education and regional accrediting groups (Eurich, 1985, pp. 89–95). Moreover, individual courses approved for either graduate or undergraduate credit are now given by more than two hundred noncollegiate organizations (Eurich, 1985, p. 80). Compare this $45 billion training figure, plus the cost of the corporate colleges, with the combined budget of about $164 billion for all of higher education in the 1991–92 academic year (U.S. Department of Education, 1992), and it is clear that corporate education represents a large financial investment in the development of people.

Industry's approach to learning, however, is significantly different from that of higher education. In many colleges and universities the teaching-learning process seems to be a given, a process that faculty and administrators believe they intuitively understand because they have been performing it for a long time. In industry, however, ongoing research is conducted into how people learn, not only to improve what goes on in corporate classrooms, but to enhance the effectiveness of courses created for the public market. Instructors are prepared by participating in "train-the-trainer" courses in adult learning and learner-centered education and receive feedback from master teachers on their effectiveness. In marked contrast to faculty in higher education, corporate trainers expect frequent ongoing evaluation, both in terms of achievement of course objectives and the methodology used, and frequent updating of training. In the corporate classroom, course objectives are clearly stated, courses are content intensive, and time is allowed for skills practice. Student achievement is assessed in terms of how well students have accomplished course objectives. Some companies insist on grades that represent achievement and record student performances as data that will assist the companies in determining career paths or in succession planning. Others feel grading inhibits open discussion and do not keep performance records (Eurich, 1985, pp. 53–55). With the development of course modules, software, and films for the public market, corporate training has the potential to become a major profitable learning industry, in addition to saving industry large amounts in tuition reimbursement.

In higher education, it is undoubtedly true that faculty members bring to their teaching a breadth and depth of knowledge about the specific academic discipline that is not generally found in the corporate classroom. However, since teaching is what faculty do in academe, it is surprising that—except for those who have degrees in higher education, in educational psychology, and sometimes in nursing—faculty members have rarely taken even one course in pedagogy or in human learning and motivation. Chairs have a unique opportunity, therefore, to create a departmental structure that will fill gaps in what faculty know about teaching, provide skill development, and give faculty a chance to increase their effectiveness.

Colleague Observation of Classroom Teaching

Supplementing student evaluations and public documents about teaching (for example, syllabi and examinations) with colleague observations provides more accurate data for making promotion, tenure, and merit decisions.

To help faculty members make teaching effectiveness an ongoing development project, chairs must use all the strategies discussed in Chapter Five, and they must arrange for faculty to be observed and to get feedback from someone who knows the subject being taught. This can best happen when there is colleague observation of classroom teaching or of a videotape of a class. To develop their methods of instruction, faculty need to be reflective practitioners.

They must plan a class, teach it, and be given feedback. They must be empowered to experiment, based on the hypotheses they develop from integrating their experience, reading, and shared communication about teaching. They need to record the results of their experimentation, reflect on what happened, and try to understand it, so the next class and the next course can be based on a systematic plan that has grown out of past events. Faculty can grow by experiencing success, but they can also learn from failure when it occurs in an environment with classroom observation.

Faculty who resist colleague observation often say, "No one really know what good teaching is. Bad reviews of my teaching by colleagues, or the chair, may simply represent different points of view about this amorphous subject." Chairs, too, may experience discomfort, not because they have doubts about what good teaching is, but simply because they feel it may be difficult to justify, or ground in theory, whatever feedback they offer.

Chairs can begin to ground observations by identifying the three main components of teaching suggested by Arreola (1989).

Content expertise. Does the instructor know the subject matter?

Instructional delivery skills and characteristics. Is the instructor enthusiastic and able to explain things clearly, and does the instructor have the talent to motivate and the knack of holding students' interest?

Instructional design skills. Does the instructor devise experiences that induce learning, and formulate assessment to confirm that learning has occurred?

These items provide a frame of reference within which performance can be appraised.

Content Expertise

Most faculty members, senior faculty when they have kept up with advances in their fields, and new junior faculty, fresh from graduate school courses, possess content expertise. Therefore, it is the areas of delivery and design skills that provide growth opportunities for many faculty members.

Instructional Delivery Skills

Research now has much to offer to answer faculty's questions about how adults learn, what motivates them, and what methodology is most effective in achieving which class objectives. The fact that student learning is an active process—in which the information students bring to class must be examined, some of it discarded as untenable, and the bulk of it integrated with new knowledge—can no longer be ignored. Since technology and knowledge are rapidly expanding in almost every discipline, and predictions are that college graduates will change careers five or six times during their working lives, students must also be taught how to manage their own learning so that they can accept the responsibility for remaining on the cutting edge of whatever fields they enter.

The covenant faculty create with students will no longer be that faculty will try to teach students everything faculty members know about a given topic, but rather faculty will share with students the excitement in learning a particular discipline, showing them how to ask the right questions related to some selected areas of the discipline, select a methodology to answer those questions, discover overarching themes, and present the major findings. The alternative is to experience the frustration of attempting to put twenty pounds of potatoes in a two-pound sack. Faculty simply cannot cram all of the facts about a topic into students' brains. The lecture method can be an effective way of presenting the main direction a field is taking, of summarizing interesting new hypotheses about a topic, or of presenting the agenda for what students must teach themselves. Lectures can also generate curiosity about issues a discipline is struggling with and give students a view of why a field is still exciting to someone who has been in it for a number of years. And lectures can model how experts in a field attack a problem and discuss what sustains them when questions are not easily resolved. However, in most disciplines, if students are to understand and be able to apply what instructors are trying to teach, active learning must be encouraged. Instructors must supplement lectures with experiential classroom learning that will involve students. If students are to be able to think critically about issues, they must experience guided analysis and synthesis of problems.

Finally, faculty members must also develop the ability to feel comfortable in the active learning classroom (Boice, 1992). This means being able to interact effectively with people in class. It involves respect for students and a recognition that learning, which sometimes means giving up beliefs we once felt certain about, can be anxiety provoking. Faculty comfort in the classroom requires good communication skills and the ability to paraphrase (do some active listening), to raise questions that make people think, and to strongly encourage effort. Students work hard at enterprises that make them feel good about themselves. Much undergraduate education does not enhance students' self-esteem . When faculty members communicate to students their belief that the students can do good work, when feedback is specific and lets students know the concrete things they need to do to improve the quality of their work, only then will students be willing to expend the effort to improve. (See Chapter Five for an extensive sample of the rich literature on instructional delivery skills.)

Instructional Design Skills

Higher education has paid insufficient attention to instructional design. Design of a course should begin with an analysis of student needs, but this first step is often omitted in higher education although it is frequently a part of employee education in industry. When a course is designed without regard for student needs and levels of readiness, students are alienated from the beginning because they cannot integrate the new information with anything they already know. The course content is too easy, too difficult, or too alien compared to their previous knowledge.

Course objectives follow from student needs and must be specified in behavioral terms. Objectives will motivate students when they understand why achieving the objectives is valuable to them. Methods of assessing the achievement of course objectives are then selected. An example of poor selection of assessment measures would be an instructor's choosing to teach analysis and synthesis through case studies for an entire semester and then choosing a final exam that consists of questions that tap only factual knowledge.

The next step in instructional design is to decide upon the strategies the instructor will use to accomplish course objectives, in other words, methodology. What proportion of class time will be devoted to lecture, small-group problem solving and discussion, analysis of case studies, or structured role-plays? Course materials, such as textbooks, study guides, books of case studies, computer software, and audiovisual materials, are then chosen. Finally, the course is taught, and its effectiveness evaluated. Existing instructional design can be determined both from reviewing a course syllabus and discussions with the instructor.

In general, to make a department more knowledgeable about instructional design and delivery skills, chairs should first informally determine the current frequency of discussions about these two topics. Typically, instructional design is a topic few faculty members will have read about or discussed with other faculty; therefore, the chair can provide some reading material on the topics. (This chapter and Chapter Five include many recommended sources.) In particular, instructional design skills are amply illustrated in Diamond's *Designing and Improving Courses and Curricula in Higher Education* (1989), which offers assistance for every phase of the design and planning process. Another highly recommended source, though it deals with training and development in organizations rather than higher education per se, is *Mastering the Instructional Design Process*

(Rothwell & Kazanas, 1992). Topics such as setting performance objectives, developing instructional materials, and evaluating learning outcomes are as useful to academicians as they are to industrial trainers. Nonetheless, it is true that engineering, science, technical, and business faculty will identify more quickly with the situations described than will liberal arts faculty. However, as has already been suggested, industry is developing sophisticated education models from which higher education can profit. The subjects of instructional delivery and design are also worth exploring in a departmental workshop, which can be conducted by a few faculty members.

In addition, the chair should encourage conversation about instructional design and delivery skills that have worked. To measure their own effectiveness in stimulating faculty, chairs should compare the frequency and effects of such discussions before and after the pre-intervention period.

Classroom Observation and Feedback Guidelines

The following guidelines cover the general introduction of the method of observation to faculty, followed by some suggestions for handling individual observations. Once the chair has determined the frequency of peer observations in the department, he or she can start the process or improve upon an existing process by, first, providing some written material on the dimensions of teaching that can be tapped through peer observation as a supplement to student evaluations. These writings will form a basis for subsequent discussion about the method of colleague observation. Sorcinelli's guidelines (1986) for classroom observation might be used as information to which faculty can react.

Second, the chair needs to conduct several faculty meetings to discuss the topic and develop guidelines for peer observation and feedback. The chair should also establish that the approach will be tried on an experimental basis for one year. Third, volunteers who are already effective teachers experiment with the guidelines, which are then revised on the basis of what was learned. Fourth, the chair formalizes the guidelines and distributes them to faculty members for review before the department begins using these guidelines for regular peer observations and feedback. And finally, at the end of the year, the chair must evaluate how well the process is working.

Handling the Observation

Sorcinelli's excellent guidelines for classroom observation are well worth reviewing with any department members who will be conducting colleague observations. Sorcinelli (1986, pp. 38–39) suggests that the observer and the instructor hold a pre-observation conference in which the observer gathers information about the instructor's goals for the class, how the students will have prepared for the class and what they will expect, and the instructor's teaching style. I also suggest that faculty members will be more receptive to observation if they have some ownership and investment in the process and will benefit in some way from the observation. One way to ensure ownership and subsequent benefits is to take a list of teaching behaviors, such as those included in *Teaching Analysis by Students* (Erickson, 1974) or Centra's sample student and classroom observation forms (1993), and ask the instructor to select a few of these items as a focus for attention and feedback. Since instructors are likely to choose items that they feel they handle well, the observer will be able to supply some positive feedback. As pointed out in the discussion of the way the chair could model being the subject of classroom observation, receiving feedback about teaching strengths will also make it easier for the instructor to accept observations about one or two areas that need improvement. Next the observer can review Sorcinelli's presentation of the characteristics of good teaching to know specifically how these skills and techniques can be observed.

Although some observers go to a class with a teaching evaluation form in hand, another effective procedure is to record a running account of whatever happens, quoting verbatim when particularly significant comments are made by the instructor or students. From my perspective, it is particularly important to separate observation from judgment and inferences. If observation is done accurately, the instructor cannot argue with it; whereas inferences made about what is observed can be questioned because people look at what happens from different perspectives. I remember a faculty member whom I observed who started his class by asking the question, "What has happened this week that is going to affect us economically?" In order to answer this question, students would have had to read the business section of a newspaper or magazine, or watch a news program on television, but they had not done so, and nobody volunteered an answer. The instructor's comments were, "What do you people do with your time? You read those pornographic magazines. You read *Playboy* and those sex magazines. You don't read *Fortune*; you don't read the *Wall Street Journal*. Why are you wasting your time and your parents' money by going to college?" There was a small amount of uncomfortable laughter. People slumped in their seats, and their eyes were lowered to their notes. The faculty member asked other questions for which no one had an answer. He then spent sixteen minutes reading an article from the *Wall Street Journal*. Sixteen minutes is a long time to be read to in a college classroom unless an instructor wants to demonstrate dramatic oratory, the beauty of language, or an analysis of a logical sequence of ideas. It is a long time to listen to an instructor's reading of an article from the *Wall Street Journal*. A number of students became inattentive and passed notes to each other. Several shifted in their seats and began to play hangman's noose in the back rows, making sotto voce comments.

I also observed that, at one point in the class, the instructor took up the problem of inflation and the effect it had on the poor. The example he chose was how prices had gone up in areas of the

Midwest when extensive flooding had made goods unavailable. He explained how donated food and clothing and building materials go into the black market, and how predators take advantage of the flood victims. One student with genuine concern in his voice asked, "Can't somebody do something about that when prices are raised too high?" Although it was now just five minutes before the end of class, student interest was at its highest during the class period.

Handling the Feedback Interview

After my observation of this instructor, I began my feedback interview with a discussion of the point at which students were deeply engaged and what he had done to involve them, taking a recent event that all had heard about and with which they could identify and using that human interest story to illustrate inflation and its effects. This demonstrated that I could see some of the positive approaches he had used, which had gotten students involved in what could have been a dull presentation. The instructor was pleased that what he had done was seen as positive and genuinely appreciated, but he seemed unaware, initially, of the relationship between his behavior and the arousal of such a high level of student interest. However, because what was pointed out was very positive, he was then able to accept some responsibility for less positive student behavior during other parts of the same class.

It is much easier to give feedback that is pure observation, than to deliver an evaluation based on your judgment. The instructor I observed did not disagree that the things I reported were what had happened in class; he was unaware, however, of the impact his behavior had on the students. It is a common experience for any instructor to be unaware of all that is happening in the classroom at any given point in time. When an observer reports what was recorded, and what the effect was on the dynamics of the group, it is then possible to find out whether this was the outcome intended.

When I asked about the impact he wanted to have on students when he read the *Wall Street Journal* article, the instructor told me his students never read the newspapers and magazines they are supposed to read. "Therefore," he said, "I read to them as a way of letting them know that if they don't do the reading, they will have to listen to me read to them." Also, since they were unable to answer his questions, he felt he should scold them. He then volunteered that they were highly resistive; he had scolded them before, but they still were not doing the reading. When I asked what other approaches he could come up with that might get them to do the reading, he initially indicated that it was hopeless because students just do not bother keeping up with the business news. I agreed with his perception, but asked again, "Given that this is true, how could one structure a classroom situation that would increase the probability that students would read?" He then came up with a workable idea. He indicated that he could divide the class into small groups, and give each group the responsibility of reporting to the class every third week on important business news. At least, he said, several of them would have to read the business news every three weeks, and maybe they would learn something when other students presented summaries of the news in class. I reinforced the value of this idea and told him I would be very interested in seeing how it worked and would like to talk with him again in two weeks. In this case, the professor accepted the observation as accurate, developed ownership in the problem, then evaluated the strategy he had used to achieve particular goals, found it ineffective, and developed an alternate approach that would be more useful in achieving his objective.

It is hard to conduct this kind of feedback interview if an observer brings a form into the classroom and focuses primarily on evaluation rather than observing and recording what happens. If observers have recorded what they saw, how much time is spent on certain activities, and the effect the instructor's behaviors have on student behavior, they can concentrate afterwards on evaluating what occurred.

Chairs can use the following summary of the steps used in conducting a feedback interview as guidelines for observers.

Get commitment to a time, place, and agenda for the interview. For example, you might start by saying, "I want to discuss my observation of your eleven o'clock class sometime in the early afternoon. What time would be good for you?" It is important to provide feedback soon after a class has been observed, certainly that same day if possible. However, observers also need to give themselves some time to think about the observation and how the discussion will be approached.

At the beginning of the interview, engage in a minute or two of small talk. This step eases the instructor's initial tension.

Ask how the instructor felt the observed class had gone. Also, ask what things the instructor felt he or she did that were good. Reinforce these behaviors, whenever possible. Take this opportunity to celebrate the good news, then add comments about other positive behaviors. Faculty generally receive too little positive reinforcement about their teaching, and sincere acknowledgement of successful behavior is crucial. Be certain that the instructor understands the relationship between what he or she did and that behavior's impact on group dynamics.

Ask what things did not work well. Inquire about objectives. What was the faculty member trying to accomplish? Why did it seem not to work? Brainstorm with the instructor other strategies that might be substituted for approaches that did not work. If a problem exists, confront the individual with evidence so that it cannot be denied or ignored.

Identify the problem in terms of performance of observable behaviors. Once specific behaviors are identified, it becomes easier to develop solutions, monitor progress, and evaluate change.

Invite the instructor to develop some solutions. Remain supportive during this step and use a problem-solving rather than an accusatory approach.

If the instructor does not generate workable solutions, feel free to make suggestions. However, be certain that he or she "buys in" to the approach that will be tried.

Agree on goals and action steps that will resolve the problem. Build in timelines. Be positive and supportive about the instructor's approach to solving the difficulty. However, be realistic. Do not support a plan that does not solve the problem.

Use active listening to make sure that the faculty member understands and accepts ownership of the problem. Ask the instructor to paraphrase or summarize what has been discussed and/or the other approaches he or she is going to try in place of what did not work. (Sorcinelli, 1986, p. 40A, suggests a series of questions that the observer can ask to stimulate the discussion in the post-observation conference.)

Set a specific meeting date for a report on progress. Agree on what records the instructor will keep, based on the behaviors with which he or she is going to experiment.

Give the instructor a copy of the observation report. This report should also be sent to the chair or the appropriate departmental committees.

Giving Feedback: General Principles

When is feedback effective? The instructor who was unaware of the relationship between what he had done and his students' behavior was typical of many instructors; therefore, one of the factors that makes a feedback interview successful is pointing out effective teaching behaviors and the impact they have on a group of students. This emphasis on effective behavior also allows a respected colleague to reinforce constructive classroom teaching and is highly rewarding for the instructor.

Just as it is important to accentuate the positive behaviors observed, it is also necessary to limit the amount of negative feedback. Human beings are very vulnerable and have fragile egos. If a faculty member is doing twenty-six things wrong in a class, and the observer says, "Let me tell you about all the things you are doing wrong," and lists all twenty-six behaviors, the instructor will be fully discouraged after hearing only the first three or so. Good observers select one or two areas where there can be some fairly rapid improvement, ask instructors for their perception of the problem in just those areas, and have the instructors develop action steps for dealing with those issues.

Faculty members do need feedback about teaching, but it must be feedback that is helpful, that is positive, and that limits the number of weaknesses pointed out. Finally, observers help instructors generate alternative strategies for change. So that change can be monitored and outcome assessed, the action steps generated should be observable behaviors rather than broad generalizations.

Dealing with Poor Teachers Unresponsive to Assistance

There are times when faculty members seem to resist for years any interventions to improve their teaching. They may continue to blame the students, insist on their right to make arbitrary decisions that result in unfair treatment of students, or simply refuse to do anything to improve their teaching. Even when such individuals are untenured, if positive approaches have not resulted in any change in the desired direction, chairs clearly have to begin documenting unacceptable behaviors, interventions used, and the results. All of this activity has to be above board. A copy of any documentation that is sent to an instructor's personnel file must also be given to the instructor. During this interval when a paper trail is being established, tension between the faculty member and the chair can become quite difficult. In most institutions, even in the case of new instructors in the second year of employment on tenure track, almost two years will pass—starting with notification to the faculty member that the chair will not support renewal of contract and proceeding through the department and college promotion and tenure committees' making their recommendations and the dean's finally issuing a notice of termination—before the faculty member actually leaves the school. Maintaining a civil and courteous climate is necessary, but there is often a concerted sigh of relief when the faculty member finally departs.

Conclusion

As we saw in Chapter Four, the two most important career anchors for faculty are competence and dedication. Faculty members want to be competent and want an affirmation of their competence from those they respect. At the departmental level, observation and feedback furnish opportunities for reinforcement of faculty competence and can also provide direction for professional growth. When colleague observation is handled in such a manner that it allows faculty to enjoy their effectiveness and increase competence on the basis of meaningful feedback, then achievement of individual goals effectively matches departmental goals.

The first goal recommended for chairs after reading this chapter is to increase the quality and frequency of colleague observation following the guidelines in this chapter for observing specific behaviors and for giving both positive and negative feedback. It is important that departmental discussions be held to involve faculty in the process and that each department experiment with guidelines, checking outcomes and revising, until guidelines are working satisfactorily. A second important goal is to upgrade faculty's knowledge of instructional design and delivery skills. Chairs should provide suggested readings and opportunities for discussion of these areas and arrange for volunteers to conduct mini-workshops for other faculty.

Chapter Seven

Enhancing Commitments to Scholarship and Service

Ernest Boyer, of the Carnegie Foundation for the Advancement of Teaching, in his book *Scholarship Reconsidered: Priorities for the Professoriate* (1990), has argued that "a wide gap now exists between the myth and the reality of academic life. Almost all colleges pay lip service to the trilogy of teaching, research, and service, but when it comes to making judgments about professional performance, the three rarely are assigned equal merit. . . . We believe the time has come to move beyond the tired, old 'teaching versus research' debate and give the familiar and honorable term 'scholarship' a broader, more capacious meaning, one that brings legitimacy to the full scope of academic work" (pp. 15–16).

Scholarship has always meant something different to faculty and administrators depending upon whether they are employed in doctoral degree–granting institutions (major research institutions with multiple graduate programs), comprehensive universities (primarily undergraduate institutions, but which offer master's and first professional degrees in some fields), baccalaureate institutions (those with four-year liberal arts programs leading to bachelor's degrees), or community colleges (two-year institutions leading to an associate's degree). Recently, however, Boyer (1990) and Rice (1991) have expanded the concept of scholarship, moving away from the limited definition of a scholarship of discovery, to which the research universities adhere, to a scholarship of integration, application (or practice), and teaching. In relating "the work of the academy more directly to the realities of contemporary life," Boyer (1990, p. 13) legitimizes the different perspectives about scholarship that already exist and makes clearer the basis for developing criteria by which various aspects of scholarship can be evaluated.

In Rice's view (1991, pp. 11–15), scholarship can be pursued in at least four categories or activities.

> The *scholarship of discovery*, most often evident in medicine and the sciences, pursues knowledge for its own sake. The advancement of knowledge and the pursuit of original research has been, and must continue to be, one of the bulwarks of scholarship.

> The *scholarship of integration* "reaches across disciplinary boundaries, and pulls disparate views and information together in creative ways." This type of scholarship requires "a capacity to synthesize, to look for new relationships between the parts and the whole, to relate the past and future to the present, and to ferret out patterns of meaning that cannot be seen through traditional disciplinary lenses" (p. 13).

> The *scholarship of application*, which has a twofold function, both discovers knowledge through practice and applies knowledge, grounded in systematic or scientific research, to social problems in the world of reality.

> The *scholarship of teaching* involves transformation of knowledge so that active learning in students is stimulated. It pulls together parts of disciplinary knowledge in a way that helps students to construct meaning.

Rice (1991) has argued persuasively for the development of an academic model that better meets "the challenges posed by the immense demographic changes in our society. . . . What it means to be a scholar in American colleges and universities must be seen within this larger frame . . . the intellectual preparation of the educated citizenry necessary for making a genuinely democratic society possible. Scholarship, in this context, takes on broader meaning" (p. 17). Aware of the paradigm shift such a redefinition of scholarship requires, Rice concludes:

> We know that what is being proposed challenges a hierarchical arrangement of monumental proportions—a status system that is firmly fixed in the consciousness of the present faculty and the academy's organizational policies and practices. What is being called for is a broader, more open field where these different forms of scholarship can interact, inform, and enrich one another, and faculty can follow their interests, build on their strengths, and be rewarded for what they spend most of their scholarly energy doing. All faculty ought to be scholars in this broader sense, deepening their preferred approaches to knowing but constantly pressing, and being pressed by peers, to enlarge their scholarly capacities and encompass other—often contrary—ways of knowing [p. 6].

More than fifteen of the scholarly and professional organizations have developed statements that translate the work of Boyer and Rice into new guidelines for the specific disciplines, a comprehensive project that Robert M. Diamond of Syracuse University is coordinating. A compilation of statements from the scholarly and professional organizations will be published by the American Association of Higher Education in 1995.

When these discipline-specific guidelines have been completed, academic departments will have an opportunity to rethink and articulate what scholarship means for them. Departments need to specify a clear rationale to justify a particular endeavor as an important faculty activity, one that deserves to be recognized and rewarded. They must also determine what information could be gathered that would provide credible evidence of the quality of work to be expected and how it should be judged. Departments will also have to develop criteria by which work can be evaluated and provide guidelines for the documentation of outcomes, so that promotion and tenure committees will have objective standards on which to base decision making. Diamond's (1994) guidelines based on the new considerations will be very helpful to members of faculty promotion and tenure committees. Exhibit 7.1, 7.2, and 7.3 illustrate documentation that applies the criteria discussed here. This sample documentation was developed by several small groups at the Syracuse University Second Annual Summer Conference on Institutional Priorities and Faculty Rewards in 1993. The issues they address meet the consistent standards emerging from the disciplinary task forces in their definitions of scholarly work.

**Exhibit 7.1. Serve on Community Task Force
Appointed by Mayor.**

Rationale

Requires high level of expertise within the discipline

Can have major impact on reducing conflict within the community

Fits within institutional mission statement regarding community service

Can be used as a case study for classroom use or further research

Suggested Guidelines for Documentation Evidence

Reflective essay describing problems faced, role of faculty member, and what faculty member learned or discovered

Description of specific actions faculty member took as part of task force and reasons for those choices

Transcripts or minutes of task force meetings

Letters of commendation by task force chair or members

Written testimony from community groups who benefited from the work of the task force

Course materials developed from this case

Student interaction with faculty member's work or responses to case

Institutional or unit goal statement articulating community service mission

Committee interviews with key actors, mayor, community leaders, and so forth

Results of work of task force as evidence of impact on community (specific initiatives planned and accomplished)

Publication or dissemination of reports

Criteria

Demonstrates high level of professional expertise

Demonstrates knowledge of recent research in conflict resolution

Demonstrates strong performance as task force member

Demonstrates innovative solutions to common societal problems

Demonstrates sensitivity to various constituencies

Shows interest in results, outcomes by other communities

Arranges publication of accounts of activity in news and other media

Seeks publication of accounts in journals in discipline

Adapted from "Working Papers on Documenting Faculty Work," 1993.

Exhibit 7.2. Direct a Play (Student Production).

Rationale

Requires research, creativity, and scholarship for interpretation of the work

Requires expertise in discipline and historical frame of reference

Requires ability to make maximum use of existing resources (human and material)

Provides theory/practical application for students in cast and in other production-related roles (teaching function)

Suggested Guidelines for Documentation Evidence

Descriptive essay including a statement of artistic, intellectual, and production goals, an overview of the intellectual and production processes, and a rationale for the basic decisions that were made

Videotape of final production for external peer review

Critical reviews

Student evaluations and critique based on pre-established goals for learning

Criteria

Shows evidence of high level of expertise within discipline

Makes maximum use of existing resources

Represents innovative, ground-breaking production

Demonstrates student learning

Adapted from "Working Papers on Documenting Faculty Work," 1993.

Exhibit 7.3. Develop New High School Curriculum.

Rationale

Demonstrates ability to communicate important concepts to a diverse population

Can increase general student interest in the field

Can prepare students for further study in the discipline

Can represent a major new approach to education in the discipline

Suggested Guidelines for Documentation Evidence

Descriptive essay including statement of need, goals of the project, and rationale for approach being used

Reviews by experts in the field (college and secondary) and by teachers who are using the materials produced

The materials

Data on changes in student learning and attitudes

Data on feasibility of continued and expanded use (cost and so forth)

Criteria

Represents a major innovation

Shows quality and accuracy of content

Meets specific needs of student population being served

Has application beyond test site (is appropriate for adoption by other schools)

Can be validated by an independent review process

Adapted from "Working Papers on Documenting Faculty Work," 1993.

Writing about the features that are common to all scholarly activities recognized in promotion and tenure structures, Diamond (1993, p. 12) observes that these activities require a high level of discipline-related expertise, break new ground or are innovative, can be replicated or elaborated, can be documented, can be peer reviewed, and have significance or impact.

In the midst of all these exciting developments, academic

chairs continue to struggle with how they can increase scholarship in their departments. In the most prestigious doctoral degree–granting research universities, research and publication in refereed journals are ongoing activities, deeply ingrained in the culture. When faculty members are hired, it is usually because they have already established themselves in an area of research. As they begin their work with the university, sufficient research release time, laboratory and computer facilities, and graduate assistants are ordinarily made available to them, until such time as they are able to attract grant money or other funding on their own. Later on, the culture that places a high value on research, subtle peer pressure from colleagues who are conducting important studies, and the power and status that come from discovery and from becoming well-known in a field lead to faculty members' generating funding for research to keep their momentum going.

At the other end of the continuum that defines scholarship are community colleges. The situation here is considerably different, since teaching loads are typically fifteen credits a semester, and there are no graduate assistants or laboratories geared for research. Scholarship in such institutions is usually a matter of staying up to date in one's discipline, perhaps by taking additional graduate credits or attending conferences or workshops in an area of specialization. In community colleges, scholarship is also defined as presenting a paper at a national, regional, or local conference; conducting classroom (action) research (Angelo & Cross, 1993); developing innovations in the curriculum; or speaking to community groups.

A third group is made up of academic chairs in comprehensive institutions or baccalaureate degree–granting colleges. Because they function in an environment with few of the incentives found in doctoral degree–granting research institutions, these chairs often must seek strategies for increasing departmental scholarship. In these departments, and even in certain departments in prestigious universities, anywhere from several to most of the members of the department may not be engaged in scholarly work.

The reasons faculty members do not engage in research and publication vary. In some departments, faculty members who are heavily involved in community work or outreach programs feel it is not necessary to publish. In other departments, there are many senior faculty who were employed at a time when there was no emphasis on research. Some of them have never published; others have at one time published one or two articles; still others have had one or more articles published in the popular press. In many departments there are some faculty who had once been engaged in research but are now suffering from a lack of momentum, perhaps after some rejections by publishers or because they find they are experiencing writer's block. Some of these individuals would like to be actively writing again but cannot seem to get started.

Moreover, despite the fact that the concept of scholarship has been broadened, it is nonetheless usually expected that a written document, or some work open to peer review, will represent the outcome. However, it is precisely the act of scholarly writing that presents barriers difficult for many faculty members to overcome, but there is a process that can change the dynamics of the department so that written scholarly work can be augmented.

The task of increasing scholarly productivity has two dimensions that the chair needs to address. One intervention that can help all faculty is changing the culture of the department so that increased scholarship becomes the norm. The second intervention, which is attuned more to the individual, provides help for faculty who would like to publish because that is part of what they feel a faculty member should do, but who do not know quite how to get started. The following processes for conducting these interventions and enhancing departmental scholarship can be adapted to all institutions, including community colleges.

Changing the Culture to Value Scholarship

A serious change in institutional and departmental culture is most likely to occur when the dean makes it clear that scholarship is expected and will be rewarded. Scholarship must then be defined, either by a college educational policy committee with input from the departments or by the departments individually. Departmental definitions will need approval from a college educational policy committee to ensure some consistency of standards, then from the dean, and finally from the provost or vice president for academic affairs. A policy that requires that more faculty become active scholars is most likely to be accepted by faculty when there is an agreed-upon need: for example, when faculty understand that an increase in documented scholarship is essential if a proposal for a new graduate program is to be approved, or when faculty believe that accreditation by a disciplinary group is needed if a college is to improve its competitive position for students.

Although the dean can provide leadership by announcing, with unmistakable clarity, college policy and rewards for scholarship, such policies and rewards may be perceived as unfair by senior faculty hired at a time when effective teaching and service were the sole criteria for tenure and promotion. This perception is particularly likely in universities that have prided themselves on being teaching institutions. A statement of a new emphasis on scholarship will not be enough to increase productivity of those who feel that the rules of the game are changing, and that they were hired to teach, not write. However, many faculty do feel that one of their responsibilities as academics is to write, but they need some help in order to be productive as authors.

At this point, the chair is in the best position to provide the help that would-be writers need by generating a change in the culture of the department. In this change, the chair needs to address the process, not just the outcome, of moving from a culture in which individuals do not write to a culture in which they do research and publish results. The steps in this process may appear very simple, but in those departments where these procedures exist, most faculty members are publishing, while in departments where these procedures are not used, little research and publication is completed. Of course, as in all cultural changes, the chair needs to enlist the backing of the informal leaders of the department, so that their input and support can be developed before the chair presents plans for the following strategies to the entire department.

Begin or resurrect department colloquia. Many faculty who have not published recently, or at all, have ideas they feel they ought to be writing up for publication or developing into a research project, but somehow they do not do it. By initiating department colloquia the chair can provide the catalyst that gets the process of research and writing started. For those in the arts, substituting the word *work* for *research* will make the process applicable. Depending upon the chair's assessment of department members' current writing and research efforts, the chair may start these colloquia by inviting outside guest speakers to talk about their research or by inviting some individuals in the department to make presentations on topics in which they have expertise or to present some aspect of ongoing research. With the goal of stimulating faculty to do research, the chair can be very creative in organizing colloquia. Individuals who make presentations can be asked to answer several process questions about their work, such as, How did you become interested in this topic? What was the process you used to bring yourself from the germ of an idea to the steps you would take in doing the research? What kind of help did you get from other people in stimulating your thinking? Chairs can also ask presenters to talk about the process of writing, asking them to answer such questions as, What do you do to be productive? Do you schedule a number of hours each day? How many days a week do you write? Do you ever feel stuck or feel that what you are doing is not worth anything? If so, what effect does this have on your writing and how do you get back on track? Faculty members who are not writing often feel that the course of writing is an untroubled one and only they have difficulties. It helps them to know that others experience similar difficulties and what can be done to overcome them. If department members feel it acceptable, the chair can announce the colloquia in the university press, personally invite the dean, and strongly encourage students to attend. All of these strategies will provide good public relations for the department and enhance the importance of the event for the faculty.

After a faculty member makes a presentation at a colloquium, the chair should encourage him or her to make the next step a presentation at a local, regional, or national professional meeting. A particular conference to which a proposal can be submitted may even be suggested. Next, the chair needs to encourage faculty members to write up for publication, somewhere, what was presented. Quite often, papers are rejected because the writers set themselves up for failure by submitting a paper to a very prestigious refereed journal when they have not written anything else for years. The chair might suggest they set their expectations at a realistic level. The process of cultural change must build on success, and this can happen only when faculty's goals are realistic. The chair may also want to talk with the dean about the intended goals so the possibility of reinforcement by the dean is increased. The form of the reinforcement, perhaps a memo from the dean or an approval of travel funds, is not important. The goal is simply to ensure that the faculty members' efforts are appreciated and encouraged.

Provide support networks so individuals can talk about their research ideas with colleagues. The chair and faculty can discuss how this would work. Psychologists generally agree that reinforcement enhances creativity. The goal is to create a supportive climate that reinforces all the positive aspects of any idea. Only then can criticism be introduced. New ideas are fragile and often die aborning. Negative criticism as a first response, even a general unsupported statement such as, "That would never work!" tends to destroy pursuit of a creative idea. Since academicians are trained to be critical of both their own thinking and the thinking of others, it is easy for them to fall into the trap of premature negativity. A good principle to use in groups, one endorsed by those with expertise in problem-solving approaches, is to insist that individuals list several things that are worthwhile about an idea before they are allowed to talk about what is wrong with it. It is useful to establish similar ground rules when colleagues discuss an hypothesis or the germ of any idea they might like to pursue. The value of researching a particular concept needs to be affirmed before faculty move on to discuss concerns about its implementation. The concerns are important. It is insincere and a disservice to a colleague to be totally uncritical and encourage a research project or paper fraught with difficulties. But the point is that many faculty members have no opportunity to think aloud about their research ideas and to receive feedback from knowledgeable colleagues, and they do need a supportive climate if they are to begin such thinking.

In two departments where I offered similar suggestions, faculty did object that such an approach was not practical because their colleagues would steal their ideas. Although the level of trust in these two places was clearly a difficulty, most departments where these strategies have been tried find that both faculty interest in research and resulting productivity have increased.

Devote some colloquia to ideas in progress. This strategy expands the number of those who will provide and receive input, and it requires all the ground rules just described. Participants must discuss the value of ideas before attempting to talk about concerns if the project were implemented. An ideas-in-progress colloquium can be very encouraging to those in the department who have not done research, because they then begin to understand how concepts develop and are turned, finally, into workable hypotheses to be tested. Such colloquia encourage individuals to think more about their own work and to generate ideas to be explored.

Establish a norm that faculty will read drafts of papers and provide feedback to each other. In some departments, individuals do not ask for feedback and criticism until they have written a final draft that is as perfect as they can make it. In such cases, it becomes quickly apparent to others that any criticism is unwelcome because the writer has already invested a great deal in the final product. However, it is also disconcerting to colleagues when they are given a badly written paper, with many misspellings and grammatical mistakes, and are asked to critique it, including watching for the errors. Individuals then feel they are being asked to do major editing of a paper that has been dashed off on the spur of the moment. Drafts of papers should be shared at an early stage of development, but it is more realistic to define the feedback requested as a reaction to the feasibility of the idea.

Begin a papers-in-progress series of colloquia. The presentations in these meetings are often the final step before submitting material for publication. Sharing research with colleagues can sometimes be helpful in developing collaborative research with someone in the department or in another part of the university. Such sharing also helps graduate assistants express an interest in working with a particular faculty member. Moreover, it is good public relations for the department, especially when the dean is engaged in fund-raising or the department is trying to form an alliance with outside groups, such as an industrial or pharmaceutical group, a state or government agency, or a health service organization. It provides another useful way of reflecting the work of faculty members, even when that work has not as yet been published.

Provide a jump start by encouraging faculty who are not publishing to collaborate with those who are. For someone who has not published in a while, collaboration can be an effective way of generating excitement and reacquainting the individual with research methodology and the process of reading computer printouts and writing up results. Occasionally, chairs will denigrate any coauthored articles as worth nothing, but such an attitude is seriously misguided. Collaboration can provide a necessary step in revitalizing faculty members who had previously thought research was beyond them.

Circulate the calls of professional conferences for proposals for presentations. Most academic chairs receive a large number of requests for proposals for local, regional, and national conferences. If the chair immediately places these requests in the departmental files and just writes a memo telling faculty of their whereabouts, faculty who have not been active scholars will not take the initiative to review them for relevant topics. The chair needs to actively intervene, either by personally perusing such requests and looking for active matches between conference themes and the interests of faculty or by delegating a rotating responsibility for this search to other members of the department. Obviously, chairs will not have to do this for all faculty members, but when chairs themselves approach faculty members about submitting proposals, they empower these individuals to do something they would otherwise not have done.

Provide word-processing and computer literacy workshops. When, as director of the Office of Professional and Organizational Development at Fairleigh Dickinson, I sponsored word-processing and computer literacy workshops for faculty, the comments of those who learned the word-processing function of computers were illuminating. One instructor who began publishing again after years of writing nothing said, "Being able to rearrange my ideas so easily has had the effect of decreasing my paralysis. I used to get discouraged because I expected that when I sat down to write, beautifully formed sentences and paragraphs would flow like Athena from the head of Zeus. But instead, I would sit there staring at the blank page in a typewriter. Then, I would tell myself that I couldn't write until I felt creative, that I needed long blocks of uninterrupted time to write, and that couldn't happen until the summer vacation. The only problem was that I didn't write during the summer vacation either." Another who became more productive said, "I don't know what I'm thinking until I see what I have written. It is terribly reinforcing and pushes you on when you see your ideas on the screen in front of you." Although it is easy to assume that by now all faculty members are familiar with the basic functions of computers, particularly word processing, this is not the case. I recall a professor of history telephoning to ask if he would be embarrassed if he attended a computer workshop and saying, "I wouldn't know a computer or a word processor if I fell over one. Will I look stupid if I attend?" Thus, the wording of notices inviting faculty to attend computer workshops must be reassuring, without being condescending.

Sponsor workshops on that most private of all disabilities, writer's block. Why do some faculty members find it so difficult to write, while others are such prolific authors? Among other reasons, people who do not write say they have no time for writing, feel anxious about writing, feel it is too painful a process, feel what they could say has already been said and said better, have too high expectations, and have a tendency to procrastinate. Each of these problems can be successfully overcome using a cognitive behavioral approach. The behavioral part includes scheduling a time to write each day and adhering strictly to that schedule to establish momentum. Nothing short of an emergency should take the place of this appointment to write. And the more people write, the better they become at it. Another useful behavior is rewarding oneself for writing for a specified amount of time or completing a certain number of pages. For example, if individuals enjoy reading the newspaper, they can deliberately postpone doing this until they have written for half an hour. This technique is based on the Premack Principle, which states that naturally occurring high-frequency behaviors can be used as rewards for low-frequency behaviors.

The essence of another behavioral strategy is to reduce anxiety by monitoring one's dysfunctional thoughts and substituting realistic positive thinking for negative irrational self-messages. For example, for the negative irrational thought, I have nothing of value to write, a faculty member can substitute, I lecture and lead class discussions for forty-five hours during each course I teach. Not only am I often enthusiastic, but my students get excited about ideas I discuss. Of course, I have something to say and to write about.

To me, the single most helpful resource for increasing one's writing is Boice's (1990b) *Professors as Writers*. The value of this work is that it takes the reader by the hand and through diagnostic monitoring and self-assessment identifies the causes of specific writing problems and makes recommendations on how to overcome them. Boice also suggests using generative writing, that is, writing on a selected topic without stopping or editing. This allows creativity without the self-criticism that, when used too early in the writing process, can abort any writing effort. Boice's general interventions come from broad-based research in cognitive behavioral approaches, which have fared so well in comparative outcome studies in the reduction of anxiety and depression. Certainly, the blocks to writing are often anxiety about the act of writing and the depression faculty feel when their self-esteem falters because their writing is not going well. Moreover, the interventions are all soundly based in research Boice has conducted with faculty members who do not write but want to. His research clearly demonstrates the effectiveness of the methods. Individual faculty members can go through the steps alone, or a workshop on the interventions can be presented in the department or in the college. Success, defined as a specific increase in writing productivity, is almost guaranteed by using Boice's method.

Sponsor departmental workshops on grantsmanship. Although college and university workshops are effective methods of encouraging faculty to write grant proposals, workshops held in the department often have the effect of encouraging collaborations that might not otherwise occur. Also the representative from the grants office needs to be encouraging and supportive. In universities where faculty do not write grant proposals, it is sometimes the case that problems outside the department create the barriers. For example, in one university the grants officer was notoriously negative. When one faculty member, who had spent weeks writing her first proposal, brought it to the grants office, the first response she received was a sarcastic, "Well, at least you seem to know how to write." In another university, the provost publicly encouraged faculty to write grant proposals but had an unpublicized rule that he would not sign a proposal unless it was brought to his office two weeks before it had to be mailed out. Several faculty members told me that when they delivered a proposal, which had been reviewed by the department's research committee and by the department chair, to the provost's office, they were told, "You are giving me only ten days to read it. The rule is two weeks. I will not look at it." Clearly, procedural problems and people in the university who convey negative and conflicting messages can be a strong deterrent to faculty who are asked to write grant proposals. When chairs are aware of problems such as these, they can make the problems known as deterrents to applying for grant money. They can also keep faculty informed about obstacles they will have to document or deal with.

Make some travel money available for faculty to attend conferences. Chairs need to fund judiciously even those who do not present papers. Faculty who have not published can sometimes be stimulated intellectually by attending a conference. Ask faculty members to conduct a mini-workshop in the department upon returning so that benefit to themselves and others can be increased. Obviously, such a practice can be applied in a limited way to selected faculty when it seems as if the interest and stimulation to present a paper at a later time can be piqued.

Discuss the changing view of scholarship with faculty and with the dean. The focus for these discussions can consist of Boyer's *Scholarship Reconsidered,* Rice's "The New American Scholar," position papers from the appropriate scholarly organizations, and Diamond's (1994) *Serving on Promotion and Tenure Committees.* Such discussions might trigger faculty productivity along nontraditional but acceptable lines of inquiry.

Helping New Faculty Become Productive Scholars

Implementing suggestions from the preceding discussion can certainly create a departmental climate that will be stimulating to new faculty members. However, there are a few additional suggestions that are particularly useful in dealing with new faculty. Since

Boice's study (1992) showed that new faculty members feel uncertain about how much research and publication will be expected of them in order to gain tenure, it is important that chairs be as specific as they can be with respect to the requirements for tenure. For example, when junior faculty ask how much they will have to publish in order to earn tenure, a chair's customary response may be, "Just do as much as you can." The chair may intend this statement to be reassuring. However, the new faculty member may feel intimidated and more uncertain than before the question was asked. Chairs who are working on their leadership skills in faculty development might respond to the question by initiating a conversation to discover the source of the concern and the faculty member's needs. Has the individual chosen an area of investigation? Does the individual need some help in terms of resources from the chair? Does he or she need someone to bounce ideas off? Has he or she written anything at this point in time? If the person has already written an article, the chair might volunteer to ask a supportive colleague in the department to read the first draft. The chair could also ask if the individual needs some help in deciding where to submit the article already written or if an article submitted for publication has been rejected.

In short, the chair should be practicing the faculty development skills of active listening and of exploring in greater depth what it is someone really wants to know before he or she answers quickly in a way that seems reassuring.

The chair has mastered these faculty development skills when conversations with faculty members result in the chair's having a clearer perception about the areas of faculty concern. The dialogue should allow new faculty members to go away feeling better than before they spoke to the chair—feeling support and experiencing a reduction in anxiety.

As mentioned earlier, another significant finding of Boice's study of new faculty members was that they lacked balance in task management. Spending an inordinate amount of time preparing for each class left them feeling they had no time to devote to research, which they understood was crucial if they were to gain tenure. The quick starters in Boice's study scheduled time several days each week to work on research. Thus, a chair needs to communicate the importance of balance in task management to new faculty members. Their goal of feeling comfortable in the classroom cannot be achieved simply by perfecting their notes. In Boice's study, new faculty kept procrastinating research to a period, usually summer vacation, when there would be long blocks of uninterrupted time available to them. Yet at the end of the summer vacation between their first and second years, an average of only 4.32 verified manuscript pages had been produced. By the end of their second year on campus, an average of an additional 4.21 verified manuscript pages had been written (Boice, 1992, pp. 87–91). This information should provide helpful insights for chairs who are trying to nurture new and junior faculty so that they can become effective professional members of the department.

Motivating Faculty to Increase Service

Like scholarship, faculty service is in the process of being defined more broadly, particularly by a number of scholarly and accrediting organizations. However, and for understandable reasons, many chairs are concerned first and foremost with everyone's taking a fair share of departmental responsibility so that the work of the department can be accomplished. A chair's best strategy for gaining faculty cooperation is to develop faculty ownership in departmental goals through participative decision making. When goals are set jointly, achieving them becomes important to everyone who has been a part of the process.

Of course, there are a number of occasions when chairs do and should make unilateral decisions, particularly when deadlines are short, when the issue is unimportant to faculty, and when a departmental responsibility cannot effectively be handled in a participative fashion. An example of the latter occasion, viewed by many simply as a chore, is the requirement of representing the department on Sunday afternoons and a number of evenings at open houses for potential students. There are some faculty members, often the energetic, dynamic ones, who do a better job of attracting students; yet thoughtful chairs do not overwork them just because of their enthusiasm. Proctoring comprehensive examinations is another example of an activity that has to be performed, usually all day on a Saturday. The best approach for a chair here is to set up a schedule of rotation, notify the faculty as far in advance as possible, and be firm about everyone's taking a turn. Those faculty members who are enthusiastic representatives at open houses for student applicants might perform this service instead of proctoring the comprehensive examinations. Such assignments must be handled with discretion and an avoidance of any negative comments about any faculty member. Occasionally a chair, perhaps in desperation, will use threats of "keeping service activities in mind" when he or she makes out the schedules and assigns research release time, to get faculty to perform the duty functions. This tactic is usually a mistake, however. Although such intimidation may work in the short term, it usually backfires eventually and sometimes results in a petition by the faculty to the dean to evaluate whether the chair has the confidence of the department. If, on the other hand, the matter of departmental representation is presented in the most positive light, as an opportunity to attract more and better students, and as "something we must all take a turn at doing," it will be perceived as fairly handled and faculty members will cooperate.

On other occasions, chairs can use a consultative process, checking ahead of time with those who will be affected by the decision. However, in any instance where faculty ownership and commitment are necessary, the life of the chair will be easier if faculty together determine goals, objectives, and timelines, and clear specifications about which committees are responsible for doing what part of the work. If chairs do make unilateral decisions on matters affecting faculty, they will find it difficult to find people willing to devote time and energy to carry out these decisions.

How Is Service Defined?

If, from the chair's point of view, taking adequate responsibility for completing the work of the department is the first aspect of service, the second is determining what service includes, how important it is, and how much weight it should carry in personnel decision making. Many faculty handbooks spell out this information in detail and considerable variation exists, depending upon the missions of institutions and departments. Although in doctoral degree–granting research institutions service to the department may be given little emphasis, in community colleges, where student advising and observation of adjunct faculty consume much faculty time, the service component weighs heavily. Scholarly associations' statements about service usefully divide service activities into those that assist the institution, those that advance the profession beyond the institution, and those that contribute to the community.

Service that assists the institution includes writing grant proposals, fund raising, recruiting students and faculty, serving on committees, and providing expertise that assists the work of other institutional units, including libraries, academic and administrative offices, and support agencies. Service that advances the profession beyond the institution includes consulting; serving on committees, task forces, review and advisory boards, and councils; explaining one's discipline or research via the mass media; and providing leadership in professional organizations. Service that reaches out to the community includes contributing to public education through teaching, performance, and presentations; participating in working groups, boards, arts councils, and community events; helping to improve instruction in the primary, secondary, and postsecondary schools; and testifying as an expert in legislative and judicial settings.

This listing indicates the range of service endeavors judged to be worthy of emphasis. When service is viewed simply as activity in connection with the work of the department, service is not valued as it should be. Moreover, individual perceptions of the significance of personal service activities vary greatly. Therefore, the question of how much emphasis will be allotted to service in personnel decision making requires discussion in the department. (Such discussions obviously need to begin with whatever information already exists in the faculty handbook.) Chairs should also decide with department members how service activities should be documented, and how their outcome or effectiveness should be evaluated, and should communicate this information to the dean.

Minimizing Service Demands for New Faculty

A word about assigning service activities to new faculty is appropriate because new faculty are often young and dynamic and willing to accept whatever they are asked to do; therefore, it is easy for chairs to overburden them, causing dysfunction and impeding their gaining tenure. This overburdening can particularly affect minorities and women, who, because they are underrepresented on the faculty in general, are often asked to serve on committees. The naïve ones somehow believe that spending their time in this way will help in the tenure process. It usually does not. Chairs should discuss this issue frankly, so that new faculty will inform the chair before accepting an invitation when requests for service come from outside the department. Several studies indicate that new faculty often view their department chairs as advocates who play a significant role in communicating what is expected to achieve tenure (Sorcinelli, 1988; Turner & Boice, 1989). Understandably, then, it is particularly important that chair expectations for service assignments be kept to a minimum.

Conclusion

Chairs can stimulate scholarship that results in publications among faculty who have never or rarely published. By designing a series of department colloquia and establishing a climate that values scholarship, even in institutions other than research universities, chairs can change departmental culture so that it values scholarship. A suggested initial, achievable goal for chairs is increasing average research productivity by 10 percent for the department.

Chairs can also set a goal of involving faculty in a fair share of the work of the department. However, they must assign the work of the department fairly, selecting the most appropriate decision-making style (unilateral, consultative, or participative) for making assignments and exercising restraint in assigning tasks to new, minority, and women faculty. A further suggested goal is that chairs discuss with faculty how much emphasis should be given to service activities as listed by the scholarly organization representing the departmental discipline.

Chapter Eight

Team Building Through Supportive Communication

The last three chapters about the chair's role as faculty developer have explored many specific ways in which chairs can evaluate departmental culture and make it more conducive to achieving both faculty and departmental goals. Now we return to the kinds of abilities that make chairs effective leaders of the department. Excellent communication skills, some understanding of small-group dynamics (particularly facilitation skills used in conducting meetings), skills in motivating others, and conflict management skills are the major abilities needed in a good team leader. In this chapter, the focus will be on communication and small-group dynamics. Chapter Nine will explore conflict management.

Creating a Supportive Communication Climate

Most department chairs have well-developed communication skills in several areas. Having mastered the intricacies of their particular academic disciplines, they know how to provide information handles for students, communicating what is difficult in a way that makes it easier to understand. Many are also successful in communicating to others some of the enthusiasm they feel for their subject. Moreover, most chairs are highly effective in critiquing ideas, and the majority are impressive as they make oral presentations before groups.

Listening Actively

However, communication skills do not end with giving effective, well-organized lectures, being facile of mind and tongue, and pinpointing the flaws in another's argument. Well-developed leadership skills include the ability to listen actively. As noted earlier, an active listener has the capacity to summarize and paraphrase what he or she has heard, in order to check for accuracy of understanding. By using active listening, chairs strive to understand the speaker's ideas, problems, and emotions, expressed either verbally or nonverbally, as if the chair could view the situation from behind the eyes and ears of the speaker. An accurate understanding of what has been communicated is the first step in active listening, the next step is conveying to the speaker an ability and a willingness to see things from the speaker's point of view.

Any message has two components: the content and the feelings or attitudes that underlie the content. Speakers usually give us cues about their feelings through such nonverbal communication as facial expressions, body posture, hand movements, eye movements, breathing, pauses or hesitation in speech, and inflection and pitch of voice. In some instances, feelings are far more important than the content of what is said. As listeners, chairs should ask themselves, What is the faculty member trying to tell me? What does this mean to the faculty member? How does he or she see the situation?

Because understanding another person is far more difficult than it appears to be, it is important for chairs to check constantly to see whether they are able to comprehend the world as the faculty member views it. Understanding can be checked by repeating in the listener's own words what the speaker seems to mean.

Many individuals lack good listening skills. Often, people make a quick judgment in terms of whether they agree or disagree with what is being said. While the speaker is still talking, the listener stops paying attention and begins to mentally rehearse what he or she will say when the speaker pauses for breath. Judgmental listeners may also interrupt or complete the speaker's sentences, assuming that they already know what the speaker is going to say. Judgments may be made about the motivation behind the speaker's words or nonverbal communication, and advice or solutions to problems may be offered. Although proposing an answer to another's problem may seem like a decent human thing to do, many people talk about their problems not with the intent of asking for solutions but simply so that the listener will understand that the speaker is in pain. The speaker merely wants the listener to know what it is like to walk in the speaker's shoes. Faculty may complain about the low academic skill level of students so that a chair will understand their difficulty in teaching undergraduates. New faculty may tell a chair how busy they are in hope that the chair will appreciate how hard it is for them to find the time to write. If a chair's style has been to provide solutions when people come with problems, it will be instructive for that chair to experiment with paraphrasing what speakers have said. If they seem happy that they have been understood, a chair will know they do not want him or her to solve their problems. However, if they ask what they should do, a chair can suggest that they look at certain options or help them generate alternatives themselves so that they maximize their choices.

Simply summarizing what has been heard sometimes feels like a passive activity and may initially sound artificial to a chair. However, paraphrasing does not necessarily mean repeating a laundry list of every single item uttered or behavior observed. If a chair sees someone slam a desk drawer, clench his or her fists, pound on a file cabinet, and yell, the summary might simply be, "You're really angry!" And if the response is an emotional, "You're right. I'm furious!" the chair knows that he or she is on target. The speaker, recognizing that the listener understands the feelings the speaker is experiencing, is then often able to move on to identify the problem and solve it.

However, there are occasions when a complete listing of items might be an appropriate form of active listening. Listing everything is one way for the listener to ensure that he or she has understood instructions. For example, in September, the dean tells the chair that, for budgetary reasons, a report will be needed that includes separate calculations of the number of full-time and adjunct faculty members required to cover classes for the following academic year. To be certain that the report will be accurate, a chair might list aloud the factors he or she will have to consider to draw up the report, saying to the dean, "You want a report that will be based on an estimate of the number of courses the department will offer at on-campus locations, at off-site locations, in the Saturday College, and in both graduate and undergraduate programs. In that case, I will need to know whether the number of hours for research release time will be increased, decreased, or held constant; whether the requested sabbaticals will be approved; whether the denial of continuation for one of our faculty members will be supported; and whether we will be permitted to offer courses in the spring for the new program in human resource management that has just been approved." This may trigger the dean to say, "You will have to make judgments based on your best estimates, and that is acceptable." The chair then has a clearer idea of what the dean expects. A simple rule of thumb is that when summarizing emotions one can be very brief and very accurate; whereas when paraphrasing instructions that are not entirely clear a detailed summary may be necessary.

Active listening demonstrates respect for the speaker, because it conveys that the listener is interested in the speaker and thinks that what he or she feels is important. This is sometimes called being totally present to another person, and it is a rare experience. Even when two people talk who have not seen each other for a while, one is often looking over the other's shoulder to see who else might be passing by. Active listening also displays respect for the speaker's thoughts, without trying to change them. Moreover, such listening shows that the listener wants to understand the speaker and that the listener is the kind of person to whom the speaker can usefully talk.

Only after faculty members feel a chair truly understands their problems is it possible for them to enter a problem-solving mode with the chair. And implicit in the active listening approach is the belief that people are capable of solving their own problems. If the chair immediately jumps in to offer a solution to a faculty member's problems, the faculty member's perception is either that the chair does not truly understand the complexity of the problems, if the chair thinks the solution is so obvious, or that the chair must think the speaker is stupid because he or she could not come up with a solution when it is so apparent. Moreover, when a chair tries to solve a faculty member's problem, the person usually feels no investment in the solution or commitment to follow through on it. As a result, the person finds some reason why the chair's solution cannot possibly work in this case. It is admittedly very difficult for a chair who feels that the problems presented by faculty are really simple ones to exercise restraint and to take the time required to lead faculty to generate options, select the most viable alternatives, and apply them in the problem situations.

Empowering Others

One effective intervention a chair can use in building a strong department is to empower faculty to implement some of the creative ideas they themselves have. How does a chair do this? By knowing that having the chair really listen to what faculty are saying is a truly affirming and empowering experience for faculty. When a faculty member presents an idea, the chair can listen and ask such questions as, What would that look like? How is that different from what is the case now?

Next, the chair encourages the faculty member to perform a gap analysis, asking this series of questions: What would it take to get from here to there? What action steps would you need to put in place? How will you monitor your progress? How will you evaluate what you have accomplished? How can I help you to do that? Faculty can be very creative. Often, all they need to move on in their thinking is someone to listen to them in a way that affirms the value of an idea and helps them add an element of reality to it. The chair can do this for them.

Some chairs are reluctant to engage in such conversations because they feel faculty will ask for resources the chair cannot provide. However, faculty usually know when financial resources are scarce, and they are not necessarily expecting a chair to provide project funding. But faculty do usually want to know that the chair thinks their ideas are good ones, that he or she is willing to take faculty seriously by asking about action steps and outcomes assessment, and that he or she has confidence in their ability to go ahead and do what they have discussed with the chair.

Being Supportive

Developing good communication techniques, using active listening, and empowering faculty are skills that both create a supportive departmental climate and help it to flourish. In this climate, faculty are flexible and look for new and better ways of accomplishing their work. Individuals are challenged and thrive. Creativity is unleashed. In a supportive climate, chairs visit faculty offices frequently. It is not enough for a chair to have an open-door policy. Only a few faculty members will drop in. Those who do not often say, in voices tinged with accusation, "My chair has never stopped at my office just to chat. He or she has never asked me how my research is coming or how my classes are going." Many faculty members look for someone who will manifest interest and concern about their professional activities. Unfortunately, they often do not tell chairs that that is what they want. They assume that if chairs are interested, they will initiate conversations with faculty about what faculty are doing. This assumption that chairs will be forthcoming may be particularly true among difficult colleagues.

A department chair can create a supportive communication climate that leads to understanding and problem solving or a defensive climate that creates barriers and impedes finding solutions to problems. The story of what happened when Matt Kincaid, a faculty member, took over the job of setting up a program for faculty development is a good example of a defensive climate in a university. Needing a desk, Kincaid was authorized to go to an office furniture store owned by two alumni who supposedly discounted prices to the university. At the store, Matt asked the price of a desk he liked and was told it was $450. He then took out his business card and a university purchase order and asked what the price would be for the university, only to be told that he had already been quoted the discounted price. Kincaid felt he would rather spend the money in his budget for faculty grants than for office furniture, so he went to an estate clearance house. He saw another desk he liked for only $150, and he knew he could also save the delivery fee because his brother would help him load the desk on top of his station wagon. However, when Matt presented all this information to the officer at the university to whom he reported, the response he got was, "Matt, do you think you know more than our purchasing department?" This kind of reaction to faculty effort creates a defensive communication climate! It discourages initiative and requires that all decisions be made from the top down. Although Matt did finally purchase the desk for $150 and deliver it to the university himself, he felt that his good will and strong motivation had been somewhat diminished by bureaucratic procedures.

One of the most important themes in a defensive climate is control. In a defensive environment, a critical judgmental attitude overshadows working conditions: the individuals in charge feel certain they are right; departments are run autocratically; people are manipulated and what they say and do is often distorted; there is little personal support for faculty and their problems; and department members are made to feel inadequate. In a defensive climate, chairs continually formulate theories about faculty problems and think they have a pretty good idea, based on their own knowledge and experience, of what faculty must do to get back on track in their personal and professional lives. These chairs unilaterally set goals for faculty and a plan of action the chairs feel will be constructive. They share with faculty only their completed diagnoses of problems and recommendations for change. Although one might think such conditions could happen in industry but not in academe, this is hardly the case, and most educators are aware of autocratic chairs in whose departments faculty keep a low profile and do the bare minimum, morale is poor, and creativity is obliterated.

The dominant themes in a supportive climate are sharing and understanding. In a supportive climate, chairs attempt to understand faculty members' problems and respect their feelings and values; creativity and risk taking are encouraged. Chairs attempt to define problems rather than offer solutions. Communication with department members is clear and accurate; information is not withheld, nor are there deliberate attempts to deceive (Costigan & Schmeidler, 1984, pp. 112–113). In a supportive climate that encourages communication, faculty opinions are accepted as legitimate points of view (even when there is disagreement over the reality of a situation), and whenever it seems appropriate to do so, chairs present their own perspectives as another point of view worth considering. Team leaders often participate in formulating short-term steps faculty can take to achieve goals. Chairs of such departments present themselves to faculty as individuals faculty can talk to and as individuals who are willing to work to get department members back on track when that is necessary, as opposed to being ready to coddle and defend faculty members against criticism from the administration even when the criticism is warranted. At the same time, the chair is usually eager to act as a strong advocate for the department and stand up to the administration if necessary. Moreover, in a supportive climate, accusation and blame are minimized. When something does go wrong, instead of criticizing individuals, chairs use a problem-solving approach that looks at policy and procedures to discover how mistakes can be prevented in the future.

In quality departments in which faculty members operate as a high-performing team, feedback is valued as crucial to professional development. It occurs in a climate of trust, where the giver and receiver of feedback both recognize its value. Basic ground rules for the use of feedback are presented in Chapter Ten. However, in terms of creating a departmental culture that is supportive of feedback, a chair's responsibility is to build trust so that feedback is not misconstrued as harmful criticism. The chair also provides a model for receiving feedback by asking for feedback for himself or herself in a variety of specific contexts. As he or she models behavior, the chair should avoid defensiveness after receiving feedback and ask only questions intended to clarify the observations offered. The chair's openness in sharing information and ability to treat all faculty members in an equitable manner also create trust. When there is a greater allocation of resources to one faculty member than another, the chair clearly specifies the criteria for that decision.

Good communication that is accepting, nonjudgmental, and does not make assumptions about the other person's motivation is a necessary part of interpersonal effectiveness. When communication includes an awareness of what nonverbal messages individuals are sending to others, when there is consistency between the verbal and nonverbal message, when people are respectful of others, and a supportive climate is created, trust is established. Positive feedback is given naturally and frequently, so that faculty members feel that their accomplishments are recognized and encouraged by the chair. (Chairs might set goals for themselves of giving at least two people positive feedback every day.) The departmental culture is positive and encourages ongoing professional development.

Stages of Group Development in a Department

Much of what has been discussed so far has focused on interactions between the chair and one faculty member. Chairs also need skills for handling faculty in groups, understanding how groups develop and the behavior that can be expected at different phases in the life of a group.

When an individual assumes the role of chair, the department becomes, in effect, a new group, which must go through the stages all groups pass through before becoming fully effective as teams. This is true even when a department has been made up of the same faculty members for years, although the fact that group members have been working together all along will shorten the time it takes the group to become a fully effective team. The stages of group development are forming, storming, norming, and performing. When a chair is elected and a new group forms, members begin to redefine their goals and develop procedures for carrying out their tasks. Since faculty do not know whether having a new chair will change the way they have been doing things, they often keep feelings to themselves until they know what to expect, are often unusually polite to one another, and are tentative in their relationships as they test the water. This forming stage is what is often referred to as the chair's honeymoon period.

At the second, or storming, stage, friction arises over how tasks should be performed and by whom. Procedures for functioning together are dealt with, often indirectly, sometimes abrasively. The group tries to agree on objectives and develop the way the group will operate. Faculty members may be concerned about how much change the new chair is going to put in place and whether the new chair will exercise more control than the last chair. For example, in one department, the former chair had never written a memo but conveyed all information to the faculty orally, through the secretary. The new chair, wanting to use a more direct channel for keeping people informed, wrote memos about relevant material, placing them in faculty mailboxes. Faculty then complained about getting too many memos from the chair and recommended that all notices be placed on a bulletin board instead. The chair agreed and used the procedure faculty recommended. However, when several people missed a meeting they wanted to attend because they had forgotten to look at the bulletin board where a change in time had been posted, they displaced their anger onto the chair for not notifying them personally about the change. Much of the conflict at this second stage has a similar element of irrationality about it. Conflicts about leadership and goals are dominant themes. Some faculty members may withdraw and isolate themselves from the resulting stress and tension. In the department described earlier in which several faculty members complained that they could not sleep the night before or the night after a department meeting because of stress, the department found that disagreement erupted at meetings but took the form of personal attacks instead of debates over issues. In another department, a chair discontinued department meetings because of the stress they generated. This chair avoided conflict, but the key role that an effective chair plays during this stage is to manage the conflict, not suppress it or withdraw from it.

In the third, or norming, stage, the group collects and shares information, accepts different points of view, develops the rules (or norms) by which group members will solve problems and make decisions, and begins to develop cohesion. Cooperation and positive expressions of feeling towards one another predominate among group members. But this is also the time when dysfunctional behaviors of individuals can become established if the group accepts them. For example, two faculty members in one department continually arrived late for meetings and then demanded that any decisions made by the group before their arrival be voted upon again if they disagreed with the action taken. When the chair and the group permitted such conduct rather than confront it, they reinforced the unacceptable dysfunctional actions, which continued unabated at future meetings.

At the final, or performing, stage, the group becomes an effective, cohesive group of individuals who perform their functions well. Faculty become aware of member strengths and begin to operate on the basis of rules that were determined at stage three. When issues such as who will take which roles, what procedures will be used, how problems will be resolved, and how decisions will be made have been clarified earlier, the group can function well. However, some groups never resolve the issues of stages two and three and continue storming, tolerating dysfunctional behavior and arbitrarily applying rules for the rest of their existence or until the negative norms have been confronted and changed. If destructive conflict in a department has continued over a semester or two, it often helps to bring in an outside process consultant to assist department members in working through their strife so they can function well together.

Conducting Effective Departmental Meetings

Meetings can enhance collegiality and be used to exchange ideas, solve problems creatively, and set goals in a participative fashion. Meetings can also waste time, provide a medium for information better distributed in writing, and be occasions for suppressing disagreement, exacerbating hostility, alienating faculty, and rejecting people whose points of view represent a minority. Because so much academic work and so many academic decisions occur at meetings, all members of the academic community ought to be familiar with the following basic information for conducting effective meetings.

Planning for Meetings

There are some planning basics that are conducive to successful meetings. Selecting and reserving a room, having coffee available, and arranging chairs in a U-shape with a chalkboard or flip chart at the open end of the configuration are important, though easily neglected, parts of the planning phase. Many departmental meetings are held in a classroom with rows of theater-style seating, an arrangement that sends the message that the chair will lecture and the faculty members will listen and that sets a mood that is not conducive to dynamic interactions. If chairs have doubts about this, they will find it useful to experiment by trying a different seating arrangement and observing how interactions change.

Preparing the meeting agenda also requires planning. A chair should begin by sending a memo asking for items to be placed on the agenda. Even if only one or two people respond, the message to the faculty is that they have a chance for input. When the chair draws up the final agenda, next to each item, he or she indicates the time to be allocated to discussion and the results expected: for example,

> Item 3. Complaints from adjunct faculty about low attendance in undergraduate classes (10 minutes).
>
> *Results expected.* Several recommendations on how this attendance problem can be handled.

Usually, agenda items should be listed in order of importance. However, the item listed first may also be one that can be decided quickly. The latter format provides an opportunity for quick success, setting the stage for tackling more serious or controversial issues successfully.

Checking on Meeting Effectiveness

The chair normally leads departmental meetings, and he or she may want to use a meetings audit form periodically, to discover participant satisfaction and dissatisfaction with different aspects of the meeting. This is another way for the chair to get feedback that can be used to develop leadership skills. A meetings audit simply requires that faculty list two or three items that they liked about the meeting, two or three factors that they disliked, and two or three ways the meeting could be improved. Each attendee then rates each of his or her items on a continuum from 6, "a great deal of satisfaction," to 1, "relatively little satisfaction" (Baker, 1982, pp. 52–54). A standard meetings audit form can be prepared and used at meetings as often as the chair feels the technique will be useful. After taking an audit, it is helpful for the chair to share the results with the faculty at the next meeting and ask for their advice on changing those meeting aspects that people dislike. Conducting audits of meetings is another way of sharing responsibility with faculty for holding successful meetings. If faculty have an opportunity for input and are encouraged to view having successful meetings as partially their obligation, planning and conducting effective meetings becomes everyone's assignment. It should be a team function.

Another intervention helpful in improving the effectiveness of meetings is called stop action. This strategy allows meeting participants to detach themselves from the content of a meeting in order to look at what is happening between individuals. If a meeting seems to be going nowhere, or if individuals are making personal attacks instead of sticking to the issues, the chair simply calls, "stop action." Next, the chair asks faculty to disengage themselves from the meeting, share their observations about what is going on among participants, and ask if that is what they want to be doing at this point in the meeting. A chair needs to be patient with this intervention, since faculty members often have difficulty disengaging themselves from the content, particularly when emotions are high or when they are not yet skilled observers of meeting dynamics, or process. The stop action intervention may also be attempted when group involvement is minimal, and the chair wants to discover why many people are silent about a topic the chair thought would engage all of them. Such an intervention heightens awareness of meeting dynamics and encourages openness and discussions about change that faculty would like to bring about.

Task and Leadership Functions in Groups

For a group to function effectively, attention needs to be given to two roles for which both the group leader and members have responsibility; these roles are the task and maintenance functions, or behaviors. Task roles achieve the goals for which the group is organized. Although the issues discussed at departmental meetings may change from month to month, they all deal with handling the concerns of the department. Maintenance roles contribute to the group's being in good working order and deal with small-group relationship dynamics, that is whether all individuals feel respected by the group, have a sense of inclusion, and feel free to express their opinions.

Task roles include carrying out the functions of the *initiator*, who defines problems and suggests strategies for solving problems; the *clarifier*, who clears up confusion; the *summarizer*, who pulls together related ideas; and the *consensus seeker*, who checks with the group to see how much agreement has been reached. Maintenance roles include carrying out the functions of the *harmonizer*, who attempts to reduce tension and reconcile disagreements; the *encourager*, who accepts others and their contributions; and the *gatekeeper*, who facilitates the participation of others. Meeting participants should also be aware of such individual roles as the *blocker*, who is stubbornly resistive and negative; the *recognition seeker*, who boasts and acts superior; the *dominator*, who tries to manipulate the group; and the *avoider*, who resists passively. Although these roles were first described in 1948 by Benne and Sheats, the same language has been used by many writers in the intervening years to describe the various ways people function in groups.

Unless a chair pays attention to the dynamics of group functioning and the task and maintenance roles, attempts to achieve group tasks will bog down. Further, when decisions are reached, there will be little commitment to them on the part of those who feel their opinions were not taken seriously, and these same faculty members will be unwilling to work to implement decisions that were made or to accomplish departmental goals. Since many chairs complain that they cannot get faculty to do their fair share of the work of the department, they might look at the way decisions are made and goals set to discover whether they have used a process of participative decision making to develop commitment. If some faculty do not participate in discussions at meetings, chairs should poll their views directly, realizing that these faculty members need to be listened to.

Until department members become skilled in small-group dynamics, at which time all members become responsible for task and maintenance functions, the chair may want to assign some of the responsibility for effective meetings. A chair can demonstrate interest in productive meetings by asking two faculty members to be accountable for task and maintenance functions. The assignment of the task leader during the meeting is to record information on a flip chart and keep track of assignments and after the meeting to prepare and circulate minutes. The task leader also assists participants by summarizing points of agreement, helping participants decide what approach they will use to solve a problem, reminding them not to criticize during the idea generation stage of brainstorming, helping them keep on the topic, and trying to get closure when there is little disagreement but people are talking a lot. The maintenance or relationship leader tries to keep abrasive members from alienating themselves from the group by paraphrasing what they have said or asking them to explain or elaborate on a point they have made. In addition, the maintenance leader tries to ensure broad participation by bringing quiet members into the discussion. Since silence often means disagreement rather than agreement, everyone needs to be given a chance to express an opinion. When faculty members are silent, looking at them as another individual speaks, occasionally nodding or smiling, includes them and makes it easier for them to contribute.

Chairs can rotate the task and relationship responsibilities among faculty members from meeting to meeting. Such assignments will pique the interest of group members, and the responsible faculty members' reporting back to the group at the end of the meeting will also supply feedback to the participants on their role in discussions. Obviously, this is an important time for the chair to ensure that the climate is supportive, with more positive than negative feedback furnished.

Problem Solving and Decision Making in Groups

The tasks addressed at departmental meetings generally have to do with implementation of the departmental mission, and the goals and objectives that flow from that mission, though faculty members may not view what they are doing as necessarily related to any formal mission statement. The specific meeting topics will vary as members of the department focus their attention on increasing their resources or managing cutbacks, so they can live within a reduced budget; recruiting students and faculty; evaluating the curriculum (which includes developing new programs and phasing out others); developing and reviewing standards for admission and evaluation of students; encouraging ongoing professional development for faculty; enhancing faculty scholarship, however it is defined by the department and the institution; mentoring of new faculty; and evaluating faculty for personnel decision making. These issues are a few of the many that absorb the time and attention of department members.

In addition, on occasion, seemingly unimportant issues can create emotional turmoil in a department. One such problem for a large management and marketing department was the allocation of office space. Many chairs have experienced something similar to this as they redistributed space when new faculty were hired, when other disciplines were combined with theirs to form new departments, or when their departments moved to new quarters. A factor such as office space may take on an exaggerated symbolic importance, particularly when faculty members feel that they are unappreciated and have not been given enough recognition in the department or that they have been treated badly and want past injustices to be eradicated.

The management and marketing department had been split

between two different campuses of a university, teaching both graduate and undergraduate courses at both campuses, but as the result of a strategic planning committee's recommendations, the entire department was directed to move to one campus. Two years earlier, department faculty had been assigned offices in several different buildings because there was not enough room in any one building. Several faculty members were angry at that time, and were still angry, because they had been assigned, arbitrarily it seemed and without consultation, to offices that were too cold in the winter and extremely hot and without air conditioning in the summer. Assistant professors had sometimes been given large offices; full professors, small offices. Some of the office furniture was shabby; wooden desks with deep gouges in their tops were distributed without regard for any discernible criteria.

So, when it was announced that the department would be relocated to the new site, with more adequate space so the faculty could all be together in the same building, the important question became how office space would be assigned this time. It had been rumored that some of the new offices would have windows and some would not, and there was concern that this disparity might not be taken into consideration. Some faculty members argued privately that rank and seniority should be the basis for assignment of space. However, the chair had been heard to comment that productive junior faculty should be given prime space to encourage them to remain with the university. The issue was not discussed publicly until a faculty member raised the question at one of the few departmental meetings called by the chair. In response to the question, the chair indicated that who occupied which office was not important and that he did not expect faculty to engage in petty fights about the topic. Afterwards, several faculty members stated privately that they would be reluctant to express their points of view after the chair's comments.

When problems like this remain undiscussed, further undercurrents of dissatisfaction will appear in a department. If the chair makes a decision without involving the faculty, none of them will be satisfied. Characterizing disagreement about the problem as nothing more than a petty squabble may keep faculty quiet for a while, but anger will smolder below the surface and may erupt in unexpected ways.

Although serious tensions already existed in this department, a straightforward problem-solving approach with an outside facilitator was used without difficulty to resolve the issue of office assignments.

The first step was to encourage faculty to describe the current situation, which simply meant identifying the symptoms of the problem. The first symptom faculty described was their dissatisfaction with the inadequacy of office space under the current arrangements. Faculty spent time discussing the extreme heat and cold of their offices, the personal physical and medical problems that made some offices particularly unsuitable, the shabby furniture, the way the offices were spread among several buildings, the fact that faculty had had no input into assignment of space, and the fact that they were not sure what criteria were used in space allocation.

Their lack of input and uncertainty about allocation criteria identified an important part of the basic problem. Defining the problem is a significant part of the problem-solving process. Moreover, the way in which a problem is formulated will determine the answers that are generated. When a problem is formulated as a how-to step, that formulation usually creates greater objectivity among those who must find solutions. The goal of any formulation is to put the problem "out there," so that the group is able to work collaboratively in problem solving rather than competitively, with some individuals trying to convince others that a single position is the correct one. The management and marketing faculty could now develop a clear definition of the problem with which everyone could agree. They determined that the problem was how to allocate office space so that faculty are satisfied that an equitable process and fair criteria have been used.

Next, they were asked to generate alternative solutions to the problem. In many situations, a group chooses a solution to a problem too quickly, both because it seems as if it might work and because group members are eager to reduce the tension that problems generate. However, an early solution may not be a good choice because the group has not explored the full range of options open to it. So, a strategy is needed to prevent the group's choosing from a limited number of options. One easy and effective way to accomplish this is to ask group members to brainstorm solutions, generating as many options as they can think of. The ground rules are that, during the idea-generating stage, all suggestions are written on a chalkboard or flip chart and no one may make any positive or negative comments about any alternative suggested. No suggestion may be regarded as foolish, since seemingly unworkable ideas may trigger creative thinking in others, and maximum participation is thus encouraged because participants know their suggestions will not be criticized. Some of the alternative criteria generated by the management and marketing faculty for allocation of office space were rank, seniority, rank and seniority together, sex (females get first choice), medical or physical problems, productivity, years in the department (new faculty get first choice), amount of time typically spent in the office, a smoking habit (smokers get offices with windows), and previous service as department chair. Faculty also suggested holding a lottery, making trade-offs (first choice goes to those who handle certain undesirable service activities or those willing to give up travel money for three years), rotating offices every two years, and bidding on offices (based on what faculty would exchange for the best offices).

In the next step, faculty identified three or four of the most viable options and considered the advantages and disadvantages of each one and the probable effect on the rest of the department. Two alternatives emerged as preferable choices: rank and seniority together, which would solve some problems since there were a number of full professors, and a lottery, strongly urged by one associate professor who felt that too much fuss was being made about office space. During the discussion, one new junior faculty member said he felt uncomfortable because, under the current arrangement, he had a better office than most of the senior faculty, and he was perfectly satisfied that senior faculty have the offices with windows. That comment seemed to influence the group. Finally, consensus developed and the criterion chosen was rank and seniority together.

The meeting could have ended here, but since problem solving also requires that the solution be tried for a period of time and then evaluated, faculty decided to try this approach for three years. After two years, the chair would poll the department to discover how well the arrangement was working and whether anyone wanted to make any changes. If not, the criterion of rank and seniority would remain in effect. At the end of the meeting, there was considerable joking about the process they had used and the decision they had made. But faculty left the meeting quite satisfied with the fact that their input was being taken seriously and that they had determined the criterion that would be used.

The steps that appeared in this example can be simply summarized.

Identify the symptoms. Define the problem.

Generate many alternatives.

Consider the pros and cons of the most viable options.

Select an alternative everyone can live with.

Experiment by trying this solution for a designated period of time.

Select one or more people who will accept responsibility for reporting back to the group on how well it is working, evaluating its effectiveness in terms of specified criteria.

If the solution works or can be tinkered with to make it work, agree to continue it for an indefinite period.

The purpose of problem solving is not for individuals to win points but to find the best possible solution to a problem. The role of the chair is to help faculty understand the problem-solving process, to enlist their aid in making it work, and to experiment with its use until faculty become good problem solvers. All of this sounds deceptively simple. However, academicians are an independent group and enjoy divergent thinking, so agreement may not be reached easily. Also, many decisions affect different faculty members in different ways. When a particular decision is made, some gain but some lose. Input for problem solving and decision making cannot be wholly objective. The chair's goal, then, must be to have decisions made fairly and with the best interests of the department as well as of the individuals in mind.

There are times when faculty discuss a problem and all of its ramifications extensively yet are unable to come to agreement about the best way to handle it. Nonetheless, some decision has to be made. For example, say that faculty in a psychology department made up of culturally diverse experimental and clinical psychologists must decide how to use a gift of $5,000 given directly to the department by a grateful alumnus. The *nominal group technique* is a good choice of strategy in such a situation because the faculty making the decision together have very different priorities, and some are usually reluctant to express their points of view at meetings. Since the nominal group technique requires participation from everyone and ignores differences in specialization and background, it can be an effective way of decision making in many situations.

The technique requires that each faculty member write three or more possible solutions to the problem on separate pieces of paper. This step ensures the choice of a wide range of options. The chair collects each slip of paper as it is written, shuffles the paper to establish anonymity, reads each solution aloud to stimulate group members' thinking, then transfers the information to a chalkboard or flip chart, generating a list of solutions. At this point any items that some faculty do not understood are clarified. Then, each individual ranks what he or she considers to be the best three options from the master list, giving the most preferred the highest number. A first-place vote is worth three votes; a second-place vote, two votes; and a third-place vote, one vote. If a clear choice emerges on the first round, that solution is accepted. If there is no strong agreement, the ranking is repeated until a clear preference does emerge. Since all faculty members will have had an opportunity to present their ideas (without concern that they will be perceived as advancing a procedure that is best for them) and to vote, this method helps break a stalemate and is usually viewed as fair by the group.

The nominal group technique is a good strategy for leveling the playing field and including the thinking of all faculty when, because of differences in rank, seniority, productivity, or ethnic background, some are reluctant to express ideas. Although this method of decision-making does not develop the total commitment that comes with striving for consensus, it has the advantage of including all points of view and is particularly useful when groups cannot reach consensus. Because everyone participates in the idea generation stage, it is different from ordinary discussion and voting, in which some group members will typically be silent, participating only in the voting at the end. For additional information on the use of the nominal group technique, chairs will find P. C. Nutt's *Making Tough Decisions* (1989) a good source.

Decision-Making Styles

The chair's attention to the process by which decisions are made in a department is important. Many departments vote on most decisions, with a simple majority winning. Although this is a very democratic procedure, the minority feel excluded and will often undermine decisions reached, passively dragging their feet when actions need to be taken. One department with which I consulted was so conflict ridden, still at the storming stage after years of having the same chair and the same faculty, that the chair decided all of their meetings would be conducted according to *Robert's Rules of Order*. Although *Robert's Rules* is fine for a faculty senate in which a large number of people come together as a recommending body, it is not generally useful when the number of participants is reasonably small. There were only eighteen faculty members in this department. Typically, after issues had been voted on, people who lost felt angry, and the telephones were very busy after each meeting, with each small group expressing strong criticism of the behavior of the other small groups. The department became more and more fragmented, and voting as a method of decision making seemed only to make things worse. A team-building intervention helped them select more constructive methods of decision making and conflict resolution.

In addition to using the nominal group technique, chairs can use seeking consensus as a way to minimize fragmentation. Consensus is not the same as unanimity. Unanimity occurs only when everyone is in agreement about the course of action to be taken. In decision making by consensus, people have the opportunity to express their views and to try to persuade others. When this method is used effectively, individuals really listen to what is said, do some paraphrasing, and understand all points of view. The group reaches consensus when one point of view is preferred over the others. Under these circumstances, those who disagreed initially are often willing to go along with the rest of the group and accept commitment for carrying through on the decision. The pivotal points are trust that the group is taking the position it does for the well-being of the department, not for selfish interests, and the understanding that everyone's views are listened to and respected, even if the group disagrees with them. The major advantages in seeking consensus are that it enhances group cohesiveness and increases commitment to decisions. The biggest disadvantage of reaching consensus is that it is a time-consuming process—some wag once suggested that, when a group operates entirely on the basis of reaching consensus, all meetings should be held with participants standing up. Therefore, chairs must be selective about which issues are worth this investment of time.

Of course, the chair may also make unilateral decisions. The advantage is that a decision can be made quickly, and this style is useful in emergencies as well as in situations that do not need faculty commitment to be successful and that are of little consequence to department members. Hiring an excellent candidate as departmental secretary, granting a faculty member an emergency leave to return to his native country because a parent is seriously ill, and permitting a bright, high-achieving undergraduate to take a graduate course are all unilateral decisions that do not necessarily require group decision making.

Another approach, consultative decision making, occurs when a chair makes a decision only after obtaining input from those faculty who will be affected by the decision. It is important, under these circumstances, to be sure that faculty recognize that the chair is not simply tallying votes but will be making the decision himself or herself after securing the points of view of those who will be influenced by the decision. If this point is not clarified, faculty will feel the chair has simply gone through the motions in talking with them about what needs to be decided. Consultation does broaden the base of information needed and lets faculty members know the chair values their opinion. However, it also takes time.

Encouraging Disagreement as a Basis for Sound Decision Making

There are many times in the life of a department when decisions represent premature closure. A recommendation is made. Faculty think it sounds fine and agree quickly. Besides, they know the agenda is heavy today. Only afterwards do they recognize that the decision was a mistake. If it can be undone quickly, no harm is done, but this is not always the case. Part of the chair's task as group leader is to encourage discussion of all sides of an issue before a decision is made, particularly when the chair recognizes that some individuals who disagree are not making their positions known.

The problem of whether to continue the old rules established by a department regarding the allocation of travel money is an example of a seemingly simple question. If the rule has been to fund anyone who presents a paper at a conference, and someone proposes that money be given instead to faculty who will benefit from attending a conference even though they do not present a paper, some faculty members will gain while others, who counted on travel money, will lose. If the person who makes the recommendation presents the idea as an unselfish gesture ("I have been receiving money to attend conferences for many years now; others have not received any funding, and I would like to give them a turn"), it is hard for other faculty to argue against the proposal. However, if the chair feels that this suggestion is, in fact, not supported by many, the chair might ask the individual who made the suggestion to give all the reasons that support the idea and then ask someone else to be the devil's advocate and present all the reasons why the idea should not be carried out. The presentation of reasons, both pro and con, frees all faculty to present their views, because they are no longer risking standing alone if they take an opposite point of view. Ideally, after full disclosure of different aspects of the issue, consensus will be reached. The important point here is that the chair deliberately encourages disagreement, so that faculty do not feel trapped into voting in a way that does not represent their point of view. Moreover, from this example can be extracted a good principle for chairing a meeting. The role of the chair is to manage conflict, not necessarily resolve it. Whenever a group seems to be reaching closure after exploring only one side of an issue, the chair can ask someone to articulate the opposite side of the question. That individual is then empowered by the chair to disagree, and does not have to risk the disapproval of others when he or she presents a point of view at variance with theirs.

When an individual offers an idea that is in disagreement with what seems to be a majority viewpoint, a group's usual response is first to try to persuade the person to change his or her mind. If that does not work, the individual is then often ignored, an event tantamount to rejection by the group. The person who feels rejected often uses nonverbal cues to indicate his or her feelings at that point. The faculty member may move his or her chair out of the circle or, as in a case I mentioned before, deliberately stare out of the window, thus withdrawing from the discussion. When this happens, that person's commitment to the final decision is lost, and chairs must recognize that they cannot count on that person to support whatever decisions are made. People can become outcasts, always withdrawing from discussions, when the chair does not pay immediate attention to individual reactions at meetings.

It is particularly hard for a group to know how to handle highly critical comments made by a difficult colleague. One of the more effective ways is simply to paraphrase what the individual has said, and perhaps ask him to elaborate or give examples. The message the chair is giving this person is that his input is valued, that he has a right to disagree with others, and that the chair wants to try to understand his point of view. It is then more likely that a collaborative decision will be made, one with which the difficult colleague can agree.

Conflict at a meeting is often unpleasant, and chairs often indicate that conflict is swept under the rug in their departments rather than dealt with directly. However, conflict can truly be a creative tension resulting in a comprehensive decision that addresses more elements than a decision reached without conflict. Conflict, then, can enrich a discussion. It certainly increases the energy level of a group when it occurs. Since conflict can be such a positive force, chairs must learn to manage it successfully so that it broadens discussions and results in better decisions, and that is the subject of the next chapter.

Conclusion

The nature of communication in a department has a significant effect on the way that department functions. Good supportive communication establishes trust, makes faculty members feel a sense of inclusion, and creates a high level of cohesiveness. Methods of problem solving are used in appropriate ways. Conflict is managed, not suppressed. Feedback is given freely and is accepted without defensiveness. Supportive communication also increases the probability that faculty's individual professional development will assist the department to achieve its goals.

It is suggested that chairs set a goal of creating a supportive communication climate in the department by practicing active listening at every opportunity, modeling the constructive use of feedback, empowering others rather than solving their problems for them, and using problem-solving approaches that include appropriate decision-making styles and that focus on problem resolution rather than laying blame. A second suggested goal for chairs from this chapter is to increase the effectiveness of departmental meetings and enhance the positive reactions of the faculty to decisions by planning meetings well, auditing meeting effectiveness, using task and maintenance leaders at meetings, and experimenting with the problem-solving tools and interventions suggested in this chapter.

Chapter Nine

Managing Conflict

The possibility of conflict is normal whenever people interact. Conflict can occur when people want different things, but must settle for the same thing (Coombs, 1987): for example, when some department members want to develop a new major to reflect a shift in faculty strengths to that area and others do not because current resources would then be stretched in a direction that does not represent their interests. Conflict can also occur when two people want the same thing but must settle for different things: for example, when two instructors want to teach the same advanced- or graduate-level course that, according to enrollment projections, can be offered only once a year. If the instructors take turns, each teaching the course once every two years, the time it will take them to keep up with the literature in a specialized area combined with class preparation time will be excessive for such infrequent teaching. In either type of conflict, if self-interests overshadow mutual interests, the likelihood is that each individual will attempt to use power instead of persuasion to resolve the issue. And in either circumstance, if the bond between the people in conflict is not strong, the relationship will be destroyed. For a chair, the task is to preserve departmental stability, which cannot exist when faculty are fragmented one from the next, clique against clique.

By the very nature of their academic preparation, faculty have been trained to be critical of other perspectives, to be skillful in defending their own professional and personal points of view, and to function most effectively in isolation. What many faculty members have not learned is how to make interpersonal conflict productive.

The chair, therefore, often finds that faculty members competing for the same, often limited, resources will indicate what they want, and if they do not get it, will try to enlist other faculty members and even students in their cause. They may line up arguments of seniority, publications, educational background, political correctness, or simply moral rectitude to bolster their positions. Sometimes, they will go to a dean or provost to complain. Occasionally, they will write memos to the president, with copies to everyone else in the academic hierarchy.

Because conflict can be so unpleasant, faculty and chairs alike frequently avoid it. If, however, the causes of conflict go unresolved, that conflict occasionally erupts at a department meeting in abrasive or sarcastic remarks or in particularly venomous statements to or about a colleague. Often, witnesses to such behavior may become so uncomfortable that they resolve privately to find ways of preventing similar outbursts from occurring again. Because of all these harmful effects, it is clear that a chair cannot allow conflict to escalate to the point where it erodes and fragments departmental relationships. Although conflict cannot always be resolved, it must be managed.

Conflict is not, in and of itself, destructive. It can be used creatively to broaden our understanding, increase our options, and generate the high energy levels that increase our participation and commitment to a group decision. In constructive conflict, faculty cooperate and support each other's ideas. Open to considering the merits of opinions different from their own, they limit disagreements to the issues and do not attack personalities. They understand the usefulness of conflict and manage it effectively, assuming that disagreements stem from sincere involvement and believing that discussion of different ideas will result in a better solution.

In disruptive conflict, the climate is competitive, and win-lose situations are created. Faculty become convinced that they alone are right and look only for reasons that will bolster their positions rather than general information, which might turn out to support their opponents' ideas. Enlisting others in their personal causes becomes more important than finding the best solution for the group's problem (Wood, 1977).

Conflict Management Strategies

There are five basic ways of dealing with conflict: avoidance, accommodation, use of power, negotiation, and collaboration. *Avoidance* is characterized by physical or emotional withdrawal; the existence of a conflict is recognized, but the issues are not confronted. When one faculty member is sharply critical of another at a department meeting, the one who has been criticized may stop participating for the rest of the meeting. He or she may feel angry and maligned because the criticism was personal but may not discuss those feelings. Therefore, although peace is apparently maintained by avoidance, the problem has not been solved and may occur again.

Accommodation occurs when an individual tries to preserve harmony at all costs, and it usually involves sacrificing one person's interests and needs in order to satisfy another's. Sometimes, for example, chairs will emphasize their role of serving the department to the extent that they spend a disproportionate amount of time trying to please all the faculty. One chair had a habit of spending $50 out of his own pocket for wine and cheese to be served at departmental meetings. "Otherwise," he said, "faculty won't attend." Although in the short term, things run smoothly for this type of department chair, in the long term, he or she may feel disappointed when faculty do not respond by accepting their share of departmental responsibility.

A third strategy for managing conflict is *competition*, or the use of power. Individuals set up win-lose climates and often use formal rules to accomplish what they want. This was the attitude articulated by a very political faculty member when he said, "Rules are made to be used against your enemies." Faculty may also cite seniority, rank, specialized experience, or some other extenuating condition as a reason to get what they want. Although this strategy often helps someone to put his or her interests ahead of others', after a time the others resent it and may join forces against the competitive person.

Negotiation is the first of the five conflict strategies that concerns itself with the needs of both parties. In this strategy, each person is willing to give up some of what is wanted in order to gain something else. The disadvantage is that people often remember what it was they had to give up and feel a resentment that may trigger other conflicts. When the number of advanced courses is limited, for example, those faculty members who are allowed to teach their preferred courses may have to pay the price of teaching them during undesirable time slots. Driving home late at night, faculty may feel taken advantage of and resentful.

Collaboration, the last conflict resolution strategy, requires individuals or groups to try to reach an agreement that satisfies both their own and the other's interests and goals. Individuals take a team approach and use methods such as brainstorming to come up with a creative solution to the problem, so that everyone becomes a winner. Instead of attacking each other, together they attack the problem. Faculty openly indicate their real needs, and the group searches for a solution that will satisfy everyone. The problem-solving approach used by the faculty members concerned about allocation of office space (described in Chapter Eight) was collaborative because they searched together for a principle that would be fair and consistent. Rank combined with seniority, the criterion they chose, was a condition that most junior faculty would achieve later in their careers, and there was nothing arbitrary about allocation of space based on this objective criterion. Although a collaborative approach takes time and should not be used to solve every conflict, cohesion and high morale are the benefits.

Principles for Preventing Dysfunctional Conflict

Since it seems clear that conflict is normal wherever people work together, it is unrealistic to expect that academic departments will be exceptions. Chairs need to be able to manage conflict so that it can be used to expand faculty's creative thinking, and they should be aware of the following general principles for preventing dysfunctional conflict (adapted from Higgerson, 1991).

Value all department members and help them to recognize that they have your respect and esteem. Create a climate of trust. Much of the discussion in the preceding chapter dealt with creating a supportive departmental climate, characterized by open communication. Such a climate is the foundation for preventing destructive conflict.

Be thoroughly familiar with relevant university policy found in the faculty handbook or the collective bargaining agreement. Specific policies and procedures may also be found in department documents such as minutes of meetings. The chair's role is to be consistent in applying policy. Not only does consistency prevent potential conflict, it is also a protection against accusations of arbitrary and capricious treatment, often the basis for grievance and litigation.

Ask faculty to spell out in advance of any conflict what procedures they would like to use in handling different kinds of conflict. Examples of some procedures that have come from my own work in team building with departments are:

If something bothers you, talk about it to the person involved. Do not talk to a third party before you have tried to straighten out the problem with the individual with whom there is a difficulty.

If a colleague approaches you with a problem, be willing to work on it so that you can both reach a solution that is mutually agreeable. You want to avoid a solution in which one person is the clear winner. Strive for a solution that makes both people winners.

Remember that it is all right to disagree, as long as you don't end up attacking the other personally.

The first step in this process is that each person presents his or her view of the problem. The role of the other one is to paraphrase what is heard, the emotions as well as the content of the message.

Once each person has had several opportunities to present his or her point of view and the other individual has listened actively, each should have a clearer perception of the colleague's point of view.

Now try brainstorming. This should generate many possible solutions to the problem.

When a dozen or so alternatives have been produced, check for a solution that both can live with. Be certain that both people really agree, be clear about who will do what, and set a date to meet again in about a week so that you can both check to see how things are going.

A general rule in the department might be that if a colleague talks about other members of the department, the first response will be, "Have you talked about this to the other person?" Many long-term conflicts that could have been resolved at an early stage fester for years because two people have not confronted each other directly.

Some of these procedures may seem simplistic. However, when I assist departments with team building, one rule participants often generate is that they will no longer listen to gossip from other members of the department but will instead ask that person to go first to the individual about whom they are complaining and try to straighten things out directly.

Some conflicts between faculty members are best handled by a departmental personnel committee that will listen to both sides and then make a judgment. There are also some simple rules to be practiced at all departmental meetings, such as to listen to all points of view, avoid abusive language, and confront the issues not the person.

Conflicts that interfere with effective departmental function must be confronted by the chair so that conflict does not become dysfunctional.

Colleagues do not have to like each other, but they have to be able to work together in a professional manner, or students and the department may suffer.

The Chair as Third-Party Facilitator

There are occasions when, for the good of the department, the conduct of faculty members cannot be tolerated. The animosity between two faculty members in a biology department, for example, had escalated to such a point that rapid intervention by a new chair was necessary. Professors Dillon and Peterson had not spoken to each other for years; moreover, their behavior was becoming increasingly hostile. If, by chance, the two happened to be walking toward each other down a building corridor, one of the two would actually pop into an empty room so that he would not have to say hello.

The incident that convinced the chair she had to intervene occurred when a new supply of cat cadavers was delivered for a comparative anatomy course. When the delivery person asked where to put them, Professor Peterson, who had ordered them, said, "Leave them in the hallway. In two weeks, we'll be dissecting the cats that are in the closet, and as soon as the closets are empty, the new order can go there." The next day, when Professor Dillon saw the cats in the hallway, he asked the secretary what they were doing there. Learning that they belonged to Peterson, he called the Maintenance Department to ask them to put the cats in the basement because they were blocking access to the telephone booth. The maintenance man, who was slightly disabled with one leg shorter than the other, then had to make a number of trips to the basement with the cats. The next day, Peterson, discovering that his cats were in the basement, telephoned maintenance to say that the cats had been put near the furnace and were going to deteriorate, so he wanted them brought back upstairs. The next day, Dillon telephoned to get the cats out of the hallway because they were blocking traffic. The cats had made two round trips from hallway to basement when finally the director of campus facilities telephoned the chair of biology to say, "When you people get together and decide what you want me to do with those cats, let me know, but we're not going to come back again until you have made a final decision."

To manage the conflict, the new chair decided to try third-party facilitation, the use of negotiating skills to help others resolve problems or reach agreements. This approach builds on creating a supportive communication climate, as discussed in the preceding chapter. Active listening and problem-solving skills and helping faculty in conflict to negotiate clear contracts about what each wants from the other are also part of this process. Most chairs can develop all the skills needed in third-party facilitation. Chairs in a single institution could do so collaboratively, meeting in small groups and using this book as a guide. In these meetings, they could also role-play third-party facilitation (in groups of four, with one person acting as an observer), developing practiced skills to carry back to their departments.

Although a variety of models exist for third-party facilitation, a good initial approach calls upon the chair to speak to each of the dissenting parties separately. The chair indicates that he or she knows a conflict exists, that the parties' behavior is interfering with their performance and the effectiveness of the department, and that the chair wants to propose an approach for managing their disagreement. If one or both say that nothing will work, the chair asks if they would be willing to make an attempt, since things cannot continue as they are. The chair arranges a meeting, in the chair's office or on some other neutral ground, at a specific time when the parties have no classes or other excuses to avoid the interview or leave before it is over. At this meeting, the chair repeats the basic message that the department is suffering from the parties' conflict and that a procedure will have to be developed so that the department can function well once again. The chair also reiterates that there is a process that will probably work for managing their problem.

The chair then describes the first step, which is for each person to look at the problem through the eyes of the other. If, as in the biology department example, the conflict has been going on for many years, the chair will probably need several interviews to bring the participants to the point of managing their disagreements. The chair may begin by asking each of the conflicting faculty to say how he or she feels about the conflict—not the specific areas of disagreement, just how being in conflict makes each of them feel. The chair asks that they avoid blaming or accusing and simply share their feelings about the existence of the conflict while the chair tries to understand their perspectives by paraphrasing what they say. The chair also explains that they will be asked to do the same kind of active listening in a few minutes. While the parties to the conflict are talking, the chair maintains good eye contact with the person who is speaking, nodding when this is appropriate and summarizing after every few sentences. The paraphrase should include a summary of the feelings expressed by the speaker's nonverbal language as well. After one person has spoken and the chair has finished paraphrasing, the other person expresses his or her feelings about the conflict. It is probable that both individuals will talk about how unpleasant, inconvenient, and intrusive the conflict is to their professional and personal lives. But regardless of what ideas are expressed, the chair simply summarizes what is said, showing interest as each person speaks and demonstrating active listening, but remaining objective and nonjudgmental and not siding with one individual or the other. If the parties do not say how unpleasant their conflict is for them, the chair might offer that statement to see if they agree with it.

Once the faculty members have described how the conflict interferes with their lives, and the chair has agreed that the conflict must be painful, the chair helps the faculty members identify a small aspect of the problem that they can work on together. This part of the problem should be something that is not too stressful, so that they have a fair chance of finding an effective way of handling it and experiencing a success in conflict management that they can build on. For example, if each finds it unpleasant to avoid the other when they happen to meet on campus, after some discussion they might agree to say hello to each other. That might seem too basic, but if the chair were to ask them to resolve something highly stressful for both of them, that attempt would be unsuccessful because each person would have too much invested in the stressful situation.

One way for the chair to identify an area that does not provoke too much stress is to ask each faculty member to rate some conflict situations on a continuum that runs from 0 to 100, measured in subjective units of discomfort (SUDs). Zero means a situation causes no anxiety or discomfort; 100 means it makes you so uncomfortable you could pop out of your skin. The chair asks both individuals to write down two or three low-anxiety situations in which they find their conflict is disruptive and to give each situation a SUD rating. The chair can then choose an area that both have rated as a low-discomfort area as a suitable topic on which they can begin their discussions. If the individuals choose totally different problems, the chair can select a problem on one person's list and ask the other person how high that problem would be on his or her SUD scale, continuing until a low-stress situation that they can both work on is identified.

Once the low-stress problem area is chosen, the chair explains the following ground rules, which rest on the idea of confronting the problem not the person. If the parties see the problem rather than each other as the enemy, it will be easier for them to come to agreement. (These ground rules are an adaptation of Guerney's 1977 work on relationship enhancement.)

Ground Rules for the Speaker

Each individual will be asked to present his or her perception of one selected aspect of the problem. Each person is undoubtedly angry, and it is all right to express some of that anger. However, the personal pronoun "I" must be used, so the individual speaking accepts responsibility for the feeling or perspective being described, and the pronoun "you" must be avoided, or at least, may not be used to make accusations or lay blame. No assumptions are to be made about the motivation of the other person. No one is to say, for example, "You did this because you wanted to get back at me for. . . ." The speaker must try to focus on his or her feelings about issues, that is, the point of the dispute itself. He or she will speak for only a minute or two before pausing so that the listener can use active listening to summarize what has been heard.

Ground Rules for the Listener

The task of the listener is to put himself or herself in the other person's position, to look at what is being presented through the speaker's eyes, and to use active listening to summarize what the speaker has said. No questions may be asked. No judgments or corrections may be made, even if the listener believes that the speaker has the facts wrong. If the speaker does not agree that the summary was accurate, the listener tries summarizing again. As clarification, the speaker may repeat what he or she has just said. If the listener is still not on target, the facilitator summarizes the statement.

Ground Rules for the Facilitator

The role of the facilitator is that of coach and role model. The facilitator may praise either of the parties when they have expressed something that was difficult or when they have shown improvement in trying to express or summarize a thought or emotion. The facilitator may say, "Foul" (with a smile), when someone breaks the rules that have been set up. And it is the facilitator who suggests that the individuals switch roles when the speaker seems to have adequately, if not exhaustively, covered the problem as viewed from one perspective. The facilitator may also suggest suitable places for the listener to interrupt with a summary, not letting the speaker cover so much ground that the listener will find it difficult to remember all that has been said.

Agreeing to Work on the Problem

Once both individuals have had several opportunities to express their perspectives, it is time for the facilitator to help the parties identify the problem as objectively as possible, and using the "how to" syntax described earlier. For example, how to identify who owns a problem and when an intervention is appropriate is a relevant issue for the two faculty members in the biology department. Was it Dillon's problem that the cats ordered by Peterson were placed in the hallway? If they were really blocking access to the telephone booth, perhaps the chair or the secretary could have informed Peterson and asked for his solution. Or perhaps Peterson could have been helped to recognize that his temporary solution of placing the cats in the hallway might create a problem for those using the hallway. Although the core problem is the antagonism between the two, if some of the abrasive behavior could be diminished, the real issues could then be managed as the two behaved in a more rational manner toward each other.

After both individuals agree on a problem that can be resolved, they might be asked to use brainstorming to generate alternative solutions. The usual rules of brainstorming hold here: the parties generate a number of options, choose a couple of viable alternatives that both parties can live with, determine the criteria they will use to decide whether the chosen alternative works, and set a specific period of time during which they will try it. A date is then set for another meeting with the chair to check how the selected option is working. The chair might even end the interview by asking the faculty members if, as a favor to him or her, they will acknowledge each other's presence when they meet in the hallway. The chair should remark on the real progress that has been made, if this is true, and how pleased the chair is about their willingness to manage the conflict.

Once the disputants reach some understanding of each other's point of view and arrive at some agreement about how each will behave in a specific situation, one step has been taken in the direction of managing the conflict. When they meet the following week, the chair can determine whether they are ready to move on to managing another area of their conflict.

There are several other points chairs should learn about facilitation behavior. A facilitator must not take sides with either party; however, he or she does not have to be neutral about the issues, particularly when they involve unprofessional behavior. In the biology department conflict, one faculty member had repeatedly advised students not to take a course with the other because, he said, the other faculty member did not have the appropriate academic credentials to teach certain courses. A deliberate attempt to diminish the reputation of a colleague is certainly unprofessional behavior that cannot be tolerated in a department, and the chair must reinforce those ethical principles.

The job of the facilitator is also to keep the discussion issue oriented. However, the parties' feelings cannot be ignored. Whereas personal attacks are totally unacceptable, expression of emotions is appropriate. Faculty members cannot be expected to check their feelings at the door, but those feelings must not be expressed as attacks or accusatory statements. However, the chair can focus on the impact the conflict is having on performance and on departmental effectiveness. And, as suggested, the chair can help faculty members put problems in perspective by focusing first on areas where they might agree and by limiting discussion so that it deals with only one issue at a time.

Facilitators should remember that they are not judges. If the facilitator does assume the role of judge, the disputants will work to persuade the facilitator rather than to solve the problem. It is also up to the facilitator to make sure the parties fully support any solutions they have agreed upon. Occasionally, faculty members may agree because they feel worn down or because they do not want to appear difficult in the chair's eyes. However, the chair must not stop the process until both faculty members have agreed to engage in specific behaviors, and if the chair senses that someone is half-hearted about the agreement, the chair must point out the apparent hesitation and ask if that faculty member is quite ready to agree to the proposed behaviors.

Before the parties leave the interview, it is useful for the facilitator to ask them to write down what each one wants from the other person. Specifically, each person should be asked to indicate the observable behaviors he or she wants more of, less of, and the same amount or kind of. The facilitator asks both individuals to be very exact in requesting the behaviors they want and in saying why they are needed. Again, there is to be no blame in the statements. And both people, as receivers of these requests for certain behaviors, need to have a clear understanding of what is being asked of them and to indicate whether they are willing to do these things. Both individuals need to be sure they can live with the contracts to which they are agreeing. This kind of role negotiation is often helpful simply because it does get faculty to be very specific as each writes down what is needed from the other person and discovers what the other individual wants in return. Indicating the reason for the request is also important, so that the other person will understand the rationale. Finally, it provides an opportunity for each party to reinforce any existing positive behaviors by indicating what actions each would like the other to continue. Chairs may want to ask each person to sign and date the statements, so there can be no argument at a later date about what was requested and agreed to.

It is not necessary for the chair to intervene personally in all the problems that arise between individuals in the department. Indeed, chairs may not know about some of them. Also, as was mentioned in Chapter Eight, an elected departmental personnel or policy committee can often make decisions when faculty are in disagreement. For example, a chair could handle the first conflict situation cited in this chapter, in which two faculty members wanted to teach the same advanced- or graduate-level course that could be offered only once a year, through third-party facilitation or through referral to the departmental personnel committee. A less-than-ideal resolution of the problem would assign the faculty members to take turns in teaching the course. However, faculty members could also agree to trade courses, if there is another course both want to teach and only one has been teaching it on a regular basis. Each would then teach a desirable course once a year that both would like to teach. As another option, the department might find it reasonable to offer a new undergraduate course in the desirable area. The instructors could then take turns teaching the graduate and undergraduate sections of the same course. Yet other options might be generated if the committee and the two faculty members did some brainstorming together. The chair or the committee might try to find out what needs both instructors satisfy by teaching the desired course and to discover whether such needs could be fulfilled in some other way. Referring such problems to the department personnel committee reduces some of the stress on the chair. It also gives other faculty members an opportunity to practice their negotiation skills. Moreover, when the chair is an untenured assistant professor, a situation that seems to be happening with greater frequency in comprehensive universities, it may be politically astute for the chair not to create an adversarial relationship with a senior faculty member.

Handling Conflict Between a Faculty Member and a Student

Another kind of problem that may erupt in a department appears in the following example of a conflict between a faculty member and student. A parent telephones the dean to complain that his son was refused a make-up final examination in a course. On the day of the test, the student left a message with the department secretary that he could not take the exam because he had the flu. He has a physician's statement verifying his illness on the day of the exam, but the tenured professor has still refused to give a make-up exam. The student's father says that several other students who had missed the final exam were given the opportunity to take a make-up exam. Also, the parent says, the final exam was given a week early, and the professor has now left campus for the winter vacation. The parent complains that the professor's behavior was arbitrary and capricious. The dean requests the department chair to investigate and solve the problem. The chair telephones the professor, who says that the exam in question was not a final examination but simply the third of three tests. He has not left early; rather, he has structured his course so that there is no final examination. He admits he did give make-up exams to two other students, but each of them "was a perfect lady or gentlemen, so each deserved a make-up test."

This is an unjust situation because the professor is applying both different and irrelevant criteria in making a decision affecting three students. After listening to the faculty member's perspective, the chair's first step should be to appeal to the professor to apply the same criteria to all three students, and if this appeal does not work, the profession should be reminded that his behavior is arbitrary and capricious and would be so judged in a court of law. If the professor still refuses to change his decision, a department personnel committee's decision about the professor's unprofessional behavior might have a greater impact than the chair's decision. If obtaining a personnel committee decision is not practical because of end-of-semester time pressures, another possibility is that the chair and the faculty member could be asked to meet with the dean, who would indicate strongly that such behavior opens the professor, the chair, the dean, and the university to litigation, and that this is unacceptable. Often a faculty member will back away from an earlier decision when institutional pressures are applied. Clearly, a continuation of such behavior will require that the chair begin documenting what is happening, establishing a paper trail as a basis for termination proceedings.

When student complaints about one or two faculty members are frequent, some departments have chosen to appoint an ombudsman to deal with the problems. If there is a strong, well-respected individual in the department who can take on this position, this strategy often works and may be particularly useful in dealing with the occasional faculty member who does not respect a chair who is a woman, a member of a minority group, or an untenured faculty member. Under these circumstances, the chair could confront the individual each time, insisting that he or she behave in an ethical and professional manner, and even use institutional leverage, such as referring the matter to the dean's office. However, dealing directly with many minor skirmishes and a few major conflagrations, all with the same person, is not worth the time it takes and the psychic energy it requires. Better to save one's energy for creative enterprises. Instead of engaging in a series of confrontations, the chair can adopt the wiser strategy of appointing an ombudsman to deal with student complaints, an action that can simply be announced in a brief memo to faculty. Such an action is not an indication of weakness; it is, rather, an executive decision about how the chair's time and energy can be used most effectively. When chairs do choose to deal directly with a difficult colleague, note that it is usually better to confront the person in his or her office rather than the chair's office. Then, if the person begins to scream or become abusive, it is easy for the chair to leave, making the simple comment that he or she would like to continue the conversation when the person has calmed down.

Other problems that evoke conflict can be handled by the department as a whole, but first, the question can be raised with all department members about how they would prefer to resolve difficulties. The guiding principles should be those stressed throughout this chapter. The first principle is that conflict is not something to be avoided, but it does need to be managed so that it does not become destructive. Disagreements need to be turned into clearly formulated problems that department members as a team can resolve. Closely related to this idea is the principle that it is easier to prevent dysfunctional conflict than to deal with its aftermath. In departments in which morale is high, dysfunctional conflict is greatly reduced. The third principle is that the chairs need not take the complete responsibility for managing conflict onto their own shoulders. All department members should have some input into developing guidelines for managing conflict so that when conflict occurs, the chair can refer faculty to a written set of guidelines to which all have agreed in advance.

Conclusion

Chairs should always remember that constructive conflict is to be encouraged because it improves the quality of decisions that are made. Destructive conflict, which often involves a personal attack, hurts individuals and cannot be permitted. Never forget: confront the problem, not the person!

I suggest that chairs set a goal of managing conflict effectively and that they begin by familiarizing themselves with the five strategies for managing conflict: avoidance, accommodation, use of power, negotiation, and collaboration—and begin consciously choosing appropriate management strategies each time departmental conflicts occur. Setting aside time with faculty to develop procedures for managing conflict can be a second goal.

I also suggest that chairs set a goal of dealing effectively with any interpersonal conflict that is occurring between two faculty members and that is clearly dysfunctional for the department. The chair must decide whether each conflict is best handled by the chair, the departmental personnel committee, or the appointment of an ombudsman. In those cases in which the chair determines to act as a third-party facilitator, the chair can practice following the steps in this chapter, evaluating his or her progress in conflict resolution by monitoring actions taken and outcomes achieved.

Chapter Ten

Using Feedback from the Department

The previous chapters have presented the major leadership and faculty development responsibilities of academic chairs, and the goals and practical implementation steps needed to accomplish these responsibilities have been explored. A variety of strategies have been discussed that chairs can employ to involve faculty in changing departmental cultures, encouraging faculty to improve teaching effectiveness, increase scholarship, take responsibility for accomplishing the goals of the department, make meetings productive and satisfying, and develop mutually agreed upon strategies for handling conflict. Now we return to the leadership matrix introduced in Chapter Two, looking at it in greater detail as a vehicle for involving both faculty and the dean in determining what is important for the department and for giving feedback on a chair's current level of leadership skills. This use of the leadership matrix will permit chairs to receive affirmation, as well as correction, of their perceptions of what the department needs and what opportunities exist for their personal leadership development.

The leadership matrix is not constructed to be a performance evaluation instrument but to go beyond evaluation to goal setting, as many organizations are now doing in lieu of using performance evaluation instruments. In the goal-setting process, individuals generate goals with the person to whom they report, and then develop implementation steps and timelines for goal completion. Of course, these goals are also tied to mission statements, functional goals, and objectives of the department, division, and organization. Opportunities for midyear corrections are built into the process, so that the goal-setting individuals can discuss whether anything has occurred after their goals were written that would significantly affect the achievement of those goals. At the end of the year, it is relatively easy to evaluate the extent to which goals have been accomplished. How chairs can use this process for both faculty development and faculty evaluation was discussed in Chapter Four.

The leadership matrix involves a similar process to develop chairs' leadership abilities. Because this instrument plots ratings on the chair's leadership from the chair, the dean, and all the individual faculty members, it can be a catalyst for team building and for discussion between the dean and the chair and between the chair and the faculty. The nine major categories the matrix plots are leadership responsibilities not observable behaviors; however, when the matrix is discussed, chairs are encouraged to ask for examples of specific behaviors that faculty currently see or would like to see more of.

This chapter deals with the ways chairs can handle feedback from faculty via the leadership matrix. First, it examines the value of feedback and how chairs can manage the feedback process in order to derive the greatest benefit from it. Second, it demonstrates a step-by-step procedure chairs can use to conduct meetings with faculty to discuss the results of the chair's ratings on the leadership matrix. Finally, it shows how to set goals and action steps with faculty, so chairs can carry out the leadership responsibilities that are high priorities for the department.

Feedback Is a Gift

Feedback is communication to a person or a group that tells the recipient how individual or group behavior is perceived by another person and how it affects that person. Feedback can also include information about the way someone reacts to what another person does and says. When provided in a supportive climate, nonjudgmentally, and as an observation separated from inference, feedback is a valuable gift, because unless people tell us, verbally or nonverbally, how they feel about what we do, we may think we are having one effect while we produce its exact opposite. Because perceptions are very subjective, we need a frequent check to find out whether others share our perceptions. How do we know, for example, whether a lecture we are giving is really as clear as we think it is unless we ask a question to see whether students can demonstrate an understanding of what we have just taught?

One simple personal growth model, which illustrates perceptions and types of interactions between ourselves and others, is the Johari Window (Luft, 1984, p. 60), shown in Figure 10.1. (*Johari* is simply a combination of the first names of the psychologists who developed the model, Joseph Luft and Harry Ingham.) Although the labels used in the Johari Window have changed over the years, the model and language used by Hanson seems most useful to me. The Johari Window compares the things one person knows to the

Exhibit 10.1. The Johari Window.

	Known to Self	Not Known to Self
Known to Others	Arena	Blind Spot
Not Known to Others	Facade	Unknown

Adapted from *Group Processes: An Introduction to Group Dynamics* by Joseph Luft, by permission of Mayfield Publishing Company. Copyright © 1984 by Joseph Luft.

things others know to produce four possible categories for this kind of knowledge: arena, blind spot, facade, and unknown.

The arena represents those aspects of ourselves, such as emotions and reactions triggered by ongoing events, that both we and others are aware of. It includes things that can be talked about freely and also encompasses the sharing, in trusting relationships, of personal reactions to people and ongoing events. Those who create open relationships with others are said to have a large arena with respect to the overall window.

The blind spot includes those aspects of ourselves that we are not aware of but that other people may know. We convey these aspects to others by body language and other nonverbal communication that constantly tell others about such feelings as our anxiety, disagreement, or confidence in what the others are saying. The blind spot also includes information about behavior that we may not be aware of; for example, we may feel that we are open when we are actually unwilling to listen to another's point of view. The extent to which we are unaware of self and the effect we have on others determines how large our blind spot is in proportion to the rest of the window.

The facade includes what we try to hide from others, perhaps a tendency to avoid conflict at departmental meetings because we are uncomfortable in dealing with an abrasive faculty member. A chair, for example, may be concerned that a failure to handle the abrasive person effectively will be criticized as weakness or incompetence. So instead of asking a member of the department in advance for support in a confrontation with the abrasive faculty member, the chair avoids the conflict. However, unless the chair does some risk taking, he or she will never know whether success is possible, or whether others will offer support when the chair confronts dysfunctional behavior. Therefore, a person hiding behind a facade may never develop the ability to handle conflict well because he or she feels that trying to deal with friction is too anxiety provoking.

The unknown includes potential or unrecognized resources within ourselves that may come to light as new opportunities for growth occur. When we are given an assignment that stretches our abilities, we can demonstrate what we are capable of doing. For example, a faculty member who became part of a negotiating team for a faculty union found this to be an exhilarating experience because he suddenly discovered he was very good at it.

One value of the Johari Window as a personal growth model is that it visually illustrates to us how we can learn more about ourselves through soliciting feedback and thus reducing our blind spots. To see ourselves as others see us is a rare gift. But if we are not open to feedback or if we become defensive when an individual criticizes something we have done, the door is closed to any professional development that requires us to change our behavior. So we need to encourage feedback.

Obviously not all feedback is valid. However, much feedback, even though it may make us feel uncomfortable, does offer us an opportunity to learn more about ourselves, if we can get past our defensiveness. When feedback about something we have done is negative, it typically evokes anxiety in us. But instead of rejecting that feedback out of hand, we need to discover whether others who have viewed us in the same or in a similar situation make observations that correspond with the feedback we have already received. The same feedback from several people constitutes *consensual validation,* and we need to take such validated feedback seriously even if it is painful. The only acceptable response to feedback is a thank-you or a request for an example that will make the feedback more understandable. If we respond by attacking the other person (saying, for example, when our meeting management skills are questioned, "Do you think you could have handled that meeting better?"), that is probably the last time we will get feedback from that individual.

Leadership knowledge and behaviors can be viewed as existing on three rising levels: awareness, working knowledge, and mastery.

Awareness is the first step in learning. Once when I was interviewing department chairs about what they felt would be useful topics in a leadership development program, one person who had been a chair for twelve years responded, "If you had asked me that question about my own discipline, I could have told you exactly what I am really expert in and what areas represent my weak points in the field. When it comes to chair leadership, I have no idea what's out there for me to learn." Of course, I then rephrased my question to ask about his success and lack of success in concrete areas of leadership. However, the point is that, like this chair, we sometimes do not know what we do not know. Now and then, we may lack insight about how what we do affects others.

Chairs' awareness in such areas as understanding how their behavior strikes others is the first step in their building leadership knowledge and skills. Such awareness, or insight, develops from their requesting feedback and being open and nondefensive when they receive it. Once chairs have a better understanding of the effect their behaviors have on others, the next step requires that they obtain a *working knowledge* of the desired behavior or skill. This learning period requires some risk taking, since it involves trying out new behaviors. During this second stage, chairs may become aware of something they could have said or done better only after the opportunity to say it has passed. In this stage, chairs also find that sometimes they will do something really well and at other times rather badly, but this inconsistency is all part of perfecting a particular leadership skill. The final stage, *mastery*, arrives when, under most circumstances, chairs can correctly diagnose the needs of a person or situation and respond by using one of the better ways of handling it: for example, using a problem-solving approach instead of accusing or blaming.

Steps in Managing Faculty Feedback

After faculty members have completed the individual rating sheets for the nine leadership responsibilities in terms of importance to the department and the rater's satisfaction with the chair's level of skill development at this time, and the information has been transferred to the tally sheets and plotted on the matrix (see Chapter Two), the chair shares this information with the faculty and participates with them in setting goals for the chair and for the department.

Some chairs may feel that engaging in this formal feedback process will be risky, but the payoff can be great. Massy and Wilger (1994) refer to avoidance of any issues that might create conflict as "hollowed collegiality." In their study of conditions within academic departments that prevent faculty from working together to make undergraduate teaching more effective, they have written, "As perverse as it sounds, a frequently cited reason for the inability of faculty to communicate is the veneer of civility that pervades faculty interactions. . . . Unpleasantness is avoided at all costs. Unfortunately, . . . this often means that the most crucial issues facing the department never get discussed. . . . Relations may seem calm, but this calm is achieved at the expense of a common sense of purpose and community" (p. 5). Discussing feedback from the leadership matrix with department members is an example of a task that might be avoided lest conflict emerge or feelings be hurt. However, discussing results and setting goals provides a strong foundation for team building with faculty. Chairs who familiarize themselves with the steps discussed below will greatly minimize the risk element and find it easier to make the process very profitable for the department as well as for the chair.

For the leadership development process to be effective, four distinct steps are required.

Step 1: Prepare by Reviewing Leadership Matrix Results

It is important not just to look at the rating results but to gauge your reaction to them and determine appropriate responses before you hold the feedback meeting.

Review the results of the chair's, the dean's, and the faculty's ratings. Some of these results may be what the chair has expected.

Others may be a surprise. Chairs should remember that they are dealing with the perceptions that the dean and faculty have of the department and its needs, and of the chair's leadership knowledge and skills. These perceptions will also be tinged by individuals' personal and professional needs. It is difficult to know what these perceptions are unless you ask. It is difficult to manage meaningful change unless you know what is important to others.

To accomplish the review, look first at cell B, listing all the responsibilities that have clusters of ratings in that cell (which indicates both high importance and high satisfaction). This information reports on the areas that faculty members feel are important and are also going well. Chairs should enjoy this feedback! Savor the success and do not skip over this step quickly! It is important for chairs to give themselves credit for their effective handling of important responsibilities. Chairs can also spend some time thinking of how they can maintain effectiveness and satisfaction in these highly rated areas. Next, review the clusters of ratings in cell A (items of high importance and low satisfaction). These are opportunities for leadership development, and though the results here may be the most painful of all the feedback given, they provide the most useful information on faculty perceptions. This feedback is the faculty's gift because it provides direction for the chair's leadership development. It deserves thoughtful attention and requires the generation of ideas for creating change. Cell C offers information about items that exhibit low satisfaction but which faculty members also feel are not important. Therefore, department members are not necessarily concerned about change in these areas. However, the chair may feel some of these items are important even though faculty do not, and if this is true, the chair may want to share his or her reactions about this discrepancy with faculty. Finally, cell D comprises areas with which raters have high satisfaction even though they perceive them to be of low importance. Sometimes we engage in activities simply because we know we do them well. If a chair is devoting much time and energy to such areas, he or she may want to rethink that action.

Get a handle on personal reactions to this feedback. Some of the information the chair receives during this review may be very reinforcing. Other parts may create some discomfort. Chairs should detach themselves somewhat from the process, looking at the implications of the ratings as objectively as possible. For example, chairs might consider what a rating would mean if it were made about someone else or another department or another university. Also, the chair's perception may be genuinely different from the faculty's. Suppose, for example, faculty feel no need for increased faculty motivation in teaching, scholarship, or service while the chair has strong feelings that much needs to be done. Perhaps faculty are unaware that anything can be done that would work to increase their motivation. The meeting with faculty to discuss the results of the feedback is a good time for the chair to share a few painless strategies that will work.

Give some thought to what can be done to maintain areas of effectiveness and improve areas that require the use of different behaviors. Plans for maintenance and change should not be carved in stone at this point, but jot down some notes about changes that must be made, while still remaining open to the suggestions you will receive from faculty at the feedback meeting.

Decide whether to meet with the faculty or the dean first. Once you have a clear perception of what the leadership ratings mean, how faculty members perceive the departmental needs and your leadership skills, and some possible actions to take in response to this feedback, decide whether the next step will be meeting with the dean or with the faculty. This decision should be based on chairs' professional judgment and knowledge of their own situations. The purpose of meeting with the dean first is to obtain a more objective point of view about what the feedback means and to learn whether the dean shares the faculty's perceptions, what suggestions the dean may have for conducting the feedback meeting with faculty, and whether the dean agrees with the plans the chair has already generated for personal leadership development. If the chair decides to meet with faculty first, the purpose of the subsequent meeting with the dean will probably be to share information, engage in some goal setting, and perhaps present a request for the resources needed to achieve departmental and institutional goals and to increase the chair's professional development.

Step 2: Schedule the Faculty Feedback Meeting

When scheduling the feedback meeting with faculty, chairs should remember the logistical basics already emphasized: choose a two-hour block of time when everyone is likely to be free; arrange the seating in a U-shape, placing the department chair and an over-head projector at the open end of the U; serve coffee and tea; create an open climate for communication; and do not include other items on the agenda.

Step 3: Hold the Faculty Feedback Meeting

In the next step, the chair leads the faculty feedback meeting, reviewing the overall results and encouraging further feedback and explanation, and leading a discussion to define plans and action steps. Since carrying out many of the leadership responsibilities also requires positive action from faculty to improve their own performance in such areas as teaching and scholarship, these plans and actions will apply to faculty as well as the chair. The general outline for this meeting is: here are the results; these are my reactions; what will we do about it?

Thank faculty for completing the leadership matrix and providing the feedback.

Review the leadership matrix. The chair recalls the way the leadership matrix works, reviewing the significance of the two dimensions: each responsibility's importance to the department at this point in time and each faculty member's satisfaction with the chair's current level of skill development. The chair also reviews the significance of each of the four cells. Faculty will be interested in learning how this instrument can focus attention on opportunities for leadership development.

Briefly overview areas with clear-cut results. To overview the ratings, simply show the clusters of ratings in cells B and A. Name the leadership responsibilities that were rated as important to the department and as ones in which the chair's leadership development was also high or very high (cell B), and then name the leadership responsibilities that were judged as important to the department and as ones in which there are opportunities for the chair's leadership development (cell A). Also name the leadership responsibilities that fell in cells C and D, and explain that faculty will have a chance to discuss all the responsibilities and ratings in detail. (Using an overhead projector to share these results is effective.)

Chairs should note that faculty may rate all nine of the leadership responsibilities as important to the department. This is perfectly acceptable. Nonetheless, in the goal-setting discussion, faculty will have to prioritize responsibilities so that effort can be directed to three or four most critical areas. The chair should not discuss any further particulars at this point unless there are basic questions about the meanings of the cells. However, faculty should know from this overview that the chair has spent some time reviewing the data and is taking faculty feedback seriously.

Initiate a detailed discussion of the results in cells B and A. Do not be modest in reviewing the findings in cell B and asking faculty for specific examples of what you are doing that demonstrates a high level of leadership in the areas the faculty rated highly. Spending some time on important leadership areas with which faculty are satisfied is good for faculty as well as for chairs. Faculty are always a bit apprehensive about a feedback meeting, concerned that there may be too much bad news, which will embarrass both the chair and them. Starting with some positive points helps everyone feel more comfortable and ready to tackle some more difficult areas.

After the information in cell B has been savored, move on to the discussion of cell A and the opportunities for leadership development in areas of departmental importance. The greatest part of this meeting will probably be spent on cell A information. Chairs must encourage department members to consider how they can help their chair develop the needed leadership skills and how, together, the chair and faculty might make the department even more effective.

It is at this point that chairs must establish the mind set that feedback is a valuable gift. They must listen, encourage the feedback, and reflect on it before reacting to it. A chair may choose not to change behavior on the basis of feedback, but if there is consensual validation, the chair should seriously consider the need for change. Chairs must also avoid explaining or justifying past actions and should reinforce openness among faculty instead. Chairs who feel defensive should resist the urge to defend themselves and should focus on paraphrasing what is heard. Chair should make a commitment to take some action in all areas that are important to department members, particularly those areas where satisfaction with leadership is lowest. Taking notes, perhaps on a flip chart, is useful for review of what was covered, especially if a chair wants to summarize the results of the discussion and the goals set in a memo distributed to the faculty after the meeting.

Beware of behavior that interferes with the positive value of feedback. Avoid these specific kinds of defensive behavior:

Denial: the chair flatly rejects the feedback as incorrect or not applicable.

Projection: the chair says, "Yes, but . . . ," and puts the blame on other people or things.

Rebuttal: the chair concentrates on every exception, to prove the feedback is wrong.

Withdrawal: the chair stops participating in the discussion.

Assume faculty mean well; accept constructive criticism. Chairs must assume that faculty are trying to supply their honest and candid perceptions of departmental needs and a chair's leadership ability. Chairs should avoid thinking that someone is out to get them! Criticism and suggestions do not constitute a wholesale attack on the person of the chair but a commentary on the leadership needs of the department and a perception of the chair's leadership skills in a particular area. Chairs must not take constructive criticism personally, and they must not act so hurt that faculty stop making recommendations.

Help faculty supply needed helpful information. For example, ask for specific examples and avoid generalities; help faculty who have difficulty pinpointing a problem by suggesting examples and asking whether they show what the person is talking about; ask for suggestions about other or better ways or approaches than you have been using.

Use supportive communication techniques. For example, chairs should use body language to improve communication—make eye contact, lean toward the speaker, and so on. This is also an occasion to demonstrate active listening skills, restating what has been said in one's own words to indicate understanding. The formula, "What you are saying is . . . ," is useful here.

Overview each responsibility before zeroing in to discuss specific objectives. For example, chairs can overview the area of motivating faculty to teach effectively before meeting participants' planned action steps for this area, so that the steps will be formulated in the context of the total area. However, it is important to recognize that there may be times when faculty rate a leadership responsibility such as this one as unimportant, because they believe the department is doing fine in this area, while the chair may be aware of low student evaluations of some faculty and frequent student complaints about a few instructors. Chairs might also have heard the kind of casual comments faculty can make about their classes that demonstrate to an informed listener that teaching effectiveness needs to be improved. It is also true that faculty who have been teaching for twenty years or so often feel that the length of time they have spent in the classroom necessarily means that they are competent and that there is no reason for them to think about innovation in their teaching. Thus, chairs may need to deal tactfully with a discrepancy between faculty ratings and their own perception of need. While this feedback meeting should not be an occasion for a chair's critical comments about faculty teaching, the chair might say something along these lines: "Since, as a department, we are committed to making teaching effectiveness an ongoing goal toward which all of us strive, and since we have done nothing as a group lately in this area, would you list two or three goals and action steps that will help us to create and maintain high-quality teaching? For example, we could set a goal of increasing the number of teaching strategies currently used in the department from two—namely, lecture and case studies—to, let us say, five, and we might accomplish this goal by conducting a mini-workshop in our department to discuss the variety of alternate teaching methods available for teachers to use to achieve specific goals for a course." (The chair could also review the list from Chapter Five of significant topics in teaching worth discussing in the department, in order to stimulate ideas about other teaching goals and action steps.)

Identify plans and action steps for future improvement in each of the leadership responsibilities for which ratings intersect in cell A. Chairs and their faculty must decide on specific action steps and strategies to enhance the chair's leadership abilities. The goal is a development plan that details what the chair intends to do, the timetable for doing it, and the support required from department members and the institution. In reaching this development plan, chairs should:

Allow all participants to serve as sounding boards for each other's ideas so that alternatives can be tested out.

Offer any ideas they may have thought of in advance and ask for faculty members' reactions.

Seek consensus and reach agreement on the details of the action steps.

Develop plans based on their own strengths, the available resources, and realistic demands.

Ask for faculty members' help in specific ways.

Do not agree to end the meeting before participants reach an understanding of issues and expected actions. The only exception to this rule occurs when all nine leadership responsibilities must be covered and it may be necessary to postpone some of them to a subsequent meeting. The chair should also encourage department members to summarize what was discussed and agreed to. Then the chair reacts to this summary with his or her understanding of it, agreeing to it, revising it, or adding thoughts. Finally, the chair should thank faculty for discussing the issues and express his or her commitment to the action plans and appreciation for promised support.

Step 4. Follow Up

After the feedback meeting, the chair and faculty must follow up on their plans and keep open the lines of communication that were established at the meeting.

Make notes about the agreements, plans, and action steps. Although chairs do not necessarily need to develop written plans, there is an advantage to developing a written statement about the outcome of the meeting. It certainly reduces the possibility of later misperceptions about what has been discussed and agreed upon.

Schedule agreed-upon actions. Chairs must follow through on any promises they have made. In addition, they should let faculty know what they have done and what they are doing, as they go along. Chairs can ask faculty to accept responsibility for some of the goals and action steps that have been set: for example, organizing a mini-workshop on some aspect of teaching by a specific date. The item to be accomplished, the name of the responsible faculty member, and the agreed-upon date should appear on the schedule.

Ask for ongoing feedback. The formal feedback meeting is simply one scheduled event in an ongoing process. Securing immediate feedback on specific actions and accomplishments is the most effective way to influence behavior. Chairs need this information if they are to successfully modify their behavior. They need feedback on the positive as much as, or even more than, on the negative.

Provide progress reports about what is being done to achieve goals and action steps.

Feedback Meeting with the Dean

Much of the process just discussed is equally applicable for chairs' meetings with their deans. As discussed earlier, a chair may choose to meet with the dean before or after meeting with faculty. It is useful to bring to the meeting the leadership matrices on which responses from both the dean and the faculty have been plotted, so that the discussion can be based on that information.

Since the chair's term of service will be more successful if he or she has done some goal setting with the dean, this interview should be very constructive. It will give the chair information about the dean's expectations that many chairs do not receive from their deans. The dean's expectations of the chair and of the department, the dean's idea of the fit between college and departmental goals, the dean's view of the growth opportunities the position of department chair offers to an individual, and the resources the dean can make available to facilitate a chair's leadership development are all items of knowledge important to a chair's overall success. This feedback discussion will also bring the special issues the chair may be struggling with in the department and the assistance the chair may need to handle them effectively to the dean's attention.

Further suggestions for the dean's role in meetings with department chairs appear in the following chapter. While addressed to the dean, the goal-setting information presented in that chapter can also help the chair prepare for the work of defining goals.

Conclusion

More than 80 percent of the several thousand chairs with whom I have worked indicate that they do not know what their deans or faculty members expect of them and that they have not done any goal setting with their deans or department members. Ninety percent have never been evaluated in their role as chairs. The leadership matrix used in conjunction with the faculty feedback meeting gives chairs clear ways to improve their departmental leadership in areas where improvement will make a real difference for faculty and the dean. A specific goal for chairs to set after reading this chapter is to manage a faculty feedback meeting so that it not only sets appropriate goals for the chair but sets goals for faculty to improve their teaching, scholarship, and service and gives the chair some good news about current leadership behaviors that faculty appreciate.

Chapter Eleven

The Dean's Role in Developing Departmental Leadership

If departments are functioning as high-quality, fairly autonomous units, the dean's life is much easier than it would otherwise be, and he or she is freed to engage in creative activities instead of putting out brushfires. In institutions where high-quality departments exist, professional development of faculty is viewed as an important ongoing activity. Faculty teach effectively, share their successes, and view failures both as topics for problem solving with colleagues and as events from which they can learn. Each department becomes a learning environment for both faculty and students. Faculty engage in scholarly activities, which may be variously defined from institution to institution but which are characterized by peer review, documentation, and other factors cited in Chapter Seven.

There is an excitement about the work in which each department is engaged, and faculty members are supportive of each other. The chair functions as a team leader. Decisions are made participatively, so that department members feel committed to the direction the department is taking and are, therefore, willing to take on their share of the work required to meet the common goals. The chair and the faculty have evolved a supportive communication climate, making departmental meetings effective and satisfying arenas for successful problem solving. When conflict emerges, disagreements are fully aired, based on the recognition that the quality of the decision making will be improved because the various facets of a problem have been explored. Dysfunctional conflict is dealt with promptly, using methods department members have previously agreed to be useful in managing conflict.

How can a dean contribute to raising the quality of academic departments so that they fulfill this vision of effectiveness? Clearly, one of the ways is working on team building with department chairs. Because deans are leaders of colleges, they are not only role models for chairs but are also responsible for developing chairs as leaders. Though an immediate investment of time is required when a dean devotes energy to developing leadership behaviors in chairs, the results include significant long-term benefits for the department, the college, and the institution.

The data I have collected from chairs lead me to conclude that chairs would be very receptive to the dean's working with them on leadership development. In workshops around the country, I have often asked chairs to devote some of their small-group discussion time to identifying the behaviors they particularly value in their deans. I have also asked chairs to complete pre-workshop questionnaires that include self-evaluations of the accomplishments and frustrations of their work. And during these workshops, I have heard spontaneous comments about the most-valued behaviors of deans. Summarizing all of these sources, I have concluded that chairs value deans who:

Frequently conduct meetings with department chairs as problem-solving meetings that address chairs' needs. They do not use such meetings simply to convey information that could as easily be communicated in writing.

Conduct effective meetings, allowing all views to be heard and knowing when to summarize and ask if the chairs are in agreement, rather than allowing the chairs to talk themselves out of a decision once they have made it.

Are supportive of chairs and do not expect them to be able to handle any and all of the problems in a department simply because they are chairs. When individual chairs have problems, the dean is available for support, discussion, and occasionally to present another perspective.

Do not allow faculty members to bypass the chair. That is, they do not grant requests or provide resources to faculty when the chair has already refused such requests. Chairs can expect that the dean will support the chair, or listen to the chair's side of the problem, or barring these actions, will act as a mediator between chair and faculty member.

Do not encourage members of departments to gossip about departmental events or to bring complaints to the dean.

Speak directly to the chair when there is a problem, rather than asking the dean's secretary to speak to the chair's secretary.

Share information with the chair before confiding it to other members of the department. Chairs do not like to hear news that affects the department from faculty members or secretaries.

Are genuinely involved in college issues and are not perceived as using an institution simply as a stepping stone in their own careers.

All of these views indicate that chairs want deans to strongly support them as leaders in their own departments and that chairs yearn to be team members with the dean as leader of the team. When a strong team has been built, with the dean as supportive leader, chairs can thrive as team leaders of their own departments. Within such a supportive context, chairs are able to accept feedback about their leadership from deans as well as from department members and others whom they respect.

Little has been done in higher education to systematically develop leadership knowledge and skills. In *Leaders for a New Era*, Madeleine F. Green (1988a), Vice President for International Initiatives of the American Council on Education, has written, "The academy has paid little systematic attention to developing its own leaders," remarking also that "higher education's relative lack of interest in developing administrative leadership is hardly accidental. Its traditions value faculty rather than administrative achievements; its culture sees administration as a necessary evil requiring little special aptitude or preparation" (pp. 1–2). The vehicle of the leadership matrix can change this institutional tradition, so that individuals can make significant contributions to their departments during their stints as chair. Moreover, when individuals return to their departments as faculty members, they will have developed important leadership skills that will continue to benefit the department, the college, and the university.

When I have asked several thousand chairs at workshops and in questionnaires when they last received some overall feedback about their work as chairs, fewer than 10 percent have indicated that they have ever been evaluated by deans in their work as chairs, have been involved in goal setting with a dean, or have a clear perception of what their dean expects of them. Deans, then, could profitably use the leadership matrix as a vehicle for discussing the dean's perspectives with chairs. The matrix creates important opportunities for giving positive feedback, verbalizing expectations, and engaging in goal setting. Since research on goal setting (Eden, 1988; Locke & Latham, 1990) strongly indicates that the goal-setting process increases productivity and accomplishments, it should be used more in higher education.

Guidelines for Useful Feedback

Feedback is a way of giving department chairs another perspective on their behavior and information about how they affect others. Just as it does in guided missile systems, feedback in institutions keeps behavior on target for achieving goals. It is a key tool in the leadership development process. Many writers make the same points about what constitutes helpful feedback, much of their advice stemming from the original National Training Lab workshops in group development, which began in 1947 and have continued to the present in Behel, Maine. From the outset, these conferences focused on personal, professional, and organizational development. The following suggestions for giving good feedback have been adapted from such sources as Bushardt and Fowler (1989) and Lucas (1992).

Feedback should describe behavior not evaluate it. Observation and inference should be separated. Moreover, when the dean focuses on describing his or her own reactions, chairs feel that they have been left free to use the feedback or not, as they see fit. By avoiding evaluative language, deans reduce the need for chairs to react defensively.

Feedback should be specific not general. Telling a chair, "You are not motivating your department to pull its weight in preparation for the accreditation visit," is probably not as useful as telling him or her, "For the accreditation visit, we will need reports from your curriculum committee that provide a rationale for a coherent curriculum and an updating of all graduate and undergraduate courses and their catalogue descriptions."

Feedback should be given with the intention of being helpful. Feedback can be destructive when it serves only our own needs and fails to consider the needs of the person on the receiving end. A discussion of the leadership matrix is not the time for the dean to tell a chair all of the accumulated problems the dean has heard about that chair. We all have fragile egos and can accept only so much negative feedback. Even if there are many leadership responsibilities in which a particular chair may be found wanting, telling that individual that few of the leadership responsibilities are being performed adequately will not bring about change in the desired direction. Success builds on success. When we want to change behavior, the way to begin is by pointing out an individual's strengths. Of course, such information must be realistic as well as positive, otherwise the chair will view the positives simply as the bait that covers the "hook"—the real, and negative, message.

Feedback should be directed toward behavior that the receiver can change. Frustration is only increased when people are reminded of some shortcoming over which they believe they have little or no control. Telling a chair that "very few department faculty appear to be doing anything in the area of scholarly work" may not be useful if the chair does not know what to do about this. Instead, in order to approach goal setting and action steps, the dean might suggest, "Let's brainstorm what strategies you might use to increase scholarly activity in your department." (Each of the chapters on leadership responsibilities also suggests strategies deans might suggest to department chairs.)

Feedback is most useful when the receiver has asked for the feedback. If a chair has not requested a dean's feedback, the dean should check to see whether the chair is open to receiving it. Chairs may be defensive and listen less when given feedback they did not request. The leadership matrix is a vehicle that allows chairs to initiate contact with the dean specifically to request feedback. It also provides an occasion for chairs and deans to discuss a chair's opportunities for leadership development, given the needs of the department at a given point in time.

Feedback should be checked to ensure that the receiver understood the intended message. Deans can verify feedback by asking department chairs to paraphrase it.

Both givers and receivers should check with others about the accuracy of feedback. Is the dean's feedback one person's impression or is this impression shared by others? The dean's feedback to a chair can best be verified by allowing the members of the chair's department to rate the chair also.

Using the Leadership Matrix

Deans should read about the leadership and faculty development responsibilities of the chair and the leadership matrix in Chapter Two. Once the dean and the chair have come to some agreement about which leadership responsibilities fall into each of the four cells of the matrix for that chair, it is important that the dean take the time to acknowledge the cell B responsibilities that are important to the department and in which the chair is effective. The dean may be tempted to take this area for granted and pass over it because no goal-setting or action steps are necessary. But chairs often receive limited positive feedback, even when they are doing an effective job, so it is valuable for them to receive reinforcement from the dean. The dean may even want to suggest that a chair with well-developed leadership skills in a certain area take on a leadership growth partnership with a chair who needs to grow in that area. Such an arrangement works particularly well if the two chairs have very disparate strengths and dissimilar areas of strengths and weakness. If the match is a good one, the dean will have created a support network that is a very constructive way of developing leadership skills.

Next, the chair and dean will look at cell A of the matrix for opportunities for leadership development in areas important to the department. Since these areas offers occasions for real personal and professional growth, they can generate the most productive part of the discussion and lead directly to goal setting, action steps, and identification of resources.

Once the dean and the chair have analyzed the tasks deemed important to leadership in a particular department, they will want to think creatively about how the chair's leadership skills are to be enhanced and what professional development resources the chair will need. Approaches suggested to chairs in earlier chapters are working with small groups of chairs in the college for the specific purpose of improving leadership skills, attending workshops, reading books and articles, viewing videotapes, listening to audiotapes, seeking out knowledgeable colleagues who are good at the skills the chair wants to develop or whose formal training gives them expertise, and working closely with another experienced chair who is willing to serve as a mentor. In addition, the institution can sponsor on-site workshops designed to help a number of chairs develop necessary skills.

Deans will find they have additional suggestions for enhancing leadership competencies. For example, deans can recommend specific "growth assignments" (appointing a chair to a particular committee or broadening an assignment for example), individual development activities, and on-the-job coaching to provide chairs with experience in applying the knowledge and skills they are in the process of mastering. Problem solving at meetings of department chairs conducted by the dean and individual coaching can be particularly useful to chairs.

Developing Chairs as Academic Leaders

In many universities, faculty elect their own chairs, and the role of the dean is simply to appoint the individual so selected. In other universities, however, deans have considerable input into the selection of chairs. In both instances, however, deans have the responsibility of making it possible for chairs to develop as leaders. The likelihood that individuals tapped for the role of chair will have leadership potential will be increased if deans make the chair position attractive enough that the right faculty members will want to serve in that role. Although making the office of chair desirable does involve a realistic reduction in the chair's teaching load and the appropriate financial remuneration, determinations usually based on the size of departments, it also requires that the dean be seen to support chairs and engage in team building with them. Thus, deans can encourage the right faculty to accept the position of department chairs by becoming aware of and developing the leadership style valued by chairs in their deans (as described earlier in this chapter), and by being seen to provide ongoing leadership development for department chairs.

Leadership Knowledge and Skills Useful for Chairs

Chairs' professional development should include acquiring communication skills, motivational skills, and chair survival skills. In addition chairs need to acquire the knowledge to be expert at the following tasks. This expertise, together with the skills just mentioned, constitutes leadership skill.

Performing chair roles and responsibilities

Motivating faculty to increase scholarship in the department

Improving the quality of teaching in the department

Improving the performance of poor teachers

Motivating difficult colleagues

Motivating midcareer faculty

Orienting and socializing new faculty to the requirements of the department

Carrying out performance counseling

Decision making in the department

Goal setting both with individuals and with the department

Managing conflict

Creating a supportive communication climate

Developing faculty commitment to the goals of the department

Getting faculty to do their fair share of the work of the department

Handling specific problems effectively

Evaluating faculty

Conducting feedback interviews

Educating chairs in these areas can best be accomplished through in-service programs for all academic chairs in the college or larger institution. Chairs could also organize themselves into an ongoing study group (Lucas, 1986) and, using a book such as this as a guide, engage in discussion and practice sessions on such issues as third-party mediation. Having a consultant meet with them once a year to help them check on their progress is useful.

Preparing Chairs to Return to Faculty Positions

Most individuals who serve as chairs do not make a career of it. Yet many chairs return to their faculty positions feeling somewhat disoriented. During their years as chair, they have often been overwhelmed with paperwork and have found their research activity sharply diminished. If they have served two or more terms as chair, the research area on which they had been working is probably no longer salient for them or sometimes for the discipline. Their power in the department diminished, they often feel displaced and unappreciated, particularly if a new chair decides to take a quite different direction from the one they formerly espoused.

It is not surprising, then, that the energy and experience of former chairs is often turned to issues outside the department and the university, with the result that much of what they learned as chairs no longer benefits the institution. Other former chairs engage in behavior highly critical of the new chair. And they have usually done little planning for the return to their lives as faculty members. When the dean and a chair engage in goal setting, the dean can raise questions at appropriate times about whether the person wants to continue as chair, and if not, what new activities the person is planning. In initiating such discussions, deans can be very helpful as catalysts, causing chairs to generate creative goals if they have not done this kind of planning on their own. Depending on the needs of the university and the talents and skills of former chairs, they can provide distinguished service on a college promotion and tenure committee or a department or college curriculum committee, take a leadership role in the academic senate, or become faculty representatives to the board of trustees.

Guiding Troubled Departments

Most departments seem to manage their affairs reasonably well, requiring little of a dean's time; others require considerable help from the dean, for a variety of reasons. The department may be preparing for a review by an outside accrediting organization, developing a curriculum for a new program or discontinuing an outdated one, or embarking on a project to satisfy a new requirement of the state department of higher education. One department may simply be in need of getting itself back on track. Another may be struggling with bitter conflict that has left faculty disorganized and incapable of moving forward.

While members of a strife-ridden department are aware that conflict has paralyzed them, they do not know how to change, and often are convinced there is no hope for resolving the conflict. Accomplishing any positive step in a department incapable of helping itself is an overwhelming task, particularly for the individual who steps into the position of chair, and a department in these straits can stagnate for years. Under these circumstances, the dean must intervene.

An effective approach for the dean is to enlist the support of the department chair and the department policy committee by discussing the issue with them first. The chair can then schedule a meeting with the department, announcing that the dean has been invited. The dean then conducts a problem-solving meeting, giving faculty examples of how their conflict has affected their performance, asking for recommendations about how they can get themselves back on track, and suggesting what he or she as dean can do to help them. It needs to be emphasized that this meeting should not be disciplinary nor an opportunity to accuse or blame faculty. It is an attempt to support faculty and offer assistance as they resolve their problems. In this spirit, telling them that all groups find themselves in conflict at one point or another and that the constructive approach is to resolve the difficulties so that the department can move forward is often helpful. Reframing the situation in this way encourages faculty, who often feel by this time that their conflict is monumental and that they are incompetent because they cannot resolve it.

One important gesture the dean can make is to offer to bring in a consultant who will engage department members in team building. However, faculty must buy in to such a suggestion, or little will be accomplished. A one- or two-day team-building meeting can help them to set and prioritize goals, look objectively at the ways they are currently functioning, develop more effective methods of handling issues, and decide who will accept responsibility for carrying out two or three of their most important objectives (Lucas, 1988). Providing for a follow-up meeting with the consultant a few months later will give faculty an opportunity to evaluate their progress and set new goals. When deans intervene in this manner, they provide leadership that makes a significant difference in the lives of the faculty who are then free of the maelstrom that is engulfing their energy and productivity.

Conclusion

When the dean uses the leadership matrix as an instrument for goal setting with chairs at the beginning of the academic year and for receiving a progress report at the end of the year, leadership and departmental issues are addressed on a regular basis. Although it does take time to meet with each chair individually twice a year in this formal fashion, the payoff is great. Once the process has been started, problems in the department are addressed by the chair on an ongoing basis, not just at times when they have gotten so out of hand that no one wants to take on the job of chair. Use of the leadership matrix ensures that the development of leadership in the college becomes a high priority.

Chapter Twelve

Survival Skills for Department Chairs

Of the many employment-related factors identified as stressful (Hellriegel, Slocum, & Woodman, 1992), three that create high levels of stress are inherent in the job of chair: role ambiguity, role conflict, and work overload. The first condition, role ambiguity, is predicted by the fact that adequate job descriptions for chairs do not always exist and that, in unionized institutions, when collective bargaining agreements do describe a chair's responsibilities, chairs within the same university may interpret those responsibilities differently. In large state universities, department governance documents are sometimes written with the intention of limiting the power of the chair, setting up an executive or an advisory committee to effect this limitation. However, such documents often leave the relationship between the authority of the chair and the committee unclear. When responsibility and authority *are* clearly established, written out, and agreed upon by both faculty and administration, stress from role ambiguity is reduced.

The second condition, role conflict, is endemic because chairs must represent faculty to the dean, and administration to the faculty. Role conflict comes with the territory. As was discussed in Chapter One, chairs elected by their colleagues may feel they must answer to faculty; chairs appointed by deans feel they serve at the pleasure of the person to whom they report. Yet, in neither case can a chair risk alienating either dean or department members. When chairs are elected by the department, they still must provide input for personnel decision making. They must also convey to faculty members the necessity of offering courses at unpopular hours and canceling classes with enrollments that are too small. When chairs are appointed by the dean with minimal faculty input, they cannot be too autocratic or the department will request the dean to review the chair's performance. Finding the appropriate line between fighting for the faculty and persuading faculty to give up certain things for the good of the institution often creates conflict for a chair. There are also the role conflicts of teacher and chair, scholar and chair, family member and chair, and social being and chair. As teachers, almost all chairs have on occasion walked into a classroom unprepared because time they had counted on for class preparation was curtailed by a crisis related to their responsibilities as chair. As scholars, they have often neglected their research because chair responsibilities frequently have a compelling urgency. As family members and social beings, they often feel torn by opposing needs, unable to give the quality time they would wish to family and friends because of chair responsibilities.

The third stressful factor is work overload. A chair's work never seems completed at the end of the day. Meetings require the chair's presence. Faculty or students need to talk with the chair. Reports of one kind or another have to be written. There are forms to be signed, correspondence to be handled, and phone calls to be returned. Role ambiguity, role conflict, and work overload all increase stress.

Stress can be either a positive or negative force in an individual's life. When stress is moderate, it is experienced as positive; life is viewed as a challenge. There is satisfaction in what is accomplished; self-esteem is enhanced. However, when stress is high and prolonged, it usually has negative effects, particularly if individuals have poor coping mechanisms. Stress has been implicated as one factor in all of the major illnesses. It is also a cause of many minor illnesses, such as regular patterns of headaches, digestive problems, and backaches. It can result in feeling drained at the end of the day and waking up tired after a full night's sleep. It can increase the amount of alcohol individuals consume. Moreover, frequent cynical statements about higher education and life in general, as well as irritability with family, friends, and colleagues, are symptomatic of excessive stress. It is also clear that the effect of stress is cumulative. When there are many changes in an individual's life during a short period of time and adequate methods of coping have not been developed, a heavier toll is taken than if single episodes of stress had occurred over a longer time span. Given the dangers to individuals' physical and emotional well-being when excessive stress exists, and the real stress that comes with the territory in chairing a department, how can chairs cope? In reducing stress to an optimal level, there are three systems in which one can intervene: behavioral, somatic, and cognitive. We will look at each in turn.

Behavioral Strategies for Managing Stress

Management of stress begins with establishing priorities in life: If I were living in the best of all possible worlds, what would my life be like? What would I be doing then that I am not doing now? What would be eliminated from my life that is a hassle today? What would I like to have accomplished five years from now? Chairs can ask themselves such questions, formalizing the answers by writing out goals, action steps, and timelines that will provide direction, a way of monitoring progress, and an opportunity to assess outcome.

Chairs' next step is to discover exactly how they are spending their time right now. People often resist this step, saying it is "too much trouble," when actually they are afraid to confront the truth. Chairs should record what they are doing with the hours of their day, half an hour at a time, using their appointment books and information from their secretaries. They should also record how they use the time between scheduled appointments. Chairs should keep track of their time for three days, or a week if they want a complete picture that includes a weekend, then create groupings that best describe how they are spending their time. Here are some typical groupings:

- Development of leadership ability
  Practicing leadership skills
  Reading and discussing leadership concepts
- Faculty development
  Improving teaching
  Increasing scholarship
  Getting faculty to do their fair share
  Enhancing service
- Role as teacher
  Preparing for classes
  Teaching
  Preparing exams
  Grading exams and papers
- Role as scholar
  Doing professional reading
  Doing one's own scholarship
  Researching
  Writing
- Contacts with students
  Advising
  Mentoring
  Handling correspondence (such as letters of recommendation)
- Meetings
  Chairing departmental meetings
  Attending department chair meetings conducted by the dean

　　Chairing or attending committee meetings (divide by
　　　purpose)
* Networking
　　Networking with administration
　　Networking with faculty
　　Networking with professional staff
　　Networking with students
* Paperwork
* Socializing (indicate groups or individuals)
* Spending time with family and friends (specify individuals)

　　These categories are not listed in order of importance because
that will vary from chair to chair. The chair's purpose in using them
is simply to obtain an accurate picture of how he or she is currently
spending limited time.

　　After completing a record of how their time is spent, chairs
should go back and look at their five-year goals and action steps.
The question they must now confront is, are they spending their
time in ways that will help them to reach their long-term goals? If
not, how can they rearrange their lives so that there is greater con-
gruence between their goals and the way their time is spent? Chairs
should ask themselves what insights emerge as they look at the
way they are using time. If there is a poor match between the direction they want their lives to take and what they are now doing,
they need to ask what interventions they can make to reduce the
dissonance, and the stress.

　　For example, a simple but often observed mismatch occurs
when chairs find that scholarship must be put on the back burner
for a three- or four-year term. The problem becomes how to
increase the time spent on research and writing and reduce the
time spent on what chairs refer to as administrative trivia. One
direct approach chairs can use is to hang a sign on the office door

that says, "Involved in research between 9:00 and 11:30 A.M. *Do not disturb unless there is a serious emergency!*" Chairs who feel they simply could not do this should remember that they are role models for faculty. If chairs do not take the time to do their own scholarly work, they cannot easily encourage faculty to increase scholarship in the department. Chairs should also think of what will happen to them personally if they do not allocate time to scholarship. When they finish their terms as chair, they will have to begin again as scholars. They will have to catch up on the literature. Even worse, their area of expertise may no longer be meaningful.

Notice that this change requires that chairs make an intervention. They may have to enlist the dean, the department secretary, and faculty members in their cause, advising these others of what they are going to be doing and what constitutes an emergency. They may have to delegate some authority to faculty who can deal with student problems while the chair is working on scholarship. Whatever it takes, if that action increases the time the chair can spend achieving long-term goals, the chair should do it.

Most chairs in workshops ask for practical recommendations on time management. Time management does not mean working harder; it simply means using your time more effectively in ways that you want to use it. Some interventions that chairs have often found useful follow.

Begin the day with a short planning session. Review your commitments for the next day, week, or month and set timelines for task completion.

Make a to-do list, prioritizing items. Do the most important tasks during your high-energy periods. For most chairs, this usually means doing the hardest things first. Handle routine items at the end of the day, when you are tired and less creative. Eliminate unimportant tasks, even if you are good at them.

Break large tasks, such as comprehensive reports, into smaller, manageable parts with individual deadlines. Confronting small pieces of a project is not as anxiety provoking as undertaking the entire project. Breaking tasks into small sections makes it is less likely that chairs will postpone the work. When an individual postpones tackling a task, avoidance is reinforced. If even thinking about doing a large project raises anxiety, stopping thinking about the task will suddenly reduce anxiety. A sharp reduction in anxiety is extremely rewarding, so avoiding, or even avoiding thinking about, the task is reinforced. When a behavior is reinforced, it will occur more frequently. The conclusion for chairs is obvious. Do not procrastinate. Plunge right in and do it!

Handle most pieces of paper only once. Write notes on incoming mail relating to what you will say when you write your response. Skim professional material. Do not use high-energy time to read unimportant notices.

Never do a task that someone else can do. Delegate. Faculty members and a secretary can often handle responsibilities that burden a chair. Ask individuals to whom work is being delegated how they will go about completing the assignment; do not tell them step by step how to handle it. Decide whether their approach is sensible, reinforce good ideas, ask for a progress report, and check outcome. Some time may be required initially to train people, but the long-term gain can be great.

Learn to say no. Chairs cannot do all the things that others would like them to do. Learn to discriminate the essential from the unessential.

Take a lunch break or leave your office to take a walk to renew your energy. People who are overtired are not effective.

Review your to-do list at the end of the day. Evaluate your effectiveness. Give yourself credit for what you have handled well. Ask yourself what you might have done differently with those items that did not go as you had planned.

Add other time management ideas of your own. Use those time management strategies that work best for you.

Goal setting, checking for and removing any dissonance

between what you want to accomplish and how you are currently using your time, and time management are all effective behavioral approaches to stress management. Many of the conflict-reducing tactics discussed in Chapter Nine, such as employing problem-solving approaches instead of blaming and accusing, involving faculty in developing methods for handling conflict, and using third-party facilitation, are also useful behavioral strategies for reducing stress, as is creating the open and supportive communication climate described in Chapter Eight.

Reducing Stress Through Somatic Interventions

The second broad system that needs to be addressed in stress reduction is the somatic, or physiological. The human body suffers when stress is severe and prolonged; daily use of relaxation methods can effectively reduce tension, thus protecting the body from the deleterious consequences of stress. The most widely used somatic approach is the highly effective method of progressive relaxation. This alternate tensing and relaxing of the large muscle groups in the body is a skill that needs to be practiced for optimal relaxation effects. A progressive relaxation session begins with tensing then relaxing the feet and toes; calves; thighs; buttocks; stomach; lower back; chest; upper back; right hand, forearm, and upper arm; left hand, forearm, and upper arm; shoulders; neck; jaws; eyes and nose; forehead; scalp; and finally, all the muscles at once. Individuals who feel pain in the neck and shoulders at the end of a day's work often find that taking stretch breaks—in which they tense and relax the specific muscles of the neck and shoulders and do head rolls—is a useful way of preventing such pain.

Since breathing-related symptoms are often part of the anxiety that occurs when we are stressed, another somatic intervention is deep breathing, taking several slow, deep breaths. Sometimes called the calming response, this approach reduces heart rate, blood pressure, and muscle tension (Fried, 1993). Another approach to stress reduction is aerobic exercise. Studies that compare the effectiveness of exercise with that of other relaxation techniques are somewhat limited. Although what research there is suggests that exercise has a smaller effect on stress reduction than other forms of relaxation, there is evidence that it alleviates depression (Lehrer & Woolfolk, 1993). Since individuals often become depressed when they are under a high level of stress, exercise can be useful for coping with stress-related symptoms.

Reducing Stress Through Changing Dysfunctional Thoughts

The third system of intervention for stress reduction is cognitive and deals with what we say to ourselves about circumstances in our lives. Although it is usual to blame situations or other people for our stress, what we say to ourselves about events triggers much of the stress we feel. Therefore, interventions in this system deal with changing the dysfunctional thinking that leads to stress reactions.

Although some generalization of stress reduction methods across the behavioral, somatic, and cognitive systems is possible, it is generally agreed that there are greater specific effects of stress reduction when the methodology is specific to the system addressed (Lehrer & Woolfolk, 1993, p. 510). For instance, if a chair's stress has been induced by negative thoughts, it will not help much if he or she simply tries to relax. Instead, intervention must take place in the cognitive system. For example, say that during one morning, two tenured faculty members in turn refuse your request that they teach an 8:00 A.M. class next semester, a class the dean has requested your department to offer at this early hour; you hear that some equipment was stolen from the lab during the lunch hour when a faculty member was supposed to have locked it but did not; the dean telephones to tell you that there was no representative from your department at the Sunday afternoon open house; a faculty member fails to show up for a 10:00 A.M. class; and two students come to you to complain. You might react by saying, "This whole department is falling apart." However, although each of these occurrences is distressing, they are not symptoms that the department is falling apart. If they were, you would be justified in feeling greatly stressed. But once you create a label that is both negative and an overgeneralization, you can feel as stressed as if a situation were really true. Such negative thinking is often based on an arbitrary inference. We begin with a logical statement, such as, "I will telephone the person who was supposed to be at the open house yesterday to find out what happened. If there is no good reason for her absence, I will certainly let her know that she let the department down." We then start thinking about the other incidents we have to check out, and if then we tie them together and look at nothing else, even though this relational view is unjustified, our stress level rises sharply.

Dysfunctional thoughts contribute to making us ineffective. Take a fairly simple example from the earlier list of time management skills. I suggested that procrastination often has anxiety as its base and that one way for chairs to manage the anxiety is to break a task into its component parts and then adhere to timelines for completing each part. The dysfunctional thinking that is often found in individuals who procrastinate often goes like this: This is an important project in terms of getting what we need for the department. If I rush, I won't do it right. It will take a long stretch of time to complete it. I really do not have the time to do it. I will tackle it next week when I have finished some of these other things on my desk. But next week comes and goes, and the project has not yet been begun. Constructive self-talk might sound like this: This is an important project, and I want to do it well. I will divide the project into its logical parts. Then I will know which areas require additional information. I can ask my secretary to gather that information, so that I will have it ready when I need it. I will set timelines that allow a sufficient period for the information to be entered on a word processor and for me to review it. I will allocate an hour a day to complete each portion of the report and not let anything keep me from doing it. I will feel really satisfied when I can give this report to the dean because it will provide the basis for her approving what I need for the department next year.

At the end of each segment of work, it is also helpful to remind yourself of what you have accomplished so far, rather than let anxiety rise because of how much more you have to do. This self-message can make the difference between feeling satisfaction at the end of the hour's work and feeling anxiety because you have not done all the rest of it.

Monitoring our internal dialogue is important because negative or dysfunctional thoughts are often automatic (Beck, 1993). We are not usually aware of their content, unless we check to discover what we were thinking just before we felt anxious or depressed. The task for chairs is to ask themselves, What evidence is there for the negative things I was thinking? What evidence is there against them? The idea is to change negative irrational thoughts to positive realistic ones. In the example just cited, it may be true that individuals who rush will not do the job right. However, it is not true that, if they wait until next week to do a report, they will be less rushed than if they do it gradually over a period of time. It is probable that this argument is just an excuse that allows them to postpone something that creates a certain amount of anxiety. Under a high degree of stress, individuals lose their ability to view their thoughts objectively, subject them to reality testing, and adjust the way they have been thinking so that it conforms to reality (Beck, 1993, p. 341). All of us often use ways of dealing with problems that may not be in our own best long-term interest, so we need to discover methods that will allow us to change that.

A final recommendation for coping effectively with stress returns us to the behavioral system. Chairs often say that they feel alone in the trenches. There is often no one at the college with whom they can talk when they simply want to discuss a problem, feel they cannot cope with a bureaucratic or other system, or feel the job is no longer fun. A strong personal support system, made up of high-quality interpersonal relationships, is crucial for chairs who want to overcome this loneliness. Although a high level of trustworthiness is the first requirement for all those in chairs' personal networks, chairs also need several different kinds of people to whom they can turn. A high-caliber support network should include a person who knows the system and can, therefore, listen knowledgeably and give good advice; a person who builds the chair's self-esteem and helps the chair believe he or she can succeed; a person with whom the chair can celebrate success; a person who is a good listener and supportive, off whom the chair can bounce ideas; and a person who is a critic, helping the chair think analytically about plans and enrich his or her ideas. Chairs who do not have this array of individuals in their support networks at present can make plans to identify people who can fill these needs. Such networking roles are often parts of reciprocal arrangements, and chairs can also consider serving one of these roles for someone else. When they think about it, many chairs find they use only one person, often a member of their families, to satisfy all of these network needs. Besides the fact that this habit places too great a burden on a single individual, it is difficult for one person to fill all the needed roles effectively.

For chairs who want to do some further reading about methods of reducing stress, I recommend several classics, all available in paperback (complete information is included in the references): D. D. Burns, *Feeling Good* (1980); E. M. Catalano, W. Webb, J. Welsh, and C. Morin, *Getting to Sleep* (1990); M. Davis, E. R. Eshelman, and M. McKay, *The Relaxation and Stress Reduction Workbook* (1988); H. S. Kushner, *When Bad Things Happen to Good People* (1993); M. McKay and P. Fanning, *Prisoners of Belief* (1991) and *Self-Esteem* (1993); M. McKay, P. D. Rogers, and J. McKay, *When Anger Hurts* (1989); M. Seligman, *Learned Optimism* (1992); and G. G. Scott, *Resolving Conflict: With Others and Within Yourself* (1990).

Conclusion

Chairs commonly experience stress related to the position of chair. They can simply choose a relaxation technique to alleviate stress. However, discovering and employing appropriate strategies from all three systems—somatic, behavioral, and cognitive—that partake in stress reactions is the most effective approach chairs can take to thriving, not just surviving, as a department chair.

I suggest that any stress reduction plan for chairs should include the immediate goal of learning to use their time in ways that help them to achieve long-term goals. This plan should involve identifying several five-year goals, monitoring current uses of time, and then delegating tasks and becoming more proficient in other time management skills, in order to spend more time on pursuits that do further long-term goals. A second goal for chairs is to routinely use the stress management strategies that they find work for them. Chairs should select one of the somatic strategies and one of the behavior strategies to use at least once a day, evaluating the extent to which they feel less stressed after using each intervention for several weeks. After experimenting in this way, chairs can retain the strategies that work for them. Also, whenever chairs feel stressed, they should monitor their internal dialogue following this process: ask yourself whether this is a dysfunctional thought and, if it is, change it. Ask yourself what evidence exists for and against the negative inference you have drawn. If your negative thoughts are overgeneralizations, substitute positive rational statements.

Chapter Thirteen

Personal Strategies for Strengthening Leadership Effectiveness

This book requires more than a cursory reading if it is to be an effective learning tool. It is an organized, systematic approach that encourages chairs to experiment with leadership skills, that is, to perform the action research that has been the primary thrust of this book. Action research is developing a baseline of behavior, experimenting by changing some aspects of behavior, and evaluating results which can then determine the next steps. In action research, the researcher—in this case, the chair—takes four steps. He or she collects data on some aspect of an ongoing system, provides feedback to clients (based on the data collected), alters selected factors within the system, and evaluates the results of that alteration, based on more data collection (French & Bell, 1990, p. 99).

Action Research to Determine Departmental Effectiveness

The following example illustrates how a chair might perform the four steps of action research to investigate and improve departmental effectiveness. The steps described here can be used effectively to improve the functioning of any system, such as a department, or the functioning of any individual, such as a chair.

Collect Data

A new academic chair, Professor Dennis O'Brien, observes that teaching is never discussed in the department. There is also some evidence, based on student evaluations, that the teaching of about one-fourth of the faculty members in the department is poor. In the classrooms where faculty receive low evaluations, students feel that class participation is not encouraged, organization of material is below average, and little relation exists between the tests given and the course goals. The chair has also heard faculty describe student evaluations as popularity contests. O'Brien also knows, from looking at departmental copies of grade rosters, that grade inflation is rampant. A review of course syllabi indicates that most faculty concoct a syllabus simply by listing the name of the course and the weeks of the class, numbered from one to fifteen. Next to these numbers are listed fifteen chapters from the textbook. Missing from a number of syllabi are such items as the assessment measures to be used, dates of examinations, the basis for grading, the methodology that will be used (how class time will be spent), the instructor's office hours and, sometimes, even the name of the instructor.

At this point, O'Brien has a number of options. After soliciting support from senior members of the department for some interventions to improve teaching, he can present his findings to the faculty as a whole, three-fourths of whom are tenured. (I use this example because many chairs of departments in which most of the faculty are tenured feel that they can do nothing to improve teaching effectiveness.) O'Brien can confront the faculty with his observations: syllabi are poorly constructed, student evaluations indicate that one-fourth of the faculty members are poor teachers, grades are inflated, faculty show strong resistance to any discussion of teaching, student evaluations are not taken seriously, and there is strong opposition to observation by colleagues. However, O'Brien might choose to take a less direct approach, especially since a number of department members subscribe to the myths about teaching presented in Chapter Five, particularly these two: "If you know the subject, you can teach it," and "There is no valid research about what makes teaching effective." Recognizing that a direct presentation of his data would undoubtedly provoke a defensive reaction from the faculty and subvert the needed changes, the chair decides to take a more indirect approach.

O'Brien decides to try an intervention of increasing the frequency of colleague observations of classroom teaching in the department. His thinking might be summed up this way: I believe much of what we learn as teachers is lost because it is not shared with other faculty members. Faculty in this department do not talk much about teaching, and I want to encourage their awareness about instruction. Therefore, my goal is to increase the frequency of colleague observations in the department. At present, the number of colleague observations per year in this department is zero. No one has shown any interest in being observed, and two people have made some very caustic comments about even the possibility of peer observation.

Provide Feedback to Clients

In this case, O'Brien is both the client and the one who has collected the data. Several measures indicate that teaching is inadequate for one-quarter of the department. No peer observations have taken place during the past academic year. The chair decides to set a goal of increasing the frequency of peer observations from zero to six for the first year, but recognizes that a direct approach is unlikely to work.

Alter Selected System Elements

The intervention the chair decides to use is to allow others to observe his classes, and then to encourage two faculty members who are known to be excellent teachers to do the same. He plans these action steps: (1) announce at a department meeting that he has not had any feedback on his teaching for a long time and is going to invite several colleagues to observe his classes; (2) invite two members of the department to observe a particular class that he teaches; (3) ask each of them to observe the extent to which he asks thought-provoking questions and what he does to get students to participate in class discussions or activities, so that they can tell him what he does that is effective and what he could do to make the class even better in these two specific areas; (4) set a time with each observer individually to meet to discuss the observations; (5) see each observer at the appointed time, accept the feedback non-defensively, and thank the observer (enthusiastically) for the rec-ommendations; (6) try out what has been recommended in his next class meetings and evaluate how well the suggestions worked; (7) report back on what he has tried, tell the observers how useful their feedback was, and ask them if they would like him to observe one of their classes; (8) talk informally with one or two other faculty members who are known to be effective teachers, and ask them how they feel about peer observation, telling them about his posi-tive experience and asking if they would be willing to volunteer at the next departmental meeting to have someone observe them; (9) report back to the department on how helpful the feedback was, telling them how refreshing it was to talk about different approaches in handling a topic and pointing out that he has been invited to attend the classes of the faculty who had observed his classes. As part of this last action step, he also plans to invite other faculty to try colleague observation of their classes, hoping he will have at least two and possibly four people volunteering. He plans to ask them to report back at the next meeting on how observation worked for them.

Evaluate Results

By the end of the year, after O'Brien has carried out all his action steps to alter the system, more than six colleague observations have taken place, so he has more than realized his goal. O'Brien now schedules a meeting for those who participated in the peer visita-tions. He wants to discover what they got from the experience, whether they think colleague observation is worth expanding to include more faculty members, how this expansion might be done, and how the process could be improved. One participant recommends that the observer have a preliminary discussion with the person who will be observed, so that the observer will know the items to which the teacher would like the observer to pay particular attention. Another participant recommends that observers talk together about the best way to conduct feedback interviews, so that they can evaluate what helped the process and what did not work. Perhaps these evaluations can evolve into a set of observation and feedback guidelines that will help the observation system give maximum benefit to all involved and on which the department can build during the next year. An oral report by all who participated is scheduled for the next departmental meeting (perhaps the one that begins the next academic year), at which other department faculty will be invited to participate in the program.

Team Building

Only in relatively rare instances have colleges and universities tried to foster a team-building effort between dean and chairs, or between chairs and faculty. Chapters Ten and Eleven offered a process to bring team building within the range of what is possible; however, some personal strategies must be emphasized here.

A new team needs to examine the norms by which it operates. Whenever a new individual becomes chair, a new team is created in the department, but this team cannot function effectively until department members discover whether old ways of functioning will continue or be replaced by new ones. Often faculty will fight to maintain norms that have evolved from past survival experiences. Norms are different from rules. Rules are written down in faculty handbooks and in collective bargaining agreements and reinforced in memos written by deans. Norms, however, are not written down. Faculty may disobey rules and come away unscathed, but if they violate a group norm the group sanctions them in some way. If the norm in a department is that office hours are not taken seriously, a new chair who decides to uphold the university rule that each faculty member must be available three hours a week for students will experience considerable resistance from faculty in enforcing it. Faculty will simply not show up for office hours. If questioned, they will offer some excuse and continue to be absent during this time. Or a faculty member will arrive late and leave early because, he or she says, "No students need to see me."

Faculty members may be only dimly aware of the existence of some departmental norms, so the chair must bring these norms to individuals' attention. When individuals become aware of norms they may be able to function more independently than before, instead of being shackled by invisible norms. For example, once the department has confronted the norm of keeping conflict suppressed, disagreement can be used to make more effective decisions and reduce departmental tensions. Clearly, negative norms can reduce the effectiveness of departments (Napier & Gershenfeld, 1989).

Particularly when norms, or ground rules, have not been talked about in some time, or when a new individual becomes chair, a department team needs to discuss these issues:

What is our main purpose?

How can we best accomplish our mission and what ground rules will help us achieve our goals?

How can we make our performance even better?

How do we communicate with each other, both individually and in a group?

Should we invite someone to attend one of our meetings as a process observer?

How will we make decisions?

How will we resolve problems? How will we handle conflicts?

What kind of climate do we want in our group and how can
we build that kind of climate?

Taking time to discuss these issues is part of the chair's leadership
responsibility, since these questions are basic to a group's effective
functioning. Yet, because some of the answers may appear pre-
dictable, people may resist even discussing these questions. However, once discussion begins, faculty discover that the answers are
far from obvious and that a team that sets clear ground rules can
prevent many problems from occurring. Discussion can also ferret
out the existence of negative norms, which can then be confronted
and changed. Moreover, exploration of ways the team wants to
function can result in commitment to a method of proceeding
when dysfunctional conflict erupts.

Summary of Tips for Becoming an Effective Leader

In this book, I have taken the leadership function of the chair seriously and respected the fact that chairs value autonomy and need
to choose for themselves the leadership functions they will work to
develop. If the leadership responsibilities chosen for development
meet particular identifiable needs of the department, opportunities
for change are great. New chairs often inherit difficult situations
and are given little systematic help in handling them. The material in this book provides a methodology and recommends that
chairs choose the direction they want to travel.

Much of what has been discussed may seem difficult and somewhat risky. Carrying out many of the concepts, certainly, will constitute a stretch assignment for chairs. However, creativity demands
risk taking. Also, chairs need not accomplish this change alone.
That is just one tip included in the following suggestions meant to
pull together some overarching ideas from the various chapters.

Select another chair as a learning partner. The purpose in your coming together is that you will form a dyadic support system to enhance leadership development for both of you.

Proceed systematically through the leadership responsibilities covered in this book. One activity you can undertake with your learning partner is discuss the contents of this book and support each other in completion of the leadership matrix. Set goals and action steps for one leadership responsibility at a time, then prioritize. Select no more than two or three goals at a time. Discuss your goals and action steps with your learning partner. Be certain that each of you has selected action steps that are observable, can be monitored, and have outcomes that can be assessed. Collect data, use action steps, and report back to your learning partner again. Support each other, and give feedback, but be mindful of the limited amount of negative feedback any of us can take at one time. Also, monitor the process the two of you use in your meetings. Does each of you get enough reinforcement? Do either of you feel that you cannot be completely open with your learning partner? Ask for what you want. More reinforcement? More suggestions? More feedback about particular areas that have not been addressed? Work on making the process comfortable and growth enhancing for both of you.

Create a larger support group made up of all the chairs in your college. Again, using this book as a guide, this larger group can deal with the practical problems each chair is facing. Use role-playing, discussion, brainstorming—all the strategies that will work for group members. Spend five minutes at the end of each meeting monitoring process. Each person should mention one thing that he or she got from the meeting and one thing that would improve the meeting. This is not to be viewed as criticism, just as feedback to the group. (To make the time you spend in meetings more worthwhile, try this strategy of processing meetings with other groups with whom you meet.)

View your role as that of a leader not a paper pusher. If you think you merely administer trivia, the power of self-fulfilling prophecy suggests that may be all you will accomplish as chair. Being a leader does not necessarily take more time than being an administrator. Leadership has to do with the way you view the things you do. The concepts and skills discussed in this book may be a challenge but view your years as chair as a stretch assignment. Take advantage of the challenges and opportunities for your own leadership development and departmental growth.

Create a team with yourself as team leader. Explore the department's mission, goals, policy, procedures, ways of solving problems, and handling conflict as team issues.

Set goals. Whether you choose to work with a partner, with a group of chairs, or alone in developing your leadership effectiveness, set goals. Put a *process* in operation for improving teaching effectiveness or increasing scholarship. Remember, if you do not know where you are going, you probably will not get there. Formalizing goals increases the probability that you will achieve them. Serendipity may be fun, but it is not a useful way to run a department, or a life.

Let faculty members work with you on conflict management. Use third-party mediation skills and work with others so they can also develop these skills for use in the department.

Set up a faculty workshop to present the principles of feedback for classroom observation (Weimer, 1990). Let faculty volunteers do the reading and present ideas to their colleagues. Contact your faculty development office for help in identifying readings or conducting part of the workshop. This workshop can increase the level of sophistication of the entire department about teaching, observation, and supportive feedback.

Begin to change the departmental culture. Improving teaching and increasing scholarship are two good places to begin.

Tell the dean what you are doing. He or she can then support you in a variety of ways. You need not present all the details of your group discussions, just keep the dean tuned in. You might occasionally invite the dean to one of department chair support group meetings.

Reinforce yourself. Monitor your own thinking. Negative thoughts are often automatic, and they can be paralyzing. Do you say to yourself that you have so much work to do in the area of leadership development that you feel like a slow learner? Or do you say, on the basis of monitoring your changing behaviors, that you are making real progress? The first self-message is dysfunctional because it will leave you feeling that what you are doing is painful. You will feel daunted by the amount you still have to learn. The second message, recognizing what you have accomplished, will leave you feeling reinforced. Since success builds on success, you are more likely to go on with your learning and risk taking when you feel reinforced.

Take charge of your own life or someone or something else will. Chairs do not want someone or something else to plan their lives. If you constantly do only things you are good at, you are not growing. If you have not failed lately, you have not been taking enough risks.

Developing a Leadership Portfolio

The approaches described in this book make it simple for a chair to compile a systematic account of his or her leadership contributions. Action research can be used as a model in developing a leadership portfolio that highlights a number of projects undertaken by the department under the leadership of the chair. In the material placed in the portfolio, a problem or a need is identified and the intervention methodology is described. Baseline data collected before the intervention are reported, along with an assessment of outcome and supporting data. In this method of compiling a portfolio, a chair does not describe his or her subjective feelings of success but provides substantive data for accomplishment of a project.

After serving their terms, chairs often feel that an institution's criteria for awarding merit increases and promotions do not give sufficient weight to the real contributions they have made as department chairs. Even worse, in some comprehensive universities, an assistant professor is asked to serve three or four years as chair, and the promotion and tenure committee then asks what that person has done to meet criteria for promotion and tenure, suggesting that the accomplishment of "four years as chair" counts for little. If individuals develop a leadership portfolio documenting accomplishments based on action research, their years as chair are very likely be taken more seriously.

Obviously, a conversation must take place ahead of time to establish the value of a leadership portfolio focused on achieving specific goals agreed upon by department members. The dean, the department and college promotion and tenure committees, the faculty senate, and the vice president for academic affairs might all be parties to these discussions. But the concept of leadership as service, or even of scholarship, needs to be given weight in personnel decisions. It is clear, too, that if faculty have been included in the process of completing the leadership matrix and all the other team-building processes described in this book, they will have a better appreciation of the chair's contributions to the institution, which can be given weight in promotion and merit decisions.

Conclusion

To take full advantage of the opportunities for leadership development described in this book, chairs must look at old problems in new ways and create learning environments for their departments that encourage all faculty to take risks and make experiments. Both department chairs and department members can be revitalized if they challenge themselves to learn new ways of functioning that contribute to individual growth and departmental effectiveness.

References

Altman, H. (1989). Syllabus shares "what the teacher wants." *The Teaching Professor, 3*(5), 1.

Anderson, J. A. (1988). Cognitive styles and multicultural populations. *Journal of Teacher Education, 39*(1), 2–9.

Angelo, T. A. (Ed.). (1991). *Classroom research: Early lessons from success* (New Directions for Teaching and Learning, No. 46). San Francisco: Jossey-Bass.

Angelo, T. A., & Cross, K. P. (1993). *Classroom assessment techniques: A handbook for college teachers.* San Francisco: Jossey-Bass.

Arreola, R. A. (1989). Defining and evaluating the elements of teaching. *Proceedings of the Sixth Annual Conference, Academic Chairpersons: Evaluating faculty, students, and programs* (pp. 3–12). Manhattan: Kansas State University.

Association of American Colleges. (1985). *Integrity in the college curriculum: A report to the academic community.* Washington, DC: Author.

Baker, H. K. (1982). Meetings audit: Planning for improvement. In J. W. Pfeiffer & L. D. Goodstein (Eds.), *The 1982 annual for group facilitators, trainers, and consultants* (pp. 49–54). San Diego, CA: University Associates.

Bandura, A. (1982). Self-efficacy mechanism in human agency. *American Psychologist, 37,* 122–147.

Bandura, A. (1986). *Social foundations of thought and action: A social cognitive view.* Englewood Cliffs, NJ: Prentice Hall.

Banks, J. A. (1988). *Multiethnic education: Theory and practice* (2nd ed.). Boston: Allyn & Bacon.

Banta, T. W., & Associates. (1993). *Making a difference: Outcomes of a decade of assessment in higher education.* San Francisco: Jossey-Bass.

Barber, L. W. (1990). Self-assessment. In J. Millman & L. Darling-Hammons (Eds.), *The new handbook of teacher evaluation* (pp. 216–228). Newbury Park, CA: Sage.

Bass, B. M. (1985a). *Leadership and performance beyond expectations.* New York: Free Press.

Bass, B. M. (1985b, Winter). Leadership: Good, better, best. *Organizational Dynamics*, pp. 26–40.

Bass, B. M. (1990a) *Bass & Stogdill's handbook of leadership: Theory, research, and managerial applications* (3rd ed.). New York: Free Press.

Bass, B. M. (1990b, Winter). From transactional to transformational leadership: Learning to share the vision. *Organizational Dynamics*, pp. 19–31.

Bass, B. M., & Avolio, B. J. (1990). The implications of transactional and transformational leadership for individual, team, and organizational development. In W. A. Pasmore & R. W. Woodman (Eds.), *Research in organizational change and development* (Vol. 4), (pp. 231–272), Greenwich, CT: JAI Press.

Bass, B. M., Waldman, D. A., Avolio, B. J., & Bebb, M. (1987). Transformational leadership and the falling dominoes effect. *Group and Organizational Studies, 12*(1), 73–87.

Bateman, W. L. (1990). *Open to question: The art of teaching and learning by inquiry*. San Francisco: Jossey-Bass.

Beck, A. T. (1993). Cognitive approaches to stress. In P. M. Lehrer & R. L. Woolfolk (Eds.), *Principles and practices of stress management* (pp. 333–372). New York: Guilford Press.

Belenky, M., Clinchy, B., Goldberger, N., & Tarule, J. (1986). *Women's ways of knowing*. New York: Basic Books.

Benne, K., & Sheats, P. (1948). Functional roles of group members. *Journal of Social Issues, 2*, 42–47.

Bennett, J. B. (1988). Department chairs: Leadership in the trenches. In M. G. Green (Ed.), *Leaders for a new era* (pp. 57–73). New York: American Council on Education/Macmillan.

Bennett, W. J. (1984). *To reclaim a legacy*. Washington, DC: National Endowment for the Humanities.

Bennis, W. G., & Nanus, B. (1985). *Leaders: The strategies for taking charge*. New York: HarperCollins.

Bergquist, W. H. (1992). *The four cultures of the academy: Insights and strategies for improving leadership in collegiate organizations*. San Francisco: Jossey-Bass.

Bergquist, W. H., & Phillips, S. R. (1975). *A handbook for faculty development* (Vol. 1). Dansville, NY: Council for the Advancement of Small Colleges.

Bloom, B. S. (Ed.). (1956). *Taxonomy of educational objectives: Cognitive domain*. New York: Longmans, Green.

Bloom, B. S., Madaus, G. F., & Hastings, J. T. (1981). *Evaluation to improve learning*. New York: McGraw-Hill.

Boehrer, J., & Linsky, M. (1990). Teaching with cases: Learning to question. In M. D. Svinicki (Ed.), *The changing face of college teaching* (New Directions for Teaching and Learning, No. 42, pp. 41–57). San Francisco: Jossey-Bass.

Boice, R. (1990a). Coping with difficult colleagues. In J. B. Bennett & D. J. Figuli (Eds.), *Enhancing departmental leadership* (pp. 132–138). New York: American Council on Education/Macmillan.

Boice, R. (1990b). *Professors as writers. A self-help guide to productive writing.* Stillwater, OK: New Forums Press.

Boice, R. (1992). *The new faculty member: Supporting and fostering professional development.* San Francisco: Jossey-Bass.

Border, L.L.B., & Chism, N.V.N. (Eds.). (1992). *Teaching for diversity* (New Directions for Teaching and Learning, No. 49). San Francisco: Jossey-Bass.

Bourne, E. J. (1990). *The anxiety and phobia workbook.* Oakland, CA: New Harbinger.

Bowker, L. H., Mauksch, H. O., Keating, B., & McSeveney, D. R. (1992). *The role of the department chair.* Distributed by the American Sociological Association Teaching Resources Center, 1722 N Street, N.W., Washington, DC 20036.

Boyer, E. L. (1987). *College: The undergraduate experience in America* (Carnegie Foundation for the Advancement of Teaching). New York: HarperCollins.

Boyer, E. L. (1990). *Scholarship reconsidered: Priorities for the Professoriate* (Carnegie Foundation for the Advancement of Teaching). Princeton, NJ: Princeton University Press.

Braskamp, L. A., & Ory, J. C. (1994). *Assessing faculty work: Enhancing individual and institutional performance.* San Francisco: Jossey-Bass.

Brinko, K. T. (1993). The practice of giving feedback to improve teaching. *Journal of Higher Education, 64*(5), 574–592.

Brookfield, S. D. (1990). *The skillful teacher: On technique, trust, and responsiveness in the classroom.* San Francisco: Jossey-Bass.

Browne, N. (1986). *Asking the right questions: A guide to critical thinking.* Englewood Cliffs, NJ: Prentice Hall.

Bruffee, K. A. (1984). Collaborative learning and the "conversation of mankind." *College English, 46*(7), 635–652.

Burns, D. D. (1980). *Feeling good: The new mood therapy.* New York: Signet/New American Library.

Bushardt, S. C., & Fowler, A. R. (1989). The art of feedback: Providing constructive information. In J. W. Pfeiffer (Ed.), *The 1989 annual: Developing human resources* (pp. 9–16). San Diego, CA: University Associates.

Carrell, M. R., Kuzmits, F. E., & Elbert, N. F. (1992). *Personnel/human resource management* (4th ed.). New York: Macmillan.

Carroll, J. B., & Gmelch, W. H. (1992). *A factor-analytic investigation of the role types and profiles of higher education department chairs*. San Francisco: The national conference of the American Educational Research Association. (ERIC Document Reproduction Service No. ED 345 629)

Carter, D. J., & Wilson, R. (1993). *Minorities in higher education: Eleventh annual status report*. Washington, DC: American Council on Education.

Catalano, E. M., Webb, W., Welsh, J., & Morin, C. (1990). *Getting to sleep*. Oakland, CA: New Harbinger.

Center for Teaching Effectiveness Staff. (1985). *Teachers can make a difference. Sourcebook for new faculty*. Austin: University of Texas, Austin.

Centra, J. A. (1973). Self-ratings of college teachers: A comparison with student ratings. *Journal of Educational Measurement, 10*(4), 287–295.

Centra, J. A. (1993). *Reflective faculty evaluation: Enhancing teaching and determining faculty effectiveness*. San Francisco: Jossey-Bass.

Christensen, R. C., & Hansen, A. J. (1987). *Teaching and the case method*. Boston: Harvard Business School Press.

Clark, J. H. (1988). Designing discussions as group inquiry. *College Teaching, 36*(4), 140–143.

Clewell, B. C., & Ficklen, M. S. (1986). *Improving minority retention in higher education: A search for effective institutional practices*. Princeton, NJ: Educational Testing Service.

Cohen, P. A. (1981). Student ratings of instruction and student achievement: A meta-analysis of multisection validity studies. *Review of Educational Research, 51*, 281–309.

Conger, J. A. (1989). *The charismatic leader: Behind the mystique of exceptional leadership*.

Coombs, C. H. (1987). The structure of conflict. *American Psychologist, 4*, 355–363.

Cooper, J. L., Prescott, S., Cook, L., Smith, L., Mueck, R., & Cuseo, J. (1990). *Cooperative learning and college instruction: Effective use of student learning teams*. Long Beach, CA: Institute of Teaching and Learning.

Costigan, J. I., & Schmeidler, M. A. (1984). Exploring supportive and defensive communication climates. In J. W. Pfeiffer & L. D. Goodstein (Eds.), *The 1984 handbook for group facilitators* (pp. 112–114). San Diego, CA: University Associates.

Cross, K. P. (1977). Not *can*, but *will* college teaching be improved? In J. A. Centra (Ed.), *Renewing and evaluating teaching* (New Directions for Higher Education, No. 17, pp. 1–15). San Francisco, Jossey-Bass.

Daloz, L. A. (1986). *Effective teaching and mentoring: Realizing the transformational power of adult learning experiences*. San Francisco: Jossey-Bass.

Davis, B. G. (1993). *Tools for teaching*. San Francisco: Jossey-Bass.

Davis, M., Eshelman, E. R., & McKay, M. (1988). *The relaxation and stress reduction workbook*. Oakland, CA: New Harbinger.

Diamond, R. M. (1989). *Designing and improving courses and curricula in higher education: A systematic approach.* San Francisco: Jossey-Bass.

Diamond, R. M. (1993). Changing priorities and the faculty reward system. In R. M. Diamond & B. E. Adam (Eds.), *Recognizing faculty work: Reward systems for the year 2000* (New Directions for Higher Education, No. 81, pp. 5–12). San Francisco: Jossey-Bass.

Diamond, R. M. (1994). *Serving on promotion and tenure committees: A faculty guide.* Bolton, MA: Anker.

Donlon, T. F. (Ed.). (1984). *The college board technical handbook for the scholastic aptitude test and achievement tests.* New York: College Entrance Examination Board.

Eble, K. E. (1983). *The aims of college teaching.* San Francisco: Jossey-Bass.

Eble, K. E. (1994). *The craft of teaching: A guide to mastering the professor's art* (2nd ed.). San Francisco: Jossey-Bass.

Eden, D. D (1988). Pygmalion, goal setting, and expectancy: Compatible ways to boost productivity, *Academy of Management Review, 13,* 639–652.

Erickson, G. (1974). *Teaching analysis by students.* Kingston: Instructional Development Program, University of Rhode Island.

Erickson, B. L., & Strommer, D. W. (1991). *Teaching college freshmen.* San Francisco: Jossey-Bass.

Erwin, T. D. (1991). *Assessing student learning and development: A guide to the principles, goals, and methods of determining college outcomes.* San Francisco: Jossey-Bass.

Eurich, N. P. (1985). *Corporate classrooms.* Princeton, NJ: Carnegie Foundation for the Advancement of Teaching.

Feldman, K. A, (1989). Instructional effectiveness of college teachers as judged by teachers themselves, current and former students, colleagues, administrators and external (neutral) observers. *Research in Higher Education, 30,* 137–189.

Franklin, J., & Theall, M. (1989, April). Who reads ratings: Knowledge, attitudes, and practice of users of students ratings of instruction. Paper presented at the 1989 national conference of the American Educational Research Association, San Francisco.

Franklin, P. (1993, July). A *disciplinary perspective.* Paper presented at the 1993 National Conference on Institutional Priorities and Faculty Rewards. Sponsored by the Lilly Endowment and the Center for Instructional Development, Syracuse University.

Frederick, P. J. (1986). The lively lecture—Eight variations. *College Teaching, 34*(2), 43–50.

Frederick, P. J. (1989). Involving students more actively in the classroom. In A. F. Lucas (Ed.), *The department chairperson's role in enhancing college teaching* (New Directions for Teaching and Learning, No. 37, pp. 31–40). San Francisco: Jossey-Bass.

French, W. L., & Bell, C. H. (1990). *Organization development: Behavioral science interventions for organization development* (4th ed.). Englewood Cliffs, NJ: Prentice Hall.

Fried, R. (1993). Role of respiration in stress and stress control: Toward a theory of stress as a hypoxic phenomenon. In P. M. Lehrer & R. L. Woolfolk (Eds.), *Stress management* (pp. 301–332). New York: Guilford Press.

Gabelnick, F., MacGregor, J., Matthews, R. S., & Smith, B. L. (1990). *Learning communities: Creating connections among students, faculty, and disciplines* (New Directions for Teaching and Learning, No. 41). San Francisco: Jossey-Bass.

Gaff, J. G. (1978). Overcoming faculty resistance. In J. G. Gaff (Ed.), *Institutional renewal through the improvement of teaching.* (New Directions for Higher Education, No. 24, pp. 43–57). San Francisco: Jossey-Bass.

Gainen, J., & Boice, R. (Eds.). (1993). *Building a diverse faculty.* (New Directions for Teaching and Learning, No. 53). San Francisco: Jossey-Bass.

Gardiner, L. (1989). *Planning for assessment: Mission statements, goals, and objectives.* Trenton, NJ: Distributed by New Jersey Department of Higher Education.

Gmelch, W. H., & Carroll, J. B. (1993). The competing roles of department chairs. *The Department Chair, 4*(1), 17–19.

Goodsell, A., Maher, M., & Tinto, V. (1992). *Collaborative learning.* University Park, PA: National Center on Postsecondary Teaching, Learning, and Assessment.

Gordon, J. (1993). *A diagnostic approach to organizational behavior.* Boston: Allyn & Bacon.

Gray, P. J., Froh, R. C., & Diamond, R. M. (1992). *A national study of research universities: On the balance between research and undergraduate teaching.* Syracuse, NY: Syracuse University, Center for Instructional Development.

Green, M. F. (Ed.). (1988a). *Leaders for a new era.* New York: American Council on Education/Macmillan.

Green, M. F. (Ed.). (1988b). *Minorities on campus: A handbook for enhancing diversity.* Washington, DC: American Council on Education.

Guerney, B. G., Jr. (1977). *Relationship enhancement: Skill-training programs for therapy, problem prevention, and enrichment.* San Francisco: Jossey-Bass.

Guskey, T. R. (1988). *Improving student learning in college classrooms.* Springfield, IL: Charles C. Thomas.

Haines, V. J., Diekhoff, G. M., LaBeff, E. E., & Clark, R. E. (1986). College cheating: Immaturity, lack of commitment, and the neutralizing attitude. *Research in Higher Education, 25*(4), 342–354.

Hall, R. M., & Sandler, B. R. (1982). *The classroom climate: A chilly one for women?* Washington, DC: Association for American Colleges.

Halpern, D. F., & Associates. (1994). *Changing college classrooms: New teaching and learning strategies for an increasingly complex world.* San Francisco: Jossey-Bass.

Hanson, P. G. (1973). The Johari Window: A model for soliciting and giving feedback. In J. W. Pfeiffer & J. E. Jones (Eds.), *The 1973 annual handbook for group facilitators* (pp. 114–119). San Diego, CA.: University Associates.

Hater, J. J., & Bass, B. M. (1988). Superiors' evaluations and subordinates' perceptions of transformational and transactional leadership. *Journal of Applied Psychology, 73*(4), 695–702.

Hellriegel, D., Slocum, J. W., Jr., & Woodman, R. W. (1992). *Organizational behavior,* (6th ed.). St. Paul, MN: West.

Higgerson, M. L. (1991). Strategies for managing conflict. *The Department Chair, 1*(4), 1–20.

Hilliard, A. G. (1989). Teachers and cultural styles in a pluralistic society: Just what does pluralism mean? In *NEA Today* (pp. 65–69). Washington, DC: National Education Association.

Hollander, E. P., & Offermann, L. R. (1990). Power and leadership in organizations. *American Psychologist, 45,* 179–189.

Holmes, W. (1985). Small groups in large classrooms. In J. R. Jeffrey & G. R. Erickson (Eds.), *To improve the academy: Resources for student, faculty, and institutional development* (Professional and Organizational Development Network, pp. 159–162). Stillwater, OK: New Forums Press.

Howell, J. M., & Frost, P. (1989). A laboratory study of charismatic leadership. *Organizational Behavior and Human Decision Processes, 43,* 243–269.

Ilgen, D. R., Fisher, C. D., & Taylor, M. S. (1979). Consequences of individual feedback on behavior in organizations. *Journal of Applied Psychology, 64,* 349–371.

Jacobs, L. C., & Chase, C. I. (1992). *Developing and using tests effectively: A guide for faculty.* San Francisco: Jossey-Bass.

Janzow, F., & Eison, J. (1990). Grades: Their influence on students and faculty. In M. D. Svinicki (Ed.), *The changing face of college teaching* (New Directions for Teaching and Learning, No. 42, pp. 93–102). San Francisco: Jossey-Bass.

Johnson, D. W., Johnson, R. T., & Smith, K. A. (1991). *Cooperative learning: Increasing college faculty instructional productivity* (ASHE-ERIC Higher Education Report No. 4.) Washington, DC: George Washington University, School of Educational and Human Development.

Kanter, R. M. (1983). *The change masters.* New York: Simon & Schuster.

Katz, J. (Ed.). (1985). *Teaching as though students mattered* (New Directions for Teaching and Learning, No. 21). San Francisco: Jossey-Bass.

Katz, J., & Henry, M. (1988). *Turning professors into teachers.* New York: Macmillan.

Kerr, S. (1975). On the folly of rewarding A, while hoping for B. *Academy of Management Journal, 18,* 769–783.

King, P. M., & Kitchener, K. S. (1994). *Developing reflective judgment: Understanding and promoting intellectual growth and critical thinking in adolescents and adults.* San Francisco: Jossey-Bass.

Kouzes, J. M., & Posner, B. Z. (1987). *The leadership challenge: How to get extraordinary things done in organizations.* San Francisco: Jossey-Bass.

Kurfiss, J. G. (1988). *Critical thinking: Theory, research, practice, and possibilities.* Washington, DC: Association for the Study of Higher Education.

Kurfiss, J. G. (1989). Helping faculty foster students' critical thinking in the disciplines. In A. F. Lucas (Ed.), *The department chairperson's role in enhancing college teaching* (New Directions for Teaching and Learning, No. 37, pp. 41–50). San Francisco: Jossey-Bass.

Kushner, H. S. (1993). *When bad things happen to good people.* New York: Schocken Books/Random House.

Lang, C. (1987). *Case method teaching in the community college.* Unpublished manuscript. (Available from Education Development Center, Inc., 55 Chapel St., Newton, MA 02160.)

Lawrence, R. L. (1989). When they don't do the reading. *The Teaching Professor, 3,* 10.

Lee, C. (1992, October). The budget blahs: Industry training report 1992. *Training,* pp. 31–38.

Lehrer, P. M., & Woolfolk, R. L. (1993). Specific effects of stress management techniques. In P. M. Lehrer & R. L. Woolfolk (Eds.), *Principles and practice of stress management* (2nd ed.) (pp. 481–520). New York: Guilford Press.

Lewis, K. (1987). *Taming the pedagogical monster: A handbook for large class instructors.* Austin: Center for Teaching Effectiveness, University of Texas, Austin.

Little, L., & Peter, H. (1990). *Motivation and performance of older Australian academics: A pilot study.* Canberra: Australian Government Publishing Service.

Locke, E. A., & Latham, G. P. (1990). *A theory of goal setting and task performance.* Englewood Cliffs, NJ: Prentice-Hall.

Lowman, J. (1990). *Mastering the techniques of teaching.* San Francisco: Jossey-Bass.

Lucas, A. F. (1986). Effective department chair training on a low-cost budget. *Journal of Staff, Program, and Organization Development, 4*(4), 33–36.

Lucas, A. F. (1988). Strategies for a team-building intervention in the academic department. *Journal of Staff, Program, and Organization Development, 6*(1), 21–32.

Lucas, A. F. (Ed.). (1989a). *The department chairperson's role in enhancing college teaching* (New Directions for Teaching and Learning, No. 37). San Francisco: Jossey-Bass.

Lucas, A. (1989b). Using student evaluations as a tool to improve faculty teaching: Conducting the feedback interview. *Proceedings of the Sixth Annual Conference, Academic Chairpersons: evaluating faculty, students, and programs* (pp. 509–514). Manhattan: Kansas State University.

Lucas, A. F. (1990a). The department chair as change agent. In P. Seldin (Ed.), *How administrators can improve teaching* (pp. 63–88). San Francisco: Jossey-Bass.

Lucas, A. F. (1990b). Using psychological models to understand student motivation. In M. D. Svinicki (Ed.), *The changing face of college teaching* (New Directions for Teaching and Learning, No. 42, pp. 103–114). San Francisco: Jossey-Bass.

Lucas, A. F. (1991). Moving towards a shared vision or maintaining the status quo. *Proceedings of the Eighth Annual Conference, Academic Chairpersons: Improving effectiveness and efficiency* (pp. 23–35). Manhattan: Kansas State University.

Lucas, R. W. (1992). Feedback awareness: Skill building for supervisors. In J. W. Pfeiffer (Ed.), *The 1992 annual: Developing human resources* (pp. 29–36). San Diego: Pfeiffer.

Luft, J. (1984). *Group processes: An introduction to group dynamics.* Mountain View, CA: Mayfield.

MacGregor, J. (1990). Collaborative learning: Shared inquiry as a process. In M. D. Svinicki (Ed.), *The changing face of college teaching* (New Directions for Teaching and Learning, No. 42, pp. 19–30). San Francisco: Jossey-Bass.

McKay, M., & Fanning, P. (1991). *Prisoners of belief.* Oakland, CA: New Harbinger.

McKay, M., & Fanning, P. (1993). *Self-Esteem* (2nd ed.). Oakland, CA: New Harbinger.

McKay, M., Rogers, P. D., & McKay, J. (1989). *When anger hurts.* Oakland, CA: New Harbinger.

McKeachie, W. J. (1994). *Teaching tips: A guidebook for the beginning college teacher* (9th ed.). Lexington, MA: Heath.

Mager, R. F. (1984). *Preparing instructional objectives* (2nd ed.). Belmont, CA: Pitman.

Magolda, M.B.B. (1992). *Knowing and reasoning in college: Gender-related patterns in students' intellectual development.* San Francisco: Jossey-Bass.

Marienan, C. & Chickering, A. W. (1982) Adult development and learning. In N. D. Nenson (Ed.), *Building on experience in adult development* (New Directions for Teaching and Learning, No. 16). San Francisco: Jossey-Bass.

Massy, W. F., & Wilger, A. K. (1994, January). *Hollowed collegiality: Implications for teaching quality.* Paper presented at the Second American Association of Higher Education Annual Conference on Faculty Roles and Rewards, New Orleans.

Menges, R. J., & Brinko, K. T. (1986). *Effects of student evaluation feedback: A meta-analysis of higher education research.* Paper presented at the 1986 national conference of the American Educational Research Association. San Francisco.

Meyers, C., & Jones, T. B. (1993). *Promoting active learning: Strategies for the college classroom.* San Francisco: Jossey-Bass.

Miller, R. I. (1987). *Evaluating faculty for promotion and tenure.* San Francisco: Jossey-Bass.

Millis, B. (1991). Fulfilling the promise of the "seven principles" through cooperative learning: An action agenda for the university classroom. *Journal on Excellence in College Teaching, 2,* 139–144.

Milton, O., Pollio, H. R., & Eison, J. A. (1986). *Making sense of college grades: Why the grading system does not work and what can be done about it.* San Francisco: Jossey-Bass.

Moses, I., & Roe, E. (1990). *Heads and chairs: Managing academic departments.* Queensland, Australia: University of Queensland Press.

Napier, R. W., & Gershenfeld, M. K. (1989). *Groups: Theory and experience* (4th ed.). Boston: Houghton Mifflin.

National Institute of Education, Study Group on the Conditions of Excellence in American Higher Education. (1984, October). *Involvement in learning: Realizing the potential of American higher education.* Washington, DC: U.S. Department of Education.

Neff, R. A., & Weimer, M. (1989). *Classroom communication: Collected readings for effective discussion and questioning.* Madison, WI: Magna.

Noel, L., Levitz, R., Saluri, D., & Associates. (1985). *Increasing student retention: Effective programs and practices for reducing the dropout rate.* San Francisco: Jossey-Bass.

Nutt, P. C. (1989). *Making tough decisions: Tactics for improving managerial decision making.* San Francisco: Jossey-Bass.

Ottaway, R. N. (1989). Improving learning for adult part-time students. In A. F. Lucas (Ed.), *The department chairperson's role in enhancing college teaching* (New Directions for Teaching and Learning, No. 37, pp. 61–69). San Francisco: Jossey-Bass.

Palmer, P. J. (1993). Good talk about good teaching. *Change, 25*(6), 8–13.

Pearson, C. S., Shavlik, D. L, & Touchton, J. G. (1989). *Educating the majority.* New York: American Council on Education/Macmillan.

Pemberton, G. (1988). *On teaching the minority student: Problems and strategies.* Brunswick, ME: Bowdoin College.

Perry, W. G., Jr. (1970). *Forms of intellectual and ethical development in the college years: A scheme.* New York: Holt, Rinehart & Winston.

Perry, W. G., Jr. (1981). Cognitive and ethical growth: The making of meaning. In A. W. Chickering and Associates, *The modern American college: Responding to the new realities of diverse students and a changing society* (pp. 76–116). San Francisco: Jossey-Bass.

Pintrich, P., & Johnson, G. R. (1990). Assessing and improving students' learning strategies. In M. D. Svinicki (Ed.), *The changing face of college teaching* (New Directions for Teaching and Learning, No. 42, pp. 83–92). San Francisco: Jossey-Bass.

Rice, E. (1991). The new American scholar: Scholarship and the purposes of the university. *Metropolitan Universities Journal, 1*(4), 7–18.

Roper, L. D. (1992). Using computers for departmental management and faculty development. In *Proceedings of the Ninth Annual Conference, Academic Chairpersons: Celebrating success* (pp. 170–179). Manhattan: Kansas State University.

Roper, L. D. (1993). Departmental management with computers. *The Department Chair, 3*(3), 8–11.

Rothwell, W. J., & Kazanas, H. C. (1992). *Mastering the instructional design process: A systematic approach.* San Francisco: Jossey-Bass.

Roueche, J. E. (1990). The role of the chairperson in assuring faculty and teaching excellence. In *Proceedings of the Seventh Annual Conference, Academic Chairpersons: Developing faculty, students, and programs* (pp. 3–12). Manhattan: Kansas State University.

Roueche, J. E., Baker, G. A., & Roueche, S. D. (1984). *College responses to low-achieving students: A national study.* San Diego, CA: Harcourt Brace Jovanovich.

Schein, E. H. (1978). *Career dynamics: Matching individual and organizational needs.* Reading, MA: Addison-Wesley.

Schein, E. H. (1987). Individuals and careers. In J. Lorsch (Ed.), *Handbook of organizational behavior* (pp. 155–171). Englewood Cliffs, NJ: Prentice Hall.

Schein, E. H. (1990). *Career anchors.* San Diego, CA: University Associates.

Schein, E. H. (1992). *Organizational culture and leadership: A dynamic view* (2nd ed.). San Francisco: Jossey-Bass.

Schön, D. A. (1987). *Educating the reflective practitioner: Toward a new design for teaching and learning in the professions.* San Francisco: Jossey-Bass.

Scott, G. G. (1990). *Resolving conflict: With others and within yourself.* Oakland, CA: New Harbinger.

Sedlacek, W. E. (1983). Teaching minority students. In J. H. Cones III, J. F. Noonan, & D. Janha (Eds.), *Teaching minority students* (New Directions for Teaching and Learning, No. 16, pp. 39–50), San Francisco: Jossey-Bass.

Seldin, P. (1985). *Changing practices in faculty evaluation: A critical assessment and recommendations for improvement.* San Francisco: Jossey-Bass.

Seldin, P. (1991). *The teaching portfolio*. Bolton, MA: Anker.

Seldin, P. (1993a, October). How colleges evaluate professors: 1983 v. 1993. *American Association of Higher Education Bulletin*, pp. 6–8, 12.

Seldin, P. (1993b, July 21). Point of view: The use and abuse of student ratings of professors. *Chronicle of Higher Education*, p. A40.

Seldin, P., and Associates. (1993c). *Successful use of teaching portfolios*. Bolton, MA: Anker.

Seligman, M. (1992). *Learned optimism*. New York: Simon & Schuster.

Senge, P. M. (1990). *The fifth discipline: The art and practice of the learning organization*. New York: Doubleday/Currency.

Shulman, L. (1993). Teaching as community property. *Change, 25*(6), 1, 6–7.

Smith, D. (1989). *The challenge of diversity: Involvement or alienation in the academy?* (ASHE-ERIC Report No. 5). Washington, DC: School of Education and Human Development, George Washington University.

Sorcinelli, M. D. (1986). *Evaluation of teaching handbook*. Bloomington, IN: Dean of Faculties Office, Indiana University. (This unpublished 42-page booklet is also available from Mary Deane Sorcinelli, Director, Center for Teaching, University of Massachusetts, 239 Whitmore, Amherst, MA 01003.)

Sorcinelli, M. D. (1988). Satisfactions and concerns of new university teachers. *To Improve the Academy, 7*, 121–131.

Sorcinelli, M. D. (1992). New and junior faculty stress: Research and responses. In M. D. Sorcinelli & A. E. Austin (Eds.), *Developing new and junior faculty* (New Directions for Teaching and Learning, No. 50, pp. 27–37). San Francisco: Jossey-Bass.

Sorcinelli, M. D., & Austin, A. E. (Eds.) (1992). *Developing new and junior faculty* (New Directions for Teaching and Learning, No. 50). San Francisco: Jossey Bass.

Svinicki, M. (1990). Changing the face of your teaching. In M. D. Svinicki (Ed.), *The changing face of college teaching* (New Directions for Teaching and Learning, No. 42, pp. 5–15). San Francisco: Jossey-Bass.

Tichy, N. M., & Devanna, M. (1990). *The transformational leader*. New York: Wiley.

Tinto, V. (1987). *Leaving college: Rethinking the causes and cures of student attrition*. Chicago: University of Chicago Press.

Tinto, V. (1988). Stages of student departure. *Journal of Higher Education, 59*(4), 438–453.

Tomlinson, S. (1990). Writing to learn: Back to another basic. In M. D. Svinicki (Ed.), *The changing face of college teaching* (New Directions for Teaching and Learning, No. 42, pp. 31–39). San Francisco: Jossey-Bass.

Trask, K. A. (1989). The chairperson and teaching. In A. F. Lucas (Ed.), *The department chairperson's role in enhancing college teaching* (New Directions for Teaching and Learning, No., 37, pp. 99–107). San Francisco: Jossey-Bass.

Tucker, A. (1992). *Chairing the academic department*. New York: Macmillan.

Turner, J. L., & Boice, R. (1989). Experiences of new faculty. *Journal of Staff, Program, and Organizational Development, 7*(2), 51–57.

U.S. Department of Education, Office of Education Research and Improvement. (1992). *Digest of Education Statistics* (National Center for Education Statistics Publication No. 92–097). Washington, DC: U.S. Government Printing Office.

Weimer, M. G. (Ed.). (1987). *Teaching large classes well* (New Directions for Teaching and Learning, No. 32). San Francisco: Jossey-Bass.

Weimer, M. (1990). *Improving college teaching: Strategies for developing instructional effectiveness*. San Francisco: Jossey-Bass.

Wilkerson, L., & Feletti, G. (1989). Problem-based learning: One approach to increasing student participation. In A. F. Lucas (Ed.), *The department chairperson's role in enhancing college teaching* (New Directions for Teaching and Learning, No. 37, pp. 51–60). San Francisco: Jossey-Bass.

Wingspread Group on Higher Education (1993). *An American imperative: Higher expectations for higher education*. Racine, WI: Johnson Foundation.

Wlodkowski, R. J. (1993). *Enhancing adult motivation to learn: A guide to improving instruction and increasing learner achievement*. San Francisco: Jossey-Bass.

Wood, J. T. (1977). Constructive conflict in discussions: Learning to manage disagreements effectively. In J. J. Jones & J. W. Pfeiffer (Eds.), *The 1977 annual handbook for group facilitators* (pp. 115–119). San Diego, CA: University Associates.

Working papers on documenting faculty work. (1993, July). Unpublished manuscript (Syracuse University Second Annual Summer Conference on Institutional Priorities and Faculty Rewards). (Available from Robert M. Diamond, Center for Instructional Development, Syracuse University.)

Wunsch, M. (Ed.). (1994). *Mentoring revisited: Making an impact on individuals and institutions* (New Directions for Teaching and Learning, No. 57). San Francisco: Jossey Bass.

Yukl, G. (1989). Managerial leadership: A review of theory and research. *Journal of Management, 15*(2), 251–289.

Yukl, G. A., & Van Fleet, D. D. (1982). Cross-situational multi-method research on military leader effectiveness. *Organizational Behavior and Human Performance, 30*, 87–108.

Index